BUYING YOUR OWN BUSINESS

Second Edition

Identify Opportunities • Analyze Today's Markets • Negotiate the Best Terms • Close the Deal

Russell Robb

BUSINESS

Avon, Massachusetts

Published by Adams Business, an imprint of
Adams Media, an F+W Publications Company
57 Littlefield Street, Avon, MA 02322. U.S.A.
www.adamsmedia.com

ISBN 10: 1-59869-705-6
ISBN 13: 978-59869-705-6

Printed in Canada.

J I H G F E D C B A

Library of Congress Cataloging-in-Publication Data
is available from the publisher.

This publication is designed to provide accurate and authoritative
information with regard to the subject matter covered. It is sold with
the understanding that the publisher is not engaged in rendering legal,
accounting, or other professional advice. If legal advice or other expert
assistance is required, the services of a competent professional person
should be sought.

—From a *Declaration of Principles* jointly adopted
by a Committee of the American Bar Association
and a Committee of Publishers and Associations

Many of the designations used by manufacturers and sellers to distin-
guish their product are claimed as trademarks. Where those designations
appear in this book and Adams Media was aware of a trademark claim,
the designations have been printed with initial capital letters.

This book is available at quantity discounts for bulk purchases.
For information, please call 1-800-289-0963.

Contents

Acknowledgments

A number of years ago I was attending a seminar. At the end of the day, the instructor passed out a blank page with just one word at the top—DREAMS. We were asked to fill in the blank. I thought for a moment. Then I wrote down several personal dreams, one of which was to write a published book . . . someday.

It has been a formidable task in that the writing has been woven around my regular job—nights, weekends, holidays, and vacations. Needless to say, the book would not have been completed without my partner in life and my partner in this book: Leslee, my wife of thirty-seven years. Her willingness to spend the hours at the computer in order to get this to a publisher made the task easier, and the constant encouragement from my four children, all adults, kept me focused.

Others to whom I am indebted are Liza Cormier, who has been my loyal publishing assistant since 1992 when Tom West and I produced a monthly national newsletter, *M&A Today*. Some of my articles in that publication have been incorporated in this book. Liza further helped my with the extensive revisions of this updated edition of *Buying Your Own Business*. I have also relied heavily on many of my business friends, particularly those who shared with me the personal experiences described in the chapter "Case Studies of Buyers."

Finally, I am indebted to Brendan O'Neill, the assistant project manager at Adams Media, who not only encouraged me to update the first edition of this book but to embellish and enlarge this second edition.

HOW TO USE THIS BOOK

The process of buying a business is usually long and difficult. In compiling this book, I spent more time reading relevant material, talking to industry professionals, and thinking about the subject matter than actually writing. Many of the references and quotes are from businesspeople I know in the Boston area. Their knowledge of the mergers and acquisitions (M&A) business is applicable nationwide.

The outline is sequential. Because the M&A business may have terminology foreign to many readers, please reference the Glossary early and often. M&A jargon includes such colorful phraseology as "deals crater because of seller's remorse," which depicts the culture of the business.

The book was written to be anecdotal, using numerous experiences. Perhaps the most interesting reading is Chapter 27, "Case Studies of Buyers," because actual buyers share their "lessons learned." This is not an academic book, as it does not rely on theory or textbook-type explanations. The examples are true, although a few are purposely disguised.

In writing the book, I have tried to impress upon you the formidability of the task of successfully acquiring a business. Additionally, on numerous occasions I emphasize the need for professional advisers to assist you in the potential transactions, e.g., in the chapters "Use of Intermediaries" and "Your Acquisition Team."

The book discusses the trials and tribulations of acquiring small businesses, family businesses, and troubled companies. Along with pointing out opportunities, I try to point out warning signs and red flags.

Buying Your Own Business can be used as an ongoing reference. Such chapters as "Valuation Techniques," "Finding the Deal," "Picking Apart the Financials," "Negotiating," and "Letter of Intent" are how-to, nuts and bolts analyses.

From a practical point of view, the chapters on "Letters, Memos, Forms, and Contracts" and "M&A Organizations" inform you of helpful resources.

Whether buying a business at all is really worth the effort is discussed in the chapters "How and Why People Buy a Business" and "Should You Buy a Business?" It is no panacea owning a small business—surveys show that more than 30 percent of these owners work ten hours per day and 15 percent work seven days per week.

I'll cover technical advice in "Representations and Warranties" and "Legal and Tax Issues." And when it comes to advice, there is no lack of opinions, as discussed in "Why Deals Fail" and "Pearls of Wisdom."

Hopefully this book is fairly easy to read, informative, and enjoyable. Throughout the book, I have referred to and quoted from many authorities in the mergers and acquisitions business. These additional viewpoints make this book even more comprehensive.

Good luck!

NOTE FROM THE AUTHOR

This book was written for those individuals who want to buy a business, particularly a business in the lower-end of the middle market, frequently referred to as companies with sales between $3 million and $50 million. More than ever, this book is timely because of our recent business society, which no longer offers long-term employment. After numerous transfers or layoffs, many people are motivated to buy their own business to become masters of their destiny and less subject to powers beyond their control.

Having sold three small businesses of my own and having been an intermediary for buyers and sellers since 1985, I have direct knowledge of this subject. This book is an attempt to educate individual buyers so they will have a better chance to successfully buy a business.

Harvard Business School case 9-385-330, *Buying an Existing Business*, clearly summarizes the search process:

Searching for a small business to buy can be difficult; not only is there no established marketplace for these firms, but you are trying to purchase an entity created and cultivated by another individual, and you are attempting to make it mesh with your own style, character and interests—all at a price which is both fair to the seller and affordable for you.

Unlike the real estate market, which is efficient in bringing buyers and sellers together, the buying and selling of middle-market businesses is inefficient because of the need to keep most transactions confidential. Strict adherence to confidentiality prevents the information being easily obtainable or widely known. The secretiveness of selling a business causes buyers to be proactive by cold-calling owners and seeking to buy companies that are originally "not for sale."

Most readers of this book have never bought a business—which is why this book is useful. You may be competing for deals against sophisticated buyout groups that have systematized every step in the acquisition process and have a fully experienced acquisition team (e.g.: attorney, accountant, appraiser, investment banker, environmental consultant, etc.). Furthermore, these professional buyout companies have computer programs ready to crank out letters of intent, financial projections, and due diligence checklists; a database on senior and subordinated lenders; and more helpful tools at their fingertips.

As a potential business buyer, you have a formidable task ahead of you. Despite the odds, however, people successfully buy businesses. In fact, many of these individual success stories are documented here. According to Fleming Meeks and Nancy Rotenier, noted business writers, "Buying a small business can destroy your ego, ruin your marriage, wipe out your bank account. It can also be the most exhilarating thing that will ever happen to you."

Buying a business makes sense if the process is well thought out beforehand and the business is well managed afterward. Because the individual buyer cannot easily locate businesses for sale, you must try one of the following tactics:

1. Uncover companies willing to discuss the sale of their business by approaching them directly, bluntly asking: "Would you consider selling your business to me?"
2. Go to business brokers who represent companies, mostly retail, that usually have between $1 million and $3 million in revenues. He will show you his "listings" but generally will not seek out companies that fit your specific criteria.

3. Meet or visit with third-party referral sources, e.g., attorneys, accountants, bankers, leaving them your business card in hopes that they will remember to call you when they hear of an opportunity to acquire a company. They may, in turn, expect to represent you or the seller in the transaction.
4. Go to middle-market investment bankers who represent companies with sales between $3 million and $50 million to request that they put you on their e-mail list that periodically announces their new clients interested in selling.
5. Retain an intermediary for a monthly charge (usually $5,000 per month) to seek out acquisition opportunities that meet your criteria.
6. Read this book to understand the process and what makes the most sense for your needs.

Ironically, as the older population expands, more and more organizations are reducing their workforces and demanding early retirement of people between the ages of forty-five and sixty. A very large number of older adults in this early retirement still have twenty to thirty years of healthy, productive lives ahead of them. But with no work, reduced income levels, and very little guidance or social support for focusing their creativity and energies, some find themselves longing for a challenge of some kind.

Most of the individuals buying middle-market companies are in this group because such people are more apt to have the financial resources, business experience, and confidence to be successful. Furthermore, a significant number of executives from public companies who lose their jobs as a result of mergers want to buy their own companies.

Almost all buyers are curious as to "why" the seller is willing to sell his business. Whether the seller tells the prospective buyer the true story is another matter. Ideally, the buyer has a better chance of completing a transaction if the seller is under some sort of distressed situation. The jargon in the trade is *death, divorce,* or *despair.* If the owner of the company is selling strictly for *financial gain*, and does not have to sell, he probably will not sell until the buyer reaches his lofty price. Most owners of small businesses decide to sell because of some *event*. In other words, instead of planning several years in advance, the decision to sell suddenly occurs when the owner hits the wall and decides enough is enough, or Wal-Mart announces they are opening a store next to their hardware store, or their key employee decides to leave.

As a buyer of a business, you should know the various reasons that trigger the owner's decision to sell. Some adverse circumstances for business owners become prime acquisition opportunities for buyers. Remember one of the sagest buyers of companies is Warren Buffet, who frequently sees great opportunities when the value of businesses is depressed due to short-term circumstances.

As stated in the PricewaterhouseCoopers publication, *The Buying and Selling a Company Handbook*:

> *"Buying a company is an enormous undertaking. You will be faced with matters both predictable and unplanned as you approach the market, and your vigilance will make the difference between success and failure. Your commitment, of course, will serve as the foundation on which your success is built. Buying a business is unlike anything you have before encountered."*

This book will teach you the process of buying a business. Granted, you should be a self-starter with an entrepreneurial flare. With the purchase of a business you will bear much responsibility, have a lot of uncertainty, and need to rely greatly on your intuition. People buy businesses because they want the independence, they want the challenge, and/or they are bored with their previous jobs. Not only have most buyers never bought a company, they have never run one either. This book is created so that the task of acquiring a company becomes less onerous, creates more pleasure, and results in more successful acquisitions.

Good luck on your journey.

CHAPTER 1

How and Why People Buy a Business

The middle-market mergers and acquisitions (M&A) business is very fragmented. First, there are investment bankers who reach down to the lower middle market. Second, there are business brokers who traditionally sell "Main Street" America businesses, but sometimes move up to sell the lower middle-market companies ($3 million to $50 million in sales). Third, there are nationwide intermediaries such as Sunbelt Business Brokers, Inc., that have multiple offices and fill the gap between the investment banker and the broker.

Following is the terminology used for the different middlemen who can help you identify a company to buy and/or provide other services in buying a company:

Finder: A finder will identify the seller to the buyer or vice versa, but will not provide other services. For this introduction, the finder will charge a fee that should be negotiated before he or she begins contacting a potential seller. The finder merely introduces the two parties; he or she does not attempt to determine the sale price or negotiate the transaction.

Broker: Like a real estate broker, a business broker usually represents the seller. He or she identifies buyers, qualifies them, prices the business, negotiates the deal, and assists in the closing. The use of the term *business broker* implies that the businesses for sale have sales of less than $3 million and frequently under $1 million.

Intermediary: An intermediary provides all the services of a broker but addresses the middle market. An intermediary will work for either the buyer or the seller and usually tries to obtain an upfront retainer. When representing a seller, the intermediary will probably write a comprehensive selling memorandum. When representing a buyer, the intermediary will probably be involved with securing the financing for the transaction.

Investment banker: An investment banker usually works for a larger firm than an intermediary and is usually involved in larger transactions. While investment bankers are often retained as intermediaries to buy or sell companies or divisions, they also help finance deals by funding bridge loans or by actually putting up some of the capital themselves. In the latter case, they would be considered a merchant banker. They usually provide extensive analysis and deal structuring and receive additional compensation for rendering fairness opinions and underwritings. Also, investment bankers normally are securities brokers with a National Association of Security Dealers (NASD) license, and they can legally handle the exchange of securities of public companies.

The middle market is a busy place in which individual and corporate buyers are chasing relatively few owners who are willing to sell their businesses. For individuals, there are many opportunities to buy the small, less sought-after retailers, distributors, and service providers. However, as an individual, you will be competing with the following acquirers of businesses:

- Companies in fragmented industries that want to consolidate to "bulk up" in size
- Corporations that are divesting noncore businesses and using the resulting cash for more synergistic acquisitions
- Businesses in slow-growth industry segments that seek strategic fits
- Venture firms that are focusing less on startup companies and are adding more established middle-market companies to their portfolios

- Buyout firms, known as financial buyers, that have been refinanced and continue to have a voracious appetite

As a potential buyer, you should realize that most sellers of privately held middle-market companies do not know how to value their business or set a reasonable price for it. One of the most common mistakes these owners make is to apply to their small private company a price-earnings multiple similar to that of a public company in the same industry.

A public company could easily be worth 25 to 50 percent more because of its access to capital, its ability to use its own stock for acquisitions, its highly scrutinized financial reporting to the SEC, the probability that the management and directors are not a "one-man band," and so on. Unfortunately, there are few, if any, price comparables for privately held companies because when these companies are sold, the price is not public information. The real estate business is different because all transactions are public knowledge.

One of the biggest problems in buying a private company is digging out the true financial numbers and understanding the company's actual earning power. As many as 90 percent of all businesses in this country are family owned. Family companies are run differently from nonfamily businesses, and you need a keen understanding of the differences so that you can analyze them accordingly. (See Chapter 5 for further information on family businesses.)

For a buyer, the acid test of whether the business is financially viable depends on three components:

1. The owner's salary
2. Sufficient debt coverage from operating income
3. A return on investment commensurate with the level of risk

Part of the difficulty in buying a business is that the buyer and the seller have different agendas when structuring the transaction. The seller usually wants as much cash as possible at closing and wants to structure the deal so that he or she will pay the least amount of taxes. (For reasons I'll explain later, selling the stock of the company is the best way to reduce the tax impact.)

On the other hand, the buyer's goal is usually to pay the least amount of cash up front and to buy the assets of the company; this allows the buyer to write up the value of the assets and also to avoid almost all contingencies of the selling company.

Aside from these obstacles, the middle market has these characteristics:

- The resources available for buyers to identify selling companies are limited.
- It is a busy place, with many individual and corporate buyers.
- It is an environment in which it is difficult to value private companies.
- Buyers and sellers have different agendas.

To successfully acquire a business, think of the three Ps:

Process: Aside from the buyer who happens to be in the right place at the right time and perhaps buys a company from a friend or relative, most successful individual buyers diligently adhere to the acquisition process. This book in large part is about the acquisition process: the strategy, the criteria, the search, the evaluation, the financing, the negotiating, the due diligence, etc.

Professionalism: Certain markets are very efficient when it comes to available information, supply and demand characteristics affecting the price, knowledgeable buyers and sellers, etc. The stock market is an example of an efficient market. However, the market for buying and selling mid-sized companies is inefficient. Frequently the seller is selling a business for the first time (it may have been his or her life's work) and the buyer is buying a business for the first time. The seller may not reveal the real reason for selling and does not always submit all the relevant information. For these reasons, a buyer should spend the time and money to assemble an advisory team of professionals—intermediary, lawyer, accountant, appraisers, etc.—to improve the chances of successfully acquiring a company.

Persistence: In case studies of individuals who successfully acquired companies, the predominant characteristic is persistence. Many of these buyers spent eight to ten hours a day for two solid years doing legwork before they finally closed on an acquisition. Most of them had sufficient capital and were qualified buyers, but the trait that sets them apart from their peers is persistence.

Individuals who fail to buy a middle-market company may just be unlucky, or there may be other mitigating circumstances. However, if you are a qualified buyer with a solid business background and a reasonable amount of capital, you should be able to acquire a company if you adhere to the three Ps and follow the advice in this book.

WHY BUY A BUSINESS?

So if it's so difficult to buy a business, why should you bother? Part of the answer comes from the quintessential outplacement firm, New Directions. This Boston-area company advises senior executives with salaries over six figures on career movement. The president of the firm, David Corbett, and his staff help clients find another executive position or, as the name of the firm implies, redirect their vocational life in a "new direction," such as buying a business.

In a comprehensive study regarding entrepreneurs, David Corbett found that:

More than half the working population of the United States think seriously about owning their own business. At least 500,000 managers are being fired every year. For many of them, ownership is an increasingly tempting option. As a practical matter, it is unlikely that someone over sixty years old is going to have much success joining another corporation. Entrepreneurship is an attractive alternative that offers new independence and control, perhaps the ticket to trying something one has always wanted to do. The fifty-five- to sixty-four-year-old market is also the single most affluent consumer group today and many of these affluent individuals are candidates for small business ownership. Midlife seems to generate many conflicting choices. The common threads, however, seem to be a need for autonomy, control, independence, and freedom as well as a quest for self-fulfillment and self-actualization and a need to have a career that is meaningful.

The essential ingredient for success is probably the sheer will to win—the total commitment to achieve at any cost. Research shows that 60 percent to 90 percent of new ventures are created as a result of some close connection between the prior work and the new venture.

Robert Weiss, a research professor at the University of Massachusetts, asked people whether they'd work if they had inherited enough money to live comfortably. Roughly eight out of ten people said yes.

Other relevant comments in the survey were:

- Today's flat organizations offer less opportunity for bigger, better jobs. Hard work is less a guarantee for success than ever before. As a result, dissatisfaction is on the rise: 47 percent say they either dislike or are ambivalent about the company they work for.
- Work really defines who you are. So much of a person's self-esteem is measured by success at work.
- Most corporate cultures are designed to eliminate creativity. Finding the sense of mission in a big business isn't all that easy.

In his book, *New Business Opportunities*, Jeffrey Timmons, professor of Babson College and Harvard Business School, states: "Graduates of the Harvard Business School . . . long thought of as the West Point for the *Fortune* 500 . . . thrive on this entrepreneurial dream: about one-third end up working for themselves."

One can look back in time and draw various analogies between explorers in the seventeenth century, immigrants in the eighteenth century, pioneers in the nineteenth century, and entrepreneurs in the twentieth and twenty-first centuries. According to *Webster's*, an entrepreneur "organizes, manages, and assumes the risks of a business or enterprise." Historically, the term *entrepreneur* has been used to mean someone who started a company, but I believe that an entrepreneur is someone who either starts or buys a company. I also believe that the motivation of both groups is the same. Gordon Baty discusses entrepreneurs' motivating factors in his book *Entrepreneurship for the Nineties*:

1. To make a lot more money than I could with some other application of my energies during a comparable period of time.
2. To get out of a professional rut—to see ideas through to completion, to gain professional recognition, to accept responsibility for the full consequences of my ideas.
3. To be my own boss, control my own destiny, set my own hours, etc.
4. To prove to myself (my spouse, my father, my ex-boss, etc.) that I can do it.
5. To advance technology, society, etc.
6. To develop and deploy talents I feel that I have outside my area of specialization.

Buying a business satisfies many of the entrepreneurs inner challenges and psychological needs of self respect and self worth. The feeling of independence is embellished when the buyer of a business realizes that as an owner of a company he is now the master of his destiny.

CHAPTER 2

Should You Buy a Business?

Before we get any farther, it is only logical to ask the preliminary question as to whether, in fact, you should buy a business at all! This book is essentially written for individual buyers who are indeed interested in purchasing a business and looking to acquire companies with $3 million to $50 million in sales, commonly known as the lower middle market. Following is a list of typical business buyers. Which type are you?

PROFILES OF BUYERS

- Layoff: Many people in corporate America have been laid off because the competition forces businesses to downsize, or, as some executives say, "right-size." These people may have become cynical about their future with other Fortune 1000 companies, or, if they are over forty, their odds of getting another job have diminished dramatically. In this case, self-employment is a viable alternative, and so buying a business is like buying a job. In fact, one well-known intermediary actually advertises in the newspapers, "Buy a Job!"
- Second career: A number of business managers either take early retirement or are jettisoned from corporate America with a golden parachute. Some simply become fed up with corporate bureaucracy. These individuals may want to prove to themselves and to their peers that they can successfully run their own company. They have confidence in themselves and usually have a credible business or professional background.
- Entrepreneur: Today's entrepreneur is our modern-day explorer, one who is willing to take risks for adventure. A decade or so ago, most entrepreneurs were associated with startup companies. How-

ever, a more prevalent form of entrepreneurship in the 2000s is buying a business. Numerous studies show that it is much safer to buy a business than to start one. Four out of five small businesses that change hands are still in business five years later, whereas only two out of five startup businesses survive for that same time period. Many MBA programs, particularly Babson College in Wellesley, Massachusetts, feature courses in entrepreneurship.

- Former business owner: Although burnout is the number one reason owners of middle-market companies sell, these individuals often later buy another company. People in this group may buy and sell two or three businesses in their lifetime.

- Part of a group: While much less prevalent than individual buyers, groups of two or three individuals will sometimes buy a business together. We all know the problems with partnerships, so if there are multiple owners, a buy-sell agreement plus an owner's life insurance policy is imperative at the outset. Geneva Business Services has noted a recent phenomenon where three individuals who have worked together at the same company join to purchase a business, particularly if each individual brings different but complementary skills (e.g., manufacturing, marketing, and finance).

- Absentee owner: A number of individual business owners prefer to treat a company the way they would commercial real estate and take a passive role. In other words, a professional manager runs the business and the owner keeps track of the company on a weekly or monthly basis, but from a distance. It is an investment even though the owner owns 100 percent of the company.

- Lifestyle: When Country Business, Inc., of Manchester Center, Vermont, started brokering businesses in northern New England in 1978, it targeted clients ranging from executives who wanted a more satisfying career to city dwellers who wanted a quieter, more fulfilling lifestyle. Many people who buy businesses simply want a significant change in where or how they live.

- Turnaround specialists: There are people like Peter Alcock who have the talent and ability to acquire distressed companies, restructure them so they begin making money, and then eventually sell them at a handsome profit. Alcock engineered the buyout of U.S. Repeating Arms (Winchester Rifles), a $55 million company from New Haven, Connecticut, that was in Chapter 11, and later sold it to a French conglomerate. Afterward, he acquired a well-known furniture company that was having some financial difficulty. Having sold the furniture company, he later acquired a contract manufacturer and tripled sales in five years.

- Well endowed: Separate from these classifications are people who are independently wealthy and may not be under time pressure to buy a business, but they want to be their own boss, they want a challenge, they want control, and they want to build their own equity.

While these buyer profiles are broad and encompass a wide spectrum of people, there is, of course, the distinct possibility that even if a person perceives himself or herself as a qualified business buyer, this is perhaps not the case.

The profile of the individual buyer is important to understand. If you want to acquire a company, you will probably be competing against other individuals and some corporate buyers. Knowing your competition will help you beat them.

DECIDE IF BUSINESS OWNERSHIP IS FOR YOU

The founder and managing director of New Directions, Dave Corbett, initially screens his clients' ability to buy a business by asking them these five questions:

1. Should I buy a business?
2. What business should I buy?
3. How will I fund it?
4. How will I find it?
5. How do I close the deal?

You should ask yourself these questions as well. The following factors are also crucial in your decision to buy a business:

- Motives
- Ambitions
- Level of commitment
- Personal risk profile
- Financial resources
- Cooperation of family members

Buying a middle-market company is not a game for neophytes. Before going any further in the process, you'll need to do the following:

1. Conduct a self-assessment. In order to successfully buy and run a business, you must have a multitude of skills and talents. It is like being a baseball player who can play all nine positions. You should be a self-starter and a leader who takes charge and is able to execute after a reasonable analysis. You should work well with people and be totally committed to your mission. You should be capable of learning quickly and working long hours. Your family should be very supportive of your endeavor. Are you willing to do menial office jobs that in a large business you would have delegated to one of many subordinates? Is your background too limited to run a company that is totally different from your prior business experiences? I could go on and on, but the point is that this is not a game for the faint of heart.

2. Assess your credibility. Put yourself in the seller's shoes. The company is often his or her life's work. When you offer to buy a company from the founder, a high price may not be enough to persuade him or her to sell. If the owner is considering whether to entrust his or her "baby" with you, you have to convince him or her that you have the experience, knowledge, and capability to successfully run the company. The seller will want to know your objectives, your background, your skills, your financial

capabilities, and whether you have others on your acquisition team. If you are buying a company in an industry you're familiar with, you will obviously impress the owner with your relevant experience. If the seller thinks that you have credibility, the likelihood that you will be considered a top candidate will improve.

3. Enlist professional help. You will probably want to seek advice from your friends, but even more importantly, you should align yourself with experienced professional advisers. For example, you do not want to hire a lawyer who is a generalist, but rather one who specializes in such transactions. An accountant who specializes in mergers and acquisitions will find innovative ways to raise cash from the target company's balance sheet. And as one experienced buyer, Peter Alcock, said, "A good intermediary is worth his weight in gold."

4. Ask yourself: Do you have a plan? You may have the credibility and the money to acquire a middle-market company, but you also need a plan. Forcing yourself to articulate your direction and how you will undertake your search and finance the transaction will cost you some "upfront" time. However, without a plan, the search for a business to buy deteriorates into a haphazard effort whose outcome has to do more with luck than with skill.

5. Determine your ability to pull the trigger. In twenty-two years as an intermediary for selling businesses, I have seen many potential buyers lose confidence and pull back on their attempt to acquire a company. You need a lot of confidence. Successful buyers are like competitive athletes: their desire to succeed translates into quick action. One of the biggest mistakes buyers make is that once they become interested in a particular company, they stop pursuing others. However, only 50 percent of transactions that reach the letter of intent stage actually close—leaving potential buyers back at square one. Conversely, many

buyers are reluctant to make an offer by submitting a non-binding letter of intent on more than one company at a time. The bottom line: You have to act quickly and be ready to refocus your attention if a deal falls through.

6. Take a financial inventory. You'll need a significant amount of your own cash to buy a profitable middle-market company. As we will discuss later in this book, a profitable manufacturing company with $4 million in sales could require $600,000 to $700,000 of a buyer's cash. If you have less than that, you might have to buy a smaller company or an unprofitable company, or you might consider buying a company with a partner or raising equity from investors. Until you know what resources you have to invest, you will not know which companies are likely targets.

   Cash for buying the business is just part of the requirement. You will also need money to live on for the year or two in which you will be looking for a company. You'll run into expenses such as a rented office, secretarial service, travel, entertaining, and professional help.

7. Consider your tolerance for risk. Let me be a devil's advocate and pose the question of what happens to you financially if you don't succeed in buying a company. Can you get a job rather quickly, or do you have alternative financial resources to lean on? Many bankers require new owners of middle-market companies to personally guarantee the bank notes. To what extent can you financially withstand the drain if such a note is called?

8. Be ready to undertake a lot of responsibility. Purchasing a middle-market company is a huge responsibility if you stop to think of the number of people who will be dependent on you: employees, customers, vendors, stockholders, bankers, etc. You should thrive on responsibility because you will have it thrust upon you. If you have been working for a Fortune 1000 company, you have not faced the crisis

of meeting a payroll when your company is undercapitalized. As a new owner of a relatively small business, you may have personally signed the bank notes, and so you will have a responsibility to your family (and your colleagues) not to fail. If you have minority stockholders, you have a responsibility not only to protect their investment but give them a decent return on their money. Above all, if your company starts to fail, or in fact fails, you will be the person ultimately in charge.

9. Exercise patience. Buying a middle-market company usually takes a year or two, assuming you devote your full time to the project. I know a number of people who are in their fourth year of pursuing an acquisition; however, they are only working on it part-time. Many individual buyers lose patience after six months and end up taking another job. Acquiring a business is a matter of the three Ps: process, professionalism, and persistence. While it is important that you have "fire in the belly" to pursue an acquisition with vigor, it is equally important that you understand that the entire process takes patience.

10. Think about your timing. Buying a business when the economy is overheated means that you might overpay for the business and/or that interest rates on the bank notes will be high. Buying a business has some similarities to buying real estate and buying stocks. On the other hand, you can't exactly wait around until the next recession to get a great price on a business.

I've been blunt in considerations and questions not to scare you away from buying a middle-market company, but rather to successfully prepare you for such an accomplishment.

WHAT THE EXPERTS LOOK FOR IN A BUYER

Several years ago, I inquired why Godfrey Wood was the most successful broker for Land-Vest, a Boston-based real estate firm that sells multimillion-dollar estates. One of the principals of the firm told me that one reason Wood was so successful was his ability to quickly qualify the potential buyer. Because real estate brokers work on commission, they can ill afford to spend half a day showing an unqualified buyer a multimillion-dollar estate. In Godfrey Wood's case he asked: 1) Do you own a house now? 2) What other estates have you looked at recently? 3) How much capital have you available for such a puchase?

Since I am an intermediary working almost exclusively for corporate buyers and sellers, I receive telephone calls daily from individuals seeking to buy a business. While I am cordial and respectful, I cannot afford to give potential buyers an hour of my valuable time unless they pass my short evaluation test. Admittedly, the following questions are curt and project unfriendliness:

- How much equity are you willing to invest?
- Where is the money coming from?
- How can I become comfortable that this money is really available?
- Have you been a CEO of a company and/or have you previously been involved with acquiring a company?
- Would you consider paying a retainer to an intermediary for the acquisition search?

The answers to the above questions give me a quick snapshot of the buyer's profile. Just as lawyers do not accept all prospects as clients, business intermediaries also are somewhat selective. The following twelve points would be my checklist for an ideal individual buyer.

1. Is capable of investing $500,000 to $750,000 of his or her own cash in the deal.

2. Was previously involved with a corporate acquisition, either personally or for an employer.
3. Has had CEO experience or has been head of a division of a substantial company.
4. Has prepared an acquisition plan for this assignment or printed a condensed version of the plan in brochure form.
5. Has narrowed the focus to target industries.
6. Has targeted industries similar to his or her business background.
7. Is willing to sign a fee agreement with the intermediary.
8. Is willing to pay a financial retainer to the intermediary.
9. Is likely to have good personal chemistry with a seller.
10. Has already spent some time looking for an acquisition.
11. Is willing to pay a full price for the target company and does not have the characteristic of being a "bottom fisher" (one who consistently bids low).
12. Is willing to accept a company with some problems.

WHO BUYS WHICH BUSINESSES?

Geneva Business Services of Irvine, California, found that the type of buyer usually indicated how large (in revenue) a company they bought:

THE BUYERS OF COMPANIES REVENUES

GROUP	LESS THAN $3 MILLION	$3–$10 MILLION	$10+ MILLION
Individuals	44%	26%	4%
Public companies	28%	21%	17%
Private companies	11%	14%	14%
Investment groups	17%	29%	47%
Foreign companies	—	10%	18%
Total	100%	100%	100%

The figures above are self-explanatory in that individuals buy more companies under $3 million in sales than any other group.

I believe there are more companies in the United States with sales between $1 million and $3 million than there are companies with over $3 million in sales. Since I'll focus on the middle market in this book, specifically companies with $3 million to $50 million in sales, individuals (you!) play an important part in acquiring companies in this category.

ADDITIONAL COSTS BEYOND THE PURCHASE PRICE

In addition to the actual purchase price, you'll also need money for fees and other costs. The following analysis is based on a one-year acquisition search for a normally profitable manufacturing company with sales of $10 million. The figures below are very general, but the largest difference between the minimum and maximum is whether an intermediary's fee is included. (Later in the book, I'll strongly recommend that you use an intermediary.) The mean total of $278,500 is equivalent to 5.6 percent of the $5 million purchase price.

ACQUISITION SEARCH FOR A COMPANY WITH SALES OF $10 MILLION
ESTIMATED COSTS

SEARCH PROCESS (OVER ONE YEAR)	MINIMUM	MAXIMUM
Retainer for intermediary	—	$30,000
Telephone, printing, office rental	$10,000	$20,000
Travel to visit companies	$2,000	$5,000
Outside valuation advice	—	$10,000
DUE DILIGENCE		
Audit and accounting due diligence*	$10,000	$20,000
Legal†	$2,000	$5,000
Other—business/management	—	$10,000
Equipment appraisal	$3,000	$7,000
Plant appraisal	$3,000	$5,000

FINANCING		
Retainer for intermediary	—	$10,000
CLOSING COSTS		
Legal: Purchase and sale agreement	$25,000	$80,000
M&A intermediary (purchase price $5 million)‡	—	$200,000
Financing intermediary§		$100,000
Raise $2 million of nonbank debt at 2.0%	—	
Raise $1 million of equity at 6.0%		
TOTAL	*$55,000*	*$502,000*
MEAN TOTAL		*$278,500*

* The accounting due diligence varies depending on whether the company has compilations or audited statements. If it has compilations, the cost could be between $15,000 and $35,000.

† The legal due diligence varies depending on whether there is litigation that needs to be settled prior to an acquisition.

‡ The M&A intermediary's fee is based on the Lehman formula less the retainer.

§ The financing intermediary's fee is based on the following:

Debt of $2 million × 2 percent =$40,000
Equity of $1 million × 6 percent =   60,000

Total financing costs $100,000

CONCLUSION

Understanding each buyer type is essential to success in business acquisition. You will probably be pursuing companies that are also being sought after by both other individuals and by some corporate buyers. Regardless of the category in which you classify yourself, you will have formidable competition.

CHAPTER 3

Acquiring Small Businesses

*B*uying Your Own Business focuses on middle-market businesses, but it would be remiss not to devote at least one chapter to small businesses, commonly considered companies with sales of under $3 million.

THE DEFINITION OF A "SMALL BUSINESS"

According to data from The State of Small Business Report: "55 percent of all U.S. businesses have sales volume under $500,000 and 74 percent have a sales volume of less than $1 million." In terms of employees, the Small Business Administration estimates the breakdown of companies as follows:

CATEGORY	NUMBER OF EMPLOYEES	PERCENT OF BUSINESSES
Very small	1–19	89
Small	20–99	9
Medium	100–499	1
Large	500 or more	1

To go one step further, the SBA estimates that the small business market is broken down into four types of companies as follows:

1. Retail: 41%
2. Services: 34%
3. Distribution: 16%
4. Manufacturing: 9%

According to BizStats (*www.bizstats.com*), the legal structure of small businesses is as follows:

Sole Proprietorships:	72%
Limited Liability Cos.:	3%
Partnerships:	5%
Corporations:	20%

WHY BUY A SMALL BUSINESS?

The attraction of acquiring a small business is obvious: There is a wider selection of small companies, and the price of a small business is theoretically lower in real terms as well as valuation metrics than that of a middle-market company.

Lower Costs

To acquire a small company with sales under $1 million, you will probably need between $100,000 and $200,000 (unless the target company has just a few employees). To acquire a profitable company with $3 million in sales, you might need between $400,000 and $500,000.

It's More Realistic

The reasons people are very anxious to own their own business are their need for independence, the challenge, and/or the desire to involve their family in the endeavor. For some people, buying a small business is a viable option. Alternatively, the person can start a business from scratch. Historically, the failure rate is twice as high in starting a business as in buying a business.

Buying a franchise is another possibility, but the best franchises, such as McDonald's, take about a $500,000 to $1 million investment per restaurant, and the relatively unknown franchises, while considerably less expensive, may not be worth the investment. And, historically, franchise contracts have been inordinately one-sided, with a large sum of the profit going to the corporation. There are some experts who feel that the golden era of franchising might be over.

HOW TO VALUE A SMALL BUSINESS

Twenty or thirty years ago, a business with $1 million in sales seemed like a good-sized business. Today, however, it is common for a small shop to have $1 million in sales. I am familiar with a wine store in which the owner works a seven-day week, day and night, and I know a bike shop where the recordkeeping is so poor that it is very difficult to determine its actual financials.

These two examples illustrate the two major concerns in buying a small business: (1) dependence on one person and (2) lack of proper information. Aside from these concerns, the biggest problem in buying a small company is often the pricing and/or valuation. The reality is that the owner of a small business usually does not know how to value companies. So the owner often does the following:

- Uses a mythical valuation technique that some so-called authority stated, such as "one times sales."
- Receives advice from a local accountant, who may or may not be proficient in valuations.
- Bases a figure on sweat equity, or "what he has to get out of it" without any correlation to the hard numbers.
- Bases the company's earnings on what the business could earn if the owner did not "skim" (personally take money off the top).
- Compares a New York Stock Exchange company to this Main Street store, e.g., a price-earnings ratio of twenty.

When brokers represent small businesses, many of them use rules of thumb to place a value on the company. While this methodology may seem inept, it is a prudent starting point for many small businesses that have insufficient financial records. For more detailed information about these rules, contact Business Broker-age Press for its annual *Business Reference Guide*: *www.bbpinc. com*, 800-839-5085. While the guide has examples of each business specialty, such as hardware stores, insurance agencies, print shops, etc., some generalizations are as follows:

TYPE OF BUSINESS	VALUATION
Retail	30% of 12 months' sales
Service	60% of 12 months' sales
Distribution	35% of 12 months' sales
Manufacturing	50% of 12 months' sales

Naturally, the rules of thumb are merely benchmarks. The real question is, what are you really buying? Cash flow? Growth potential? Assets? Liabilities? Risks? More specifically, what are the terms and conditions of the lease, the value and life of the inventory, the condition of the furniture and fixtures, the age of the machinery and equipment, the status of the franchise or licenses, the probability of ongoing business, and the likelihood of employee continuity?

In addition, buying small companies involves higher risk than acquiring larger ones. Small companies often have the following characteristics:

- The management team consists of one or maybe two principals—the owner and/or a partner or family member. When the business is sold, the management disappears.
- Very few financial, inventory, manufacturing, or quality control systems are in place. Analysis of comparative monthly or yearly backlogs is usually nonexistent, and breakeven points and product costing figures are unavailable.
- Accounting figures are late or not provided on a monthly basis.
- Customer concentration often exceeds the 80/20 rule (80 percent of their entire business comes from only 20 percent of their customers).

A Case in Point

A few years ago a lawyer called me to see if, as an intermediary, I would be willing to sell a small custom sheet metal manufacturer. Normally I would have graciously declined the assignment; however, against my better judgment, I accepted for the following reasons:

- On $800,000 of sales, the owner was taking out $200,000.
- The business was growing.
- There was a very motivated seller.
- Including the real estate, which was assessed at $250,000, the owner was willing to sell the business and the plant for $500,000.

Below are a few facts about the business.

- The two largest customers represented 50 percent of total sales, and the top ten customers represented 90 percent of sales.
- The owner was in charge of manufacturing, designing, purchasing, quoting new business, and sales, and he sometimes delivered the orders on the company truck. He arrived at work every day at 6:30 A.M., and he hadn't taken a vacation as long as he could remember.
- The owner's wife came into the office a few hours every day. She was the principal contact for matters concerning the sale of the company.
- There was a full-time secretary who did three things: answer the telephone, type the invoices, and make out the weekly employee payroll.
- There were no computers in the office, and only after I insisted did they install a fax machine.
- The factory was in a residential area; i.e., it was a nonconforming use, and a new owner could not expand the facility.

- Almost all the machinery and equipment was fully depreciated. There were no Computer Numerical Control (CNC) machines. One machine was more than 100 years old.
- Neither the machinery and equipment nor the real estate was appraised. The financials were not audited.

When two offers for the business were delivered, the principals were too busy to consider them. The owner was in the middle of a rush job, and his wife's father had just been taken to the hospital.

This description of a small business is a true case. With the help of another intermediary, we were fortunate enough to find the right buyer, and the deal closed successfully.

Let us step back and assess the characteristics of owners of small businesses and/or startups. Rarely are they management, marketing, or financial types; rather, they are creative engineers, inventors, salespeople, programmers, and so on who are very entrepreneurial. They are often willing to work eighty-hour weeks, and they often do not have support systems such as secretaries and assistants. In many cases they are multitalented, carry much of the corporation information in their head, build close personal relationships with vendors and customers, and do not necessarily build a management team. It is common for their businesses to have heavy customer concentration and/or a few key products dependent on a limited number of suppliers. Of course, there are exceptions to the rule, but generally speaking the owner/operator *is* the business.

It is one thing to start and build a company from scratch, but it is another to buy a company when the principal asset (the owner) is leaving and what is left is a weak or nonexistent management team with few, if any, systems in place. Unfortunately, it costs a buyer almost as much in professional fees to acquire a company with $1 million in sales as it does one with $3 million in sales. It may be wiser to raise more equity up front by bringing in other investors and/or putting together an acquisition team (so you can buy a more established business) than to acquire a smaller company by yourself.

THE REBUTTAL TO THE TROUBLE OF SMALL BUSINESSES

Despite the challenges of acquiring a small business, most of the estimated 300,000 businesses that are sold annually are considered small. So why bother?

You could find a diamond in the rough. In Chapter 27, "Case Studies of Buyers," you'll find two examples of enormously successful small business acquisitions. In the case of Bailey's of Boston, Franklin Wyman bought an ice cream parlor restaurant and candy store with only $7,500 of his own money plus his partners' investment. Over twenty-three years, the sales grew from $250,000 to $4.6 million, and Wyman sold out with over $1 million profit. In another case, Tom Tremblay acquired Guardair Corporation with the financial backing of an investor group and in ten years increased sales fivefold.

Or, you could buy a small business that could make history. In his book *New Business Opportunities*, Jeffrey A. Timmons, professor at the Harvard Business School, states: "Since World War II, half of all innovations and 95 percent of all radical innovations have come from new and smaller firms. Innumerable innovations and industries began this way: the heart pacemaker, the micro-computer, overnight express packages, the quick oil change, fast food, the oral contraceptive, the x-ray machine, and hundreds of others."

In spite of Timmons's rousing statement, there is usually greater risk, albeit less costs, in acquiring small businesses because they are often less established, more dependent on one person, and subject to customer concentration and can be weak on financial controls.

RECOMMENDATIONS

Before you seek out small businesses for sale, you should think about the following things.

Make a Financial Plan

First, determine how much cash you are willing to commit—not only to the purchase of a business but also to upgrading it. If you have $100,000 to $150,000 for an initial investment in a business, you probably can expect to acquire a company with $500,000 in sales at a purchase price of $200,000 to $250,000. The balance of your equity investment will be covered through seller's financing and/or bank debt. Remember, you will be expected to personally guarantee bank notes.

Your financial capabilities will somewhat determine the size business you can expect to buy. Perhaps you have heard about books that encourage you to "buy a business with no money down." While anything is possible, the likelihood of achieving such a feat is remote unless there is something terribly wrong with the target company.

Settle on a Location

Another consideration is your geographic limitations: are you willing to relocate your home or drive an hour to the business's locale? In seeking out small businesses for sale, you can refer to the Business Opportunities section of the city newspaper, contact business brokers, and call on owners directly. The most widely used online resource is *www.bizbuysell.com*. Do not be afraid or hesitant to seek professional advice in this process even though the businesses are small.

Determine What Type of Business Is Best for You

The issues of valuation, negotiation, and due diligence are the same whether the business is large or small. Regardless of the size of the business, embrace some of Warren Buffet's critical assessments:

1. Value of company's assets both tangible and intangible
2. Risk and reward components such as predictable and stable earnings
3. The ability to understand the business without reservation

There is a temptation to consider any and all businesses that are for sale. However, you should analyze the pros and cons of the four categories as they pertain to your background, your skills, and your lifestyle.

Retail
Pros: These businesses require a fairly moderate investment compared to manufacturing and distribution businesses and are less labor-intensive than service companies. If the company has a unique concept, such as Boston Market, you can raise money and do a national rollout, opening a series of stores.
Cons: For small retailers, the long hours and six- to seven-day weeks make the commitment enormous. Many owners find it difficult to work fifty to sixty hours a week. If a retailer picks the wrong location or a significant competitor opens up a store next door, he or she is often locked into a long lease with little recourse.

Services
Pros: The U.S. economy continually shows solid growth in special services, from office cleaning to rubbish removal. If consumers' needs are met reliably and the company partially fills a void in the marketplace, the business should be able to grow nicely.
Cons: The owner/manager has to have a lot of "people skills" to work well with the multitude of employees and customers. Since the business is relationship-driven, key employees could steal customers unless there are sound noncompete clauses.

Distribution
Pros: Most distributors have 85 percent of their assets in accounts receivable and inventory. If both items turn over quickly, then concentrating on these two components of the business can lead to continued success and growth.
Cons: Distribution is a high-volume, low-margin business. It is not uncommon for both the customer and the supplier to squeeze the

margins and demand more. Distributors are very vulnerable to a recession, as the balance sheet is often highly leveraged in order to carry the necessary inventory. Furthermore, the business trend continues to cut out the middlemen and go direct to the factory.

Manufacturing

Pros: Since you are making a product of your own, you are capable of differentiating your company from the competition. There is a strong possibility that your product or process can be proprietary, giving your company a competitive advantage. Most manufacturers are less dependent on relationships and can build the business worldwide from one location: the factory.

Cons: Usually manufacturing companies are more capital-intensive because of the cost of machinery and equipment. Operating margins tend to be slim for low- to medium-tech manufacturers. Manufacturers are complex organizations, coordinating product design, procurement, production, distribution, marketing, customer service, etc., to meet just-in-time requirements of demanding customers.

CONCLUSION

Yes, acquiring a small business usually costs less than buying a middle-market company. But small businesses have less available financial information, less management in place, and a narrower customer base.

One alternative to acquiring a small business is to start your own company. But first consider the challenges of that option! Most startups fail within five years. For every two startups that succeed, three startups fail. Of course, every business segment has its own characteristic and idiosyncrasies. In retail, startups might settle for an unproven location or overpay for the store build-out. In service companies, startups usually commence with no employees and no customers. In manufacturing, startups frequently grossly underestimate the cost of obtaining and fine-tuning the production equipment and training the personnel.

Buying a small business certainly has its challenges, but historically, it is a better bet than starting your own company.

CHAPTER 4

Acquiring Businesses via the Internet

Ⅰt is unclear when buyers began using the Internet to find companies for sale. However, many people believe that Robert Brauns, founder of Marketplace Technologies, launched the first M&A Web site on the Internet, *www.mergernetwork.com*, in May 1995.

THE FIRST ONLINE ACQUISITIONS

Mr. Brauns had worked for ten years as an investment banker on Wall Street with such firms as Merrill Lynch and Lazard Freres before starting his own firm to address the needs of the middle market.

Mr. Brauns realized that the M&A marketplace is extremely inefficient and fragmented with no control clearinghouse like the stock exchange for public securities. Originally, he planned to implement an online bulletin board, but was later convinced that he should establish a Web site, especially since there was no other M&A Web site at that time. Mergernetwork.com was launched, with the help of outside investors, and the rest is history. Buyers and sellers were very skeptical about the Internet in the beginning. Now, the whole concept of marketing businesses online has been validated. However, buyers and sellers mostly use the Internet as a complementary method, not the primary method, of doing M&A transactions.

YOUR USE OF M&A WEB SITES

According to Tom West, publisher of Business Brokerage Press (*www.bbpinc.com*), which is particularly well known for their Reference Guide that has an extensive listing of Rules of Thumbs, there are five major Web sites:

Bizbuysell.com
Bizquest.com
Businessesforsale.com
Mergernetwork.com
Mergerplace.com

Many of the listings you will find online are for small companies with sales under $3 million. The last two sites are the only ones that really appeal to the M&A middle-market audience. However, when business brokers have larger companies that would be classified as the middle market, these brokers would also use the top three sites for their listings as well.

Aside from these major Web sites, there are approximately twenty-five other sites used to sell U.S. businesses. Most of these listings are for small companies below the middle-market category of $3 million in revenue. To make sure your search is successful, be sure any Web site you use meets the following criteria:

The Keys to a Good M&A Web Site

- Constantly updates with new listings and deletes inactive listings.
- Utilizes search capabilities known as automated search engines called "smart agents" that contain specific criteria (sales, geographic location, industry, etc.) which alerts users via e-mail when a target company appears on the site.
- Offers a large number of listings.
- Presents opportunities effectively.
- Ensures the quality of listings.
- Continually grows its membership.

If you come across a M&A Web site that meets these criteria, it will be a very useful tool for you to use when searching out a business to buy. One flaw to watch for: Many of the listings on these sites are purposely vague regarding the company's location by stating simply "New England," for example. If the business' location is not ideal, sellers may use this tactic to attract buyers who may otherwise have skipped over the listing.

According to Tom West, the Internet's inability to keep information private poses the biggest challenge for sellers: "The big problem is confidentiality, so I don't think middle-market intermediaries use the sites nearly as much as the Main Street brokers of small businesses. Unfortunately, the sites require more and more information and the intermediaries keep giving it to the providers of the sites, which in turn creates a loss of confidentiality. Most sellers are somewhat paranoid about the buyers discovering their business is for sale without a signed Confidentiality Agreement. The operators of the sites want to please the buyers while the intermediaries need to protect their clients, the sellers."

Information on Particular Sites

If you use either of the two largest Web sites, *www.bizbuysell. com* and *www.bizquest.com*, you log on and have various searching options:

By industry
By state
By industry and state together
By listing intermediaries who are classified as brokers

Both of these Web sites have a brief description of the business, its location by state, the asking price, and the company's annual revenues. If, for example, you were interested in all medical companies throughout the United States, you would insert the word "all states" for location, "medical" for keyword, and "all" for category. At the time of this writing, using the above criteria on BizBuySell.com yielded 383 businesses.

Another option is to access these listings through a business broker. For example, if you are just interested in businesses in Florida, go to Business Brokers of Florida (*www.bbfmls.com*). Or, through BizQuest, you could identify such brokerage firms as CBI, which covers New England (*www.countrybusiness.net*). CBI typically lists about thirty-five businesses for sale. It is the only regional business brokerage firm serving New England and Atlantic Canada with a network of thirteen company-owned offices. If the buyer has further interest, you are asked to complete a Buyer Registration Form and then if you are qualified, sign a Confidentiality Agreement.

Unless you narrow your Internet search by using specific criteria—such as industry, size, geography, and purchase price—you'll be overwhelmed by the number of listings. BizBuySell claims they are connected to more than 30,000 sellers. Even if you can identify one business to buy from these 30,000 sellers, you still might need an intermediary to help you evaluate the business, place a value on it, structure the deal, and negotiate the Purchase & Sale Agreement. Most of the businesses listed on these sites also list the brokers' Web site in the "contact broker" section, which means that you should contact the broker directly. If you particularly like that person, you can begin to build a relationship with him or her. If the business of interest is already under contract, you can inquire what other companies they might have for sale that meets your criteria.

Aside from these various Web sites, most middle-market intermediaries have their own Web sites with a description of the companies they represent. In many of these situations, the intermediaries do *not* list the annual revenues of the companies and hardly ever place a price on the business. These middle-market intermediaries generally run an auction-type sale to strategic and financial buyers and rarely sell to individual buyers unless they are backed by private equity groups.

LARGER DEALS

The various Web sites I've already listed are basically geared to smaller companies. eMergers.com, which was launched in November 1999 by TM Capital Corp., addresses the market for larger companies for sale with annual revenues from $10 million to $100 million. TM Capital was formed in 1989 when its partners acquired the investment banking division of Thomson McKinnon Securities, Inc. Their Web site (*www.emergers.com*) not only lists TM's proprietary sale mandates, but acquisition mandates from public companies. This Web site uses visual icons for each deal and constantly updates the status of each listing with information such as:

- Exclusively retained
- Descriptive memorandum prepared
- Initial offers received
- Agreement signed
- Transaction completed

According to Greg Robertson of TM Capital: "eMergers.com is designed to leverage the distribution power of the Internet to broadcast opportunities while safeguarding confidentiality."

CONCLUSION

The world of online business acquisitions is constantly growing, and the Internet continues to be an important resource for anyone looking to purchase their own company. Your best bet is to try the Web sites listed in the chapter, and if they do not meet your needs, use the "Keys to a Good M&A Web Site" to review any others you come across. While the Internet is a useful tool to identify companies for sale, it is by no means necessarily the best way, but rather just one of many resources the buyer should exploit.

CHAPTER 5

Acquiring Family Businesses

T he definition of a family business is that there are two or more members of the same family managing/working in a company in which the business is owned and run for the benefit of that family and its individual members. The average life cycle of a family business is less than twenty-five years. Fewer than 30 percent ever go beyond the second generation, with fewer than 15 percent lasting through the third generation. Given the dynamics of family businesses, you could easily assume that this category should be the number-one target area for corporate buyers.

Before discussing the opportunities and pitfalls in trying to buy a family business, it's helpful for you to understand why family businesses have such a high mortality rate.

- Taxes on the founder's estate (the top federal rate is 55 percent), without offsetting life insurance policies, often force sale or liquidation.
- Family members have trouble establishing a management succession plan.
- There are rivalries between siblings and in-laws.
- Nonworking family members depend on the business for their income.

In spite of the inherent problems with family businesses, their positive attributes are family members' loyalty, their willingness to sacrifice, and their teamwork. During a recession, family members pull together with a unique kind of durability, because they are making sacrifices for their own business. Rarely do these businesses have to worry about a team member jumping ship to the competition. Family members' trust in one another inspires a more open and communicative relationship, which in turn gives the business a competitive advantage.

Like most other middle-market companies, family businesses with sales over $1 million are approached by numerous potential buyers. If you decide to approach a family business to buy, here are a number of insights:

- While buyers should always do their utmost to determine the real reason the owner might sell the company, it is even more important to find out the reason when a family business is concerned. After all, why wouldn't a family member be the logical successor? Is there something wrong with the company? Is there something wrong with the middle management? Or does the owner really just want to cash out?

- It is particularly important that on your initial visit to the company, you obtain a breakdown of the ownership of the voting stock. You might find yourself discussing the possible sale of the company with the founder's son, who has a minority position. In spite of what the son might imply, the key person to contact in future discussions is the family member who has control. More than once, I have been misled by not talking with the key player in the possible transaction. Many times as transaction nears closing, the founder has "seller's remorse" and decides not to sell the company after all.

- Partly because they support many family members—some of whom do not work in the business—family businesses are usually run to pay out most of the profits. In fact, many family businesses are Subchapter S corporations, which by nature pay out most of the profits to the shareholders. The result is that these family businesses often do not reinvest enough of their earnings in new plants and equipment or let the earnings build up on the balance sheet.

- The more family members there are in the business, the greater the likelihood that there will be disagreement on whether or not to sell the company.

- Family members in the business should be evaluated very carefully to determine whether they should remain employed under the new ownership. Often family members would not have their position in the company if it were not for that relationship.

THE SAGA OF A FAMILY BUSINESS

A third-generation family business produced frozen pasta for supermarkets and restaurants. Annual sales were $10 million, of which $5 million was sold to one customer, a leading restaurant distributor.

The family patriarch was retired and living in Florida. His son was now CEO of the company, and his daughter and son-in-law were, respectively, in charge of sales and production. In addition, two cousins worked in the office. Business was brisk, the company was growing at 20 percent per year, and annual earnings before interest and taxes (EBIT) was $1 million. The company had been using a marketing consultant, who became alarmed when sales projections showed that in four years, 70 percent of the company's business would be dependent on the one restaurant distributor.

Under the CEO's leadership, the company decided to diversify both its product offering and its distribution channels by acquiring another food company. Because the company was a Subchapter S corporation, it paid out most of its profits to the family stockholders, leaving only $400,000 of available equity to invest in another business. After a one-year acquisition search, the company was unable to identify a target company to buy, partly because it did not have the financial or management resources to acquire a profitable company with sales of around $5 million.

Still faced with a heavy customer concentration and the resulting vulnerability of this, management decided to sell the company for $6 million. The patriarch owned nearly 55 percent of the stock. He was of the "old school" and insisted on receiving all cash at closing.

Many qualified buyers visited the company. Seven months later, one of the buyers agreed to the patriarch's terms in spite of the problem of depending so heavily on one customer. In the final analysis, however, the patriarch turned down the $6 million offer and pulled the company off the market.

Lesson Learned

A family business is a way of life, a heritage, and often the soul of the family. In this case, there were five family members working in the business plus three nonworking members receiving compensation through their ownership of stock. If the company were sold, it would be almost impossible to assure every family member a job. And what of the after-tax money—where could it be invested to give the same type of return? The family name was on every package of pasta, and the patriarch was an icon in the industry and a legacy for generations to come.

Needless to say, family businesses take special considerations. The most likely prospect to buy a family business is a family member.

THE KEYS TO ACQUIRING A FAMILY BUSINESS

There is no foolproof way to acquire a family business, because frankly it is extremely difficult. With multiple owners frequently at odds with each other, it's more difficult to have the family members agree among themselves, than agree with your offer. Here are some of my suggestions, based on my twenty-plus years of experience:

- A family business usually retains an outside adviser, such as an attorney or their accountant. Make an effort to work through this trusted councilor and when making an offer to buy the business, present your offer in person to all, or almost all, the shareholders.
- Getting to know the family owners personally is paramount as they are on the verge of parting with their family legacy and must feel comfortable and confident with the buyer.
- Acquiring a family business requires the right timing and infinite patience. In fact, it may take years, not months, of schmoozing to seal the deal.

- Prepare for the worst. The family may call off the sale at the last moment for no viable reason other than seller's remorse.

CONCLUSION

In the first deal I worked on as an investment banker, I failed to complete the sale. The company was the largest Italian bakery in New England. Sales were $4 million and essentially it was running at break-even. The company was equally owned by five Italian families, two of whom had sons working in senior positions.

After six months of hard work, I produced a letter of intent for $2 million to be paid over time. Not a bad price for a small company in a very competitive industry that wasn't making money! The five families took the letter of intent and locked themselves in a conference room for further discussion. It wasn't long before the ranting and raving began, so I left the premises knowing they would never reach a consensus. The company was never sold and, to my knowledge, the second- and third-generation owners continue to struggle, barely surviving and without hope for liquidity in the future.

The buyer and I should not only have presented the offer to the group in person, but should have explained verbally the rationale for the price and terms. While we had this conversation with the head of the family, we failed to do so with the *entire* family. And therein came our failure to acquire the family business. As noted, acquiring a family company is tricky business, but if you understand the key fundamentals, you will have a greater chance at success.

CHAPTER 6

Acquiring Service Businesses

M ost of the businesses available to acquire in the United States are service companies. Arguably retailers and distributors are service companies, albeit, they are inventory intensive requiring substantial capital. There are other companies such as car wash businesses, coin laundries, road paving companies, etc., that are also in the service category. For the purpose of this chapter, however, I'll define service companies as businesses with little or no physical assets other than computers. For these types of service companies—for example, information technology businesses, employee outsourcing outfits, healthcare services, advertising agencies, and consulting firms—people are the principal assets. Before buying a service business, you need to understand how to value and structure the purchase when the people, by far, are the company's major asset.

MANUFACTURING VERSUS SERVICES

Since 1980, the manufacturing sector has decreased substantially as the service sector has increased dramatically. Observers may think the loss of manufacturing jobs is an uniquely American phenomenon. It isn't. In fact, all the major industrial nations have seen their factory workforces shrink. Of the big four industrial nations (the United States, Japan, Germany, and the U.K.), only Germany has more than 20 percent of their civilian workforce in manufacturing. Surely, the growth of China's manufacturing sector has contributed to the loss of domestic U.S. manufacturers. The point is: you'll need to at least consider buying a middle-market service business simply because there are so many more of them for sale.

Advantages of Service Companies

- There is recurring revenue with ongoing customers. Once a satisfied customer is on board—whether with a dentist or a landscaping firm—the relationship is usually secure even when threatened by a lower price offered by a competing firm.
- The type of service firms we are addressing in this chapter have modest capital equipment requirements—wages are the principal expense.
- Expansion and geographic rollout merely require leasing another office(s) in another location and adding more personnel.
- U.S service businesses such as engineering firms and callcenters are infrequently impacted by foreign competition but conversely, they can easily offshore their work requirements to countries like India and Ireland where English is their common language. An annual salary for a computer operator in the United States might average $62,000 compared to $6,000 in India.

Of course for every advantage an opportunity presents, there is a disadvantage. Following are the reasons acquiring service companies can sometimes be problematic.

Disadvantages of Service Companies

- Service companies are largely dependent on their management team and their employees. If the entire management team of a consulting business walked out the door, the company might not recover. On the other hand, if the top management team at the Hershey Company left, the business would be hurt, but customers would continue to buy their chocolate bars.
- Service companies are more difficult to grow. To double sales, for example, the company would probably have to double their employees. In manufacturing, where labor often represents 20 percent of the product cost, doubling sales is more doable.
- After owning a service business, it is not easy to "cash out" when selling. The norm in selling a service company is to

receive 50 percent of the purchase price in cash at closing with the balance paid over the next three years depending on retention of key accounts and key employees. Service companies are difficult to sell because the buyer only has accounts receivable to leverage the purchase price. (Unlike manufacturers, service companies do not have machinery and equipment and inventory to leverage.)

- A larger service company has a greater inherent infrastructure. Its larger size will stabilize the business with hundreds of customers and as a result, the company will be less dependent on the retiring CEO.

KEY ELEMENTS IN BUYING A SERVICE COMPANY

The valuation multiples and transaction structures of service companies varies widely across industry sectors. Using industry comparables is essential, as a temporary staffing firm might have a substantially lower EBIT multiple than a consulting firm. Further, a small $2 million service firm could be hugely dependent on the owner/CEO to bring in new business and would sell for 3.5 multiple of EBIT, while a $20 million service firm could sell for a 7 multiple of EBIT. The size of the service company affects the multiple of EBIT.

With service companies, there is almost always a contingent portion of the purchase price. It can be based on one or several factors such as the following:

- Retention of key employees
- Retention of key customers
- Performance milestones based over two to three years measured by certain criteria (such as an earnout in order to satisfy the seller's lofty price expectations)

Perhaps the most important point in buying a service company is to retain the top management by including these managers in the sale process. In essence, without them you might be buying a "pig in the poke." Let's say there is an investment management firm that advises high-net-worth people on their securities. The founder wants to retire. There are five key investment managers between forty-five and fifty-five years of age who each have various portfolios amounting to $400 million. As the buyer, you might structure a deal whereby you buy 100 percent of the company and "give" 25 percent of the stock to the five key managers. In return, these five managers will sign a five-year noncompete and a five-year employment contract. In addition, you derive a formula whereby over the next ten years, these managers will buy you out, thus assuring you of your exit plan. Obviously, you will have to safeguard yourself with the unexpected by having certain rights such as "puts and calls" on the stock.

There have been some fabulously successful service firms that started with very little capital such as Dun & Bradstreet (a credit service) and Paycheck (a payroll service). From a buyer's perspective, the key ingredient is to carefully structure the transaction so a sizeable portion of the purchase price is paid over time from recurring revenues of the business.

CHAPTER 7

Acquiring Troubled Businesses

B uyers are often tempted to acquire underperforming companies because the potential sellers are usually motivated to, and often will sell for, a very reasonable price. However, buyer beware! Companies do not find themselves in trouble overnight; it usually develops over several years. Some of the following characteristics would indicate that the company is in trouble:

- Negative book value
- Rapidly declining earnings or negative earnings
- Default of the bank loan covenants
- Inability to meet debt obligations
- Rapidly running out of cash

The obvious initial question you should ask is why the company is in trouble. The answer may surprise you. For example, it is possible to have a good company with a bad capital structure caused by too heavy a debt load. Given the alternatives, it is usually better if the target company has financial problems than if it has operating problems, because the former are easier to overcome than the latter.

Unless you have previously turned a company around and/or acquired a company, you should not undertake both events at the same time. Successful acquisitions are difficult enough in the best of circumstances, let alone trying to execute a turnaround at the same time. If you're thinking about buying a troubled company, however, the following items are usually the critical issues:

- Large fixed-debt payments to the secured lender vastly limit available working capital for daily requirements.
- Products or services are poorly marketed.
- The company lacks sufficient critical mass to gain the necessary economies of scale.
- The company is poorly managed.
- Employees are not properly trained or motivated.

Regardless of the company's problems, if you are experienced in the target company's industry and/or experienced in turnarounds, you have an opportunity to buy a company at a very favorable price.

PRICING THE TROUBLED BUSINESS

As you will find in Chapter 9, "Valuation Techniques," if companies are losing money at the EBIT level, it is reasonable to acquire them at book value or adjusted book value or book value plus goodwill, because there are no earnings to capitalize.

However, there are some troubled companies that are earning a reasonable amount at the EBIT level (5 to 10 percent of sales) but have such a heavy debt load that principal and interest payments result in a deficit before taxes. In such a case, if there is a negative net worth, the seller probably would be willing to sell you the business for only $1 if you assumed all the debt, including trade and interest-bearing debt (commonly known as accounts payable and bank debt). However, in some cases, even book value may be too generous. Alternative acquisition structures could include an earnout arrangement or a payout based on a 5 to 10 percent royalty on sales. You would have to read the covenants of the loan agreement before entering into such an acquisition, as the bank may prevent the sale of the company unless the debt is paid off prior to the change of ownership.

UNCOVERING THE PROBLEMS

Some common reasons a company may be in trouble include the following:

- Poor management
- Loss of key people
- Lack of focus
- Inappropriate or inadequate financial structure (could be over-leveraged or undercapitalized)
- Product problems, including quality, functional, or technical obsolescence, or lack of responsiveness to market needs
- Operating problems or inefficiencies, such as capacity underutilization and unfavorable business economics due to raw material prices, labor rates, geographic locations of plants and warehouses, and an unreasonable burden of parent company overhead
- Customer problems, including a loss of a key customer or poor or deteriorating customer relationships
- Market problems due to a declining market or market price level or a paradigm shift in the market
- Litigation problems, which could be environmental or patent-related

Another item to consider when buying troubled companies is whether you want to keep the current management in place. If the company is losing money on an operating basis, chances are you will not want most of them around after the acquisition. Actually, it is easier to replace poor management than to radically change a poor manufacturing system. It could be important to have a non-compete agreement with the sales manager as well as the owner because, after their jobs are terminated, they may be tempted to work for the competition. One of the keys to a successful turn-around is maintaining your core customers. You need the steadiness of repeat business while you rebuild your customer base.

In many cases, the owner of the troubled company also owns the plant and/or office in which the company operates. If your intention is to move the business, then not only will the owner be out of a job but he will be left with an empty building. The owner may be more agreeable to selling the troubled company at a loss if he or she is able to enter into a favorable lease for three to five years on the building.

FIXING THE PROBLEMS

Paramount in the analysis of whether or not you should buy a troubled company is to identify not only the problems but also how to rectify them. You will need to spend significantly more time in due diligence than when buying a healthy company, both before and after the letter of intent. You may initially think you're getting a good deal, but after a little digging you may find otherwise. For example, conceptually, buying a business with no money down and the assumption of debt sounds fine. In reality, it may be an awful deal.

A PROFESSIONAL'S ADVICE

Ellen Ledley Korpi of Newton Advisory Resources (newtonadvisory@comcast.net) is a consultant who focuses almost entirely on companies out of control and/or near a crisis point. The major trouble areas she addresses are: 1) accounting irregularities; 2) liquidity squeeze; and 3) poor communication with the CFO and their lenders.

Korpi conducts due diligence for troubled businesses on behalf of clients interested in acquiring these companies. She is mindful of specific issues that arise out of purchasing these troubled companies; such issues are described in the following article published by *M&A Today*:

Customer loyalty: The business owner often brings key customers on board, but the nurturing of customer relationships is frequently passed down the chain of command. The key relationships may be relegated to the sales department—but the company runs the risk of key salespeople leaving the company. It is crucial to understand who owns those relationships, because they are the ones who need to be tied to the future of the business in some way to assure the customer base remains intact.

Accurate records: The title of CFO or Controller does not guarantee that a person understands accounting. Often, the senior financial person began at the company as a bookkeeper, doing the books by rote. Their promotion might have less to do with skill set and more to do with longevity and the owner's perception of loyalty.

As a result, you'll need to scrutinize all financial metrics. For example, a client of mine with books audited by an outside firm was forced to write down inventory by nearly 80 percent. A write down is when the value of the products are substantially depreciated as if they are worth very little. Such a writedown is often the result of fraud, but can also be due to poor accounting and inadequate financial management.

Inventory valuation seems to be a challenge for many companies. Often, there is no cycle counting or other value testing except at year end. Manufacturers may not have accurate recordkeeping, with sloppiness often associated with allocating proper material pricing, labor, and/or overhead costs. Timeliness of recordkeeping seems a particular challenge, especially in the receiving process and in the appropriate writeoffs of damaged goods, scrap, theft, etc. An audited balance sheet does not fully protect against this problem.

These companies are often missing basic good practices such as frequent cash reconciliations, clean cutoff dates, wire confirmations, and cash flow planning.

Understanding of performance: Many business owners believe that financial statements are something they are forced to produce for the IRS and capital providers. What they fail to recognize is that the financial statements are the key to how the company is performing. The entrepreneur often neglects to analyze the numbers and fails to read crucial signals that could flag problems much sooner than when finally discovered. For example, in the case of the entrepreneur who was forced to write down inventory by 80 percent, his sales had remained approximately flat for five years but his inventory value had grown by a factor or five. Clearly, the entrepreneur either committed fraud or had no idea what was happening at the business. The official story might have been that "we have more sales than we can handle; the problem is insufficient working capital to service the sales." The real story might be that the expense structure is out of control, the workmanship is shoddy, and the company's primary competitive edge to its customers is its lax collection policies.

The lack of discipline in monitoring performance metrics inevitably leads to poor efficiency management.

Outside professionals: The owner of a stale company is likely to engage outside accounting and legal professionals who are not accomplished in their fields, who are tolerant of sloppy business practices, and who are personal friends. This laxity often manifests itself in continuing poor accounting practices and in poorly drafted contracts. In one of my transactions years ago, both a seller's attorney and business broker recently missed a technical flaw in a letter of intent that could have cost my client more than $100,000.

Work ethic and loyalty: If an entrepreneur's commitment to the business weakens, and if an entrepreneur's self-indulgent behavior becomes obvious to other employees, the employees' work ethic and loyalty will undoubtedly suffer. Often, the employees with the highest tolerance for owner's misbehavior are rewarded, rather than those who are the best performers. This phenomenon becomes a pervasive rot in the company's culture.

Contingent liabilities: In the stale company, the more dysfunctional the behavior of the owner, the more likely there are contingent liabilities such as lawsuits from former employees. Basic human resource best practices are often missing. You may have trouble unearthing these types of liabilities.

Korpi has this advice for potential buyers of a troubled company: "Just like peeling paint should tell you that a house has more problems than meet the eye, a troubled company is likely to be worse than what you first encounter. If you buy the company, you have to buy smart. That means: a) adjust your purchase price to reflect the problems you have yet to uncover; b) put your own economic value on the assets, regardless of their book value; c) evaluate the business and market based on your own data points (preferably you are a strategic buyer); d) apply your own cost structure to determine the earnings potential; e) provide golden handcuffs to those who control the customer relationships; f) put the seller who will remain with the company on a short leash with clearly defined expectations; and g) be cynical in order to sniff out the underlying problems that will become apparent after the fact."

UNDERSTAND WHAT YOU ARE IN FOR

Assuming responsibility for a troubled company can certainly be a headache. For example, as a new owner, you may deem it necessary to lay off 30 percent of the workforce so that the company will become more efficient. Or you may have to re-evaluate the company's supply chain. Many troubled companies have become complacent and continue to buy from their old-line suppliers without shopping for new, more competitive prices. A seemingly small savings in either cost of goods sold or SG&A will increase operating profits dramatically. As illustrated in the following table's Scenario One, the new owner cut the cost of goods sold and doubled his operating income from 5 percent of sales to 10 percent of sales, but the gross profit dropped from 35 to 30 percent. This can also be achieved by simply reducing the overhead or SG&A from 30 to 25 percent of sales, as seen in Scenario Two. In this case, the gross profit remains the same from the time of purchase.

	AT THE TIME OF PURCHASE	SCENARIO ONE	SCENARIO TWO
Sales	100	100	100
Cost of goods sold	65	60	65
Gross profit	35	30	35
SG&A	(30)	(30)	(25)
Operating income	5	10	10

To assess the viability of acquiring a company, you may need to hire a turnaround specialist to give you a second opinion. You'll need to address such basic questions as:

- What areas of the business are making money and what areas are losing money?
- Is the workforce skilled and competent to compete effectively with the troubled company's competition?
- How up to date is the machinery and equipment, including computers?
- If the financials are not audited, how reliable are the stated figures for receivables, payables, inventory? (Usually troubled companies have poor and unreliable financial systems, and the statements are seldom timely and up-to-date.)

You'll also need to review the company's customer base. Troubled companies often have customer or vendor concentration to such an extent that 50 percent of their sales or purchases is with one party, and the company is overly dependent on that customer or vendor.

LEGAL AND FINANCIAL IMPLICATIONS OF LIABILITIES

Naturally, if you are contemplating the purchase of a troubled company, you do not want to encounter unwelcome surprises, such as unintended assumption of seller liabilities. To avoid this situation, do not buy the stock of the company. Even if you have to pass up the tax loss, do that rather than buy stock. The amount you can take each year is limited; for example, if there is a $100,000 tax loss and you acquire the company for $500,000, you can take 10 percent of the purchase price or $50,000 as a deduction each year for two years.

The Uniform Commercial Code

Also, you do not want to purchase assets burdened with liens. In an asset purchase of a company, it is imperative to check the

Uniform Commercial Code (UCC) filings to be sure creditors have not placed liens on the assets you are about to receive. Since the company's bank will undoubtedly have tied up the assets as part of its collateral for the loan agreement, the seller must receive a release from the bank. If there is a lease involved, you will need to have the landlord assign the lease to you. If the company has the right to sublease the premises, find out if the landlord has any outstanding claims against the seller. If not, your attorney should have the landlord sign an *estoppel* certificate, whereby the landlord agrees that there are no claims pending against the seller on the lease. Otherwise, the landlord might have the right to collect these claims from you, the new tenant. As in any asset sale, be sure you are assigned all advantageous contracts, patents, trademarks, etc.

Let us assume that you have done your due diligence on the troubled company and, with some tough negotiating, you pick and choose which assets you will buy and which liabilities you will assume. The assets are free of liens with no UCC filings, and so you take title to the assets. Are you home free? Maybe not! If the seller's remaining company is forced into bankruptcy by its creditors, under the Uniform Fraudulent Transfer Act, and if it is held that the seller received less than fair value (inadequate consideration), you as the buyer would lose your claim to the assets. Therefore, if you are acquiring these assets, you probably need either an appraiser to verify their market value or a solvency opinion on the selling company.

The Bulk Sales Act

You should also comply with the Bulk Sales Act, which still exists in approximately twenty states, before assuming assets. This act was designed to protect the buyer and give some protection to the creditors of a business whose assets are being sold. In most states, the Bulk Sales Act applies only if the business has substantial inventory (this excludes most service companies). Buyer and seller comply as follows:

- The seller provides the buyer with a sworn affidavit that lists the names, addresses, and amount of debt for all the seller's creditors.
- The buyer sends each creditor a notice at least ten days prior to the sale stating that the transfer of assets is about to take place and that the buyer will also assume the corresponding payables, to be paid at closing or, more likely, as each debt comes due.

A sale can take place without compliance with the Bulk Sales Act, but the seller's creditors will be able to go against the buyer to collect their debts. If the seller's business is not excluded from the Bulk Sales Act (check with your attorney), then the buyer has two choices: either comply with the act and risk certain creditors causing a delay in the closing, or proceed with the closing without compliance but have the seller set up an escrow account to satisfy creditors that demand immediate payment. Remember, this act only applies to twenty states. By contacting any business transaction attorney in your state, he or she will be able to inform you whether the bulk sale act applies in that state or not.

CONCLUSION

Finally, there are three important considerations:

1. Determine how long the company can survive before it runs out of cash or the bank shuts it down. Plan to close the acquisition in three months, not the normal six to nine months.
2. Be sure the seller provides total disclosure, complete candor, and reliable information. If he does not, walk away from the deal.
3. Only retain advisers and attorneys who are very experienced in distressed transactions.

I'll leave you with an ominous warning from the book *The Warren Buffett Way*: "Buffett learned a valuable lesson about corporate turnarounds: they seldom succeed."

CHAPTER 8

Assessing Your Acquisition Strategy

Most individual buyers of middle-market companies take one to two years to complete an acquisition. The length of this procedure is usually a result of prior inexperience, lack of focus, and, above all, an acquisition strategy that is not thoroughly conceived.

NECESSARY CRITERIA

Many buyers are so anxious they tend to consider almost any opportunity that is presented to them. Since most buyers have difficulty seeing enough companies for sale to begin with, asking them to be more selective sounds like an oxymoron. However, the secret to success is to receive a flow of quality deal options that match your criteria and capabilities. Before we map out an acquisition strategy, let's determine the basic criteria.

Type of Business

There are basically four types of businesses:

Retail: A single retail store is somewhat limited in its future growth. Multiple-store expansion can be dynamic but is very dependent on selection of the right location and is somewhat vulnerable to extension of leases on favorable terms.

Service: Temporary employment agencies, landscapers, insurance agencies, etc., can be solid businesses, especially as service providers continually become a more significant part of the gross national product (GNP). The transferability of the business relationships is again critical for the new owner.

Distribution: Companies that act as middlemen between the manufacturer and the customer historically work on relatively low gross margins and have high turnover. Buyers have to be particularly concerned about the ability to transfer the business relationships with the seller's vendors and customers to the new owner. Owning a distribution company with a well-known brand with exclusive territorial rights is very valuable, while owning a company that distributes products with little brand recognition in an unprotected territory has questionable value.

Manufacturing: Companies in this category range from job shops, which make one-of-a-kind items; to subcontractors, which make production runs for other manufacturers; to producers of products that are sold to original equipment manufacturers (OEM); to makers of branded products that are sold to consumers. Additionally, you'll find integrated manufacturers that build items out of raw materials, and light manufacturers that do mostly subassembly work.

By far, the most sought-after type of business for middle-market buyers is manufacturing companies, especially companies that make a consumer or OEM product. There are a number of reasons for this: Business relationships are more transferable; the assets are more easily leveraged with the bank; the potential for worldwide sales are perceived to be greater; and the labor component is far less than for service businesses and usually less than for retail businesses.

Type of Industry

You usually want to stay within the industry that matches your background because of your experience, your greater credibility with the seller, and the probability of more favorable financing from your banker. For example, if your previous employer was a high-tech company, it is wiser for you to stay in the electronics industry than to pursue a totally unrelated field like the food business.

On the other hand, though, there are business buyers who seek underperforming companies and are perfectly capable of turning around businesses in almost any industry. Furthermore, some buyers who left a previous business because of corporate burnout purposely want to buy a business in a different industry.

Size

The size of your target company greatly depends on the amount of liquid cash you are willing and able to invest. A general rule of thumb is that profitable manufacturing companies with operating income of perhaps 10 percent of sales sell for approximately 50 percent of sales.

Most of the deals require 25 to 30 percent owner's equity at closing. Therefore, if you had $500,000 cash, you could expect to buy a profitable manufacturing company with sales of $3 million to $5 million. An example structure follows for a business with $4 million in sales:

Company sales	$4,000,000
Purchase price	$2,000,000
Equity	$750,000
Bank notes	$750,000
Seller's notes	$500,000
Total	$2,000,000

Location

Location is an obvious consideration that depends on your lifestyle and willingness to travel. Most individual buyers draw a twenty-five- to fifty-mile radius around their hometown. A fifty-mile radius encompasses a huge area, so start with a small radius and gradually move out. Some buyers are willing to move from their hometown in order to buy their desired business. If you plan to be an absentee owner, then closeness is not so critical.

Performance of the Target Business

Most buyers want to acquire only profitable companies, because the risks are too great otherwise. Unprofitable companies can also be too difficult for a new buyer to finance. On the other hand, some buyers prefer to buy companies that are losing money, because they can negotiate very favorable prices and terms.

BUSINESS ENTITY

As part of your acquisition strategy, it is important to choose your business entity—whether you are representing yourself as an individual, as part of a group, or as a holding company. You may wonder why your choice of entity affects the acquisition strategy. The answer is simply a matter of whether being part of a group of buyers strengthens your ability to successfully buy a company or whether the image of a holding company elevates your status for the seller. For example, one individual buyer has formed a holding company, XYZ Corporation, and has prepared a seventeen-page investment proposal. The abbreviated highlights of this proposal are as follows:

Executive Summary

XYZ intends to acquire a manufacturing company with a purchase price between $5 million and $10 million. The search is expected to take between eighteen and twenty-four months. XYZ has successfully raised equity to capitalize the company with $500,000. John Smith will lead the on-site management team. Smith has more than ten years of experience in the management and improvement of manufacturing companies as well as significant experience in the identification and evaluation of middle-market acquisition opportunities.

Management

A complete description of John Smith.

Type of Business

The reasons for pursuing manufacturing companies.

Acquisition Criteria
More detailed analysis.

Search Strategy
XYZ will seek out not-for-sale companies and will approach companies directly, with more reliance on brokers and investment bankers than is customary among buyout funds.

Financial Structure of Acquired Company
Seller financing
Bank debt
Investor debt
Liquidity
Management's carried interest

Exhibits
John Smith's resume
Individual references
Screening criteria

Obviously, a professionally documented acquisition plan such as this gives the buyer credibility and respect. It is very important that you be able to communicate this message in writing to the seller.

In addition to representing yourself as an individual buyer or representing yourself as a holding company, you could also create a group buyer. By joining forces with one or two other buyers, you can create the team approach. A team of buyers often gives the buying unit more talent, more money, and more credibility. Of course, there is a distinct possible downside if the team is not compatible, especially if the individuals have not previously worked together.

Luckily, some intermediaries work with upper-middle to senior management in order to cluster three people who can effectively buy a business together. They do not matchmake the team, but encourage people who have previously worked together to build a group that has a background in manufacturing, finance, and marketing. (We'll talk more about the use of intermediaries in Chapter 11.)

THE IMPORTANCE OF ADVISERS

The third aspect of assessing your acquisition strategy is to determine to what extent you will involve advisers, consultants, and other resources early on in the search process.

My experience is that even when an individual has $500,000 or more to invest in a business, he or she is generally reluctant to spend upfront money for advice, intermediary acquisition searches, and professional valuation opinions. With that caveat aside, the following are my recommendations:

Lawyers

Your regular family lawyer may be terrific regarding wills, trusts, real estate, and taxes, but when it comes to corporate acquisitions, it takes a special expertise. Corporate transaction lawyers are experts. Additionally, if you inform such a lawyer of your commitment to him or her for your impending transaction, he or she may be motivated to inform you of some potential companies for sale. Naturally, the lawyer has a vested interest!

Since the acquisition counsel prepares the purchase and sale agreement, it is important to predetermine some ballpark figures as to what the charge will be: $30,000, $50,000, $70,000, etc. Hourly rates generally run between $250 and $400. Don't be swayed by lawyers who charge the lowest fees, as a legal mistake in the contract can have catastrophic ramifications. On the other hand, try to negotiate a cap for the total legal expense—an amount "not to exceed $60,000," for example. This should not be onerous for a transaction lawyer.

Your lawyer should review your letter of intent. Although this document usually states that it is not binding, it is also difficult to substantially change the letter of intent after the fact. An experienced lawyer should have standard employment agreements and noncompete clauses. The lawyer should also review leases and loan agreements, and provide a due diligence checklist. It is customary for the buyer's lawyer to prepare the purchase and sale agreement and consummate the closing.

Accountants

As with lawyers, you can find specialists within the accounting community who are experts in mergers and acquisitions. They can help you analyze the selling company's financials and assist in structuring the deal. You may need to have an independent audit to verify the financial statements as part of the due diligence. All of this could cost $20,000 to $40,000.

Your accountant should be alert for any improprieties that would adversely affect you after the business is purchased. For example, the owner may have aggressively written down the inventory so that the company would pay lower taxes. If you are acquiring the stock of the company instead of the assets, the result would be that under your new ownership the profits on this inventory would be inflated, causing you, the new owner, to pay unnecessary taxes going forward.

If the accounting firm knows that you intend to retain it after the closing, it is more apt to be very cooperative in presenting you with other clients who might be willing to sell their company.

Bankers

The first source of debt capital is, of course, a bank. In addition to making a hard-nosed credit evaluation of the business by examining the company's balance sheet, cash flow statements, and business plan, the banker will be evaluating your character and background. It is quite probable that you will have to sign personal guarantees for the notes.

While most bankers in the commercial loan department usually respond to specific deals, you should predetermine your most likely bank resources by meeting them in advance. By getting a jump on the all-important selection of bankers, you will save an enormous amount of time during the critical stage of putting the deal together.

Financing is so fundamental to successfully completing the transaction that you have to sort it out early on. Therefore, you need to narrow down your list of bankers before you become knee-deep in the deal.

Intermediaries

The agent between the seller and the buyer is known by numerous titles, such as broker, investment banker, adviser, consultant, M&A specialist, dealmaker, bird dog, and finder, but for the moment we will categorize all of them as intermediaries.

Obviously, intermediaries are a great potential source of leads on companies willing to sell. You should plan to use one or more intermediaries. Their function and how to work with intermediaries most effectively will be discussed at length in Chapters 12 and 16, respectively.

However, even if you plan on using intermediaries, you should understand that this is still *your* endeavor. According to the PricewaterhouseCoopers publication, *The Buying and Selling a Company Handbook*: "Professional intermediaries and advisers have little interest in working with would-be buyers who do not know what they want to buy, do not have access to the necessary financing or are not prepared to proceed professionally." Just because you are using an intermediary to buy a business does not mean you can take a backseat in the purchasing process.

Be sure to line up your advisers early in the acquisition search, because when you start chasing deals, you will not have time to spend interviewing advisers. In assessing your acquisition strategy, I encourage you to use a transaction lawyer, a transaction accountant, and one or more intermediaries not only to help you create deal flow but give you a second opinion and/or be a devil's advocate. However, advisers do not make your business decisions. Ultimately you will be the one to decide whether you should buy a particular business and at what price, on what conditions, and on what terms.

UNDERSTAND YOUR ROLE IN THE PROCESS

In addition to choosing a team with which to work on finding and buying a business, you need to recognize what you can do in order to facilitate the acquisition of a company. There are a number of things individual buyers should consider when preparing a purchase strategy.

Narrow Your Focus

Perhaps no other matter gives more consternation to an intermediary than the inability or reluctance of buyers to focus on what kind of company they want to buy.

Most corporate refugees who want to buy a middle-market company have discarded retail, service, and distribution companies. So we are left with manufacturers as a business type. Even with some basic criteria established, such as location, size, profitable/unprofitable, high tech/low tech, there are a vast number of industry choices, from the food industry to the medical industry. While many buyers want to keep their options open, it is better if they select an industry that is somewhat related to their background. The intermediary will find it easier to qualify the buyer's credentials to the seller and to the buyer's banker. If the buyer's focus is too broad, intermediaries will be less likely to be helpful to the buyer.

Package Yourself

The most successful individual buyers tend to do a better job of packaging themselves than their peers. Whether it is preparing an investment proposal; creating a holding company; naming your investors, directors, and/or advisers; or publishing a brochure incorporating these items along with a photograph of yourself, professionalism goes a long way toward helping your cause. Some critics might retort that you can't judge a book by its cover, but to some degree this approach in gaining credibility is effective.

Differentiate Yourself

Most individual buyers I have met do not understand why I am not overly excited when they tell me that they are looking for a profitable, low-tech manufacturing company with sales between $3 million and $5 million that has a proprietary product.

Such a buyer means well and I encourage him in his courageous mission to buy a small business. But he needs to redefine his strategy in order to separate himself from the pack. What I tell the individual buyer (free advice) is usually to have a sharper focus, package himself or herself better, raise some more equity, and not hesitate to pay an intermediary for professional advice, particularly in the search process. With that, the individual usually thanks me, picks up his or her briefcase, and leaves. This scenario is perhaps the genesis of this book. No matter what I tell individual buyers in a half hour, it always seems like I have only scratched the surface.

If I have one piece of advice to individual buyers, it is to differentiate yourself from your peers. This idea will be addressed in Chapter 13, "Finding the Deal."

WHY COMPANIES ARE FOR SALE

When a profitable and growing company is for sale, your first reaction should be, why? Usually owners are very sensitive as to when the industry and/or company is peaking. If this is not the case, the following reasons for selling are possible.

No Heir Apparent

If you look around your own community and identify companies run by owners in their sixties, you could target companies that fall into this category. As you network at your golf course or the local Rotary Club, keep an eye out for elder owners of companies and then tactfully approach them on whether they would consider selling their business.

Loss of Interest and Burnout

Obviously, it is difficult to ascertain which business owners are burned out, but surveys show that this is the number-one reason owners sell. If you can keep your antennae out for business owners with this attitude, you might be on to something.

The Business Needs More Capital to Remain Competitive

Many industries are consolidating. One such industry is office copy machine distributors. With the copier business more competitive than ever, gross margins have eroded, which means that the distributors' profits are dependent on more unit volume, which creates more service contracts. It is the latter that are the primary profit generator. Many copier distributors with sales of $2 million to $4 million need more capital to buy competitively, so that they can sell competitively, so that they can get the profitable service business. This is an opportunity for you to acquire a business very reasonably and then infuse the necessary capital to allow it to grow.

Estate Tax and Liquidity Concerns

While I do not suggest that you become an ambulance chaser, a lot of family businesses fall on hard times after the founder dies. Many state business directories list companies' banks, law firms, and accounting firms. Perhaps a discreet telephone call to the company's law firm several months after the death notice would be appropriate.

Financial Offer Too Good to Turn Down

Some owners sell not because of burnout or lack of capital, but simply because the buyer's offer is too good to refuse. I know of a former president of a famous fast-food chain who desperately wanted to own a particular house. When he contacted the owner, he was told that the house was not for sale. He told the owner bluntly that he still wanted to buy the house.

The company president returned a week later. When the owner stated his price, the company president had the audacity to negotiate the price, and bought the house! The point of the story is that the difference between no and yes may be just a matter of how much you are willing to pay.

WHY AN OWNER MAY NOT SELL

How many times have you heard about business buyers who spent an inordinate amount of time attempting to acquire a company, only to have the seller back off? Heaven forbid, but you too may go though a similar experience.

One individual buyer, Paul Nechipurenko, has already acquired several businesses for himself. Nechipurenko insists on dealing through intermediaries as a way to qualify that the company is really for sale. Many individual buyers prefer to bypass the intermediary/broker if possible, because they perceive that not only will the price be less for the company, but there will be less hassle by avoiding a competitive bidding process. "Not true," says Nechipurenko, "you can waste a lot of time and effort chasing a company only to realize the seller is really not motivated to sell, or the seller has no perception of fair market value for the business." Notwithstanding Nechipurenko's beliefs, there is always the chance a buyer may get lucky when bypassing the intermediary.

Small companies often have several owners. I have seen a family business with ownership disbursed among five different members. To reach consensus with this many owners can be difficult or, in some cases, nearly impossible. Additionally, the buyer may be negotiating with the CEO, only to later realize that the CEO is not the decision maker. In this case, the board of directors has the ultimate choice in selling the company. Sometimes, the company's bank has to release a statement permitting the sale, particularly if the company's loan agreement is out of covenants.

Owners Want an Unreasonable Price or Terms

While many buyers hope to close the gap as the negotiations proceed, many sellers have valued their company based on sweat equity, or compared it to public companies on the New York Stock Exchange, or have a preconceived number in mind, such as $2 million after taxes.

There is an old expression in the M&A business: "The seller sets the price; the buyer sets the terms." When the owner sets both the price and the terms, then there isn't much room for negotiating. There is another expression in the M&A business: "The deal is not financeable." In order for a purchase to make economic sense, the buyer should have a certain return on investment. If the owner sets a very high price for the business plus wants all cash at closing, then it becomes doubtful that the business can pay for itself over a certain time period (say, five years). And finally, there is one more common expression in the M&A business: "The business is really not for sale." That means the owner's price is so high that it's inconceivable anyone would pay that price, so in reality, the owner is not realistic. For all intents and purposes, therefore, the business is not for sale.

Second Thoughts by Owner

One family patriarch withdrew the business offering after the family had paid an intermediary a $15,000 retainer to sell the company and after there was a letter of intent on the table. He said his deciding factor was a desire to protect the jobs of two third-generation family members, even though the buyer was anxious to include an employment contract for these two managers. On another occasion, an owner received the letter of intent and then never signed it. To this day, he will not take or return phone calls from the buyer. Intermediaries call these situations "seller's remorse."

From 1956 to 1958, I served in the U.S. Marines. Being discharged was a big moment, and most of us would count the days as we neared the date. Invariably there would be a few unexpected Marines who would re-enlist the week before they were to be discharged. For years, it had been the only life they had known. To be discharged was to leave the life to which they had become accustomed. As a result, a few of these Marines remained in the Corps.

This is analogous to some business owners. It is difficult to detect similar situations, unfortunately. But I can tell you that the chances of owners changing their mind about selling increases dramatically when there are multiple owners.

Owner Would Rather Leave Business to Heirs

A family business is defined as one in which there are two or more members of the same family working in the company, in which the business is owned and run for the benefit of the family and its individual members. Certainly family businesses are targets for individual buyers. Many owners sell the family business, because they need the liquidity, they secretly feel that their heir is not competent to run the company successfully, or they sense that the industry and/or the company is peaking. Nevertheless, many owners leave their company to their heirs . . . wisely or unwisely.

Capital Gains Liability the Overriding Concern

How many times have you heard an owner of a business or an owner of a large block of stock with a near zero cost basis say, "I can't afford to sell"? Of course, these people are referring to the federal capital gains tax, not to mention the individual state capital gains taxes. There are numerous ways to prepare the business for sale that will mitigate large tax liabilities, and there are ways to structure the deal that will do the same. Invariably, however, numerous potential sellers do neither, and as a result, the owner ends up not selling the company.

The Security of Owning a Solid Company

Many founders and owners have made their company their life's work. When they reach retirement age without an heir, an alternative to selling is to hire a professional manager. The thought of selling the company and reinvesting the proceeds in the stock market or real estate can be less appealing to owners who have little or no experience in these areas.

Loss of Owner's Salary from Business

The owner's rationale for not selling is often driven by the fact that he or she cannot replace the salary. It is not unusual for small-business owners to take out $300,000 to $400,000 annually. Let's assume that a company with sales of $6 million sells for $3 million. Let's also assume that the capital gains taxes are $700,000, leaving the owner with $2.3 million to reinvest. Use whatever interest rate is prevalent at the time of your reading this book and you will see that the business owner will fall way short of his or her salary. Often, there is no way the owner can come close to replicating the income with the net proceeds from the sale of the company. As an M&A intermediary, I am usually concerned when a small company owner wants to sell for financial reasons alone, because I much rather see their motivation to sell based on such reasons as death, divorce, or despair.

Frequently, potential sellers think that potential buyers should acquire their business at some exorbitant price like ten times operating income. It doesn't work that way. The M&A market is fairly efficient when it comes to pricing.

The difference of opinion on valuation between a buyer and a seller is the single largest deal breaker. The sooner the buyer can determine the seller's expectations and the reasons why, the better. This way, the buyer can allocate his or her time constructively to the target company or move on to another opportunity.

CHAPTER 9

Valuation Techniques

If you are analyzing a privately owned company, you may have to adjust or recast a number of items on the financial statements in order to understand the real earning power of the company. Business owners are highly motivated to pay the least amount of corporate taxes possible, and the extent to which they stretch to minimize tax liability runs the gamut from legitimate to marginal to illegitimate. Legitimate deductions include abnormally high salaries for the owners, above-market rent for buildings owned by a related family-owned real estate trust, and company automobiles. Illegitimate deductions include salaries for nonworking family members, pleasure trips charged as business trips, and home maintenance expenses charged to the company.

In valuing the target company, you need to ask the seller a very basic question: What is for sale? The owner will generally prefer to sell stock, since such a transaction results in a single capital gains tax. A stock sale, on the other hand, may be a disadvantage to you, the buyer, if there are depreciable assets on the balance sheet, because you cannot "step up" the value of the assets and increase depreciation charges. In addition, you will assume all liabilities resulting from previous infractions or product malfunctions. For these reasons, buyers typically value a company lower when they are required to purchase stock.

Conversely, in an asset sale, the seller will be taxed twice: once at the corporate level and again when distributing the proceeds of the sale out of the corporation. For the right to buy assets, therefore, the buyer may have to place a higher valuation on the target company. Like many things in life, there are exceptions to the rule. If the owners of a subchapter S corporation sell assets, there is only one tax, but owners of a C corporation will pay a double tax when selling assets.

Whether you buy assets or stock is only part of the answer as to what is for sale. Other considerations could include what assets, particularly real estate assets, are going to be withdrawn prior to the purchase. And, are there any obligations of the seller, particularly debt, to be assumed by the buyer?

VALUATION TECHNIQUE NUMBER ONE: MULTIPLE OF EARNINGS

For middle-market manufacturers, the multiple of earnings approach is the preferred method of valuation. For such businesses, earnings before interest and taxes (EBIT) is the standard earnings component to which multiples are applied in determining business sale prices. If EBIT shows no earnings, a multiple is sometimes applied to EBITDA and even to gross margin. EBITDA is earnings before interest, taxes, depreciation, and amortization and is higher up the income statement, just as gross margin is much higher on the income statement. A manufacturing company with lots of heavy machinery might sell for five times EBITDA or six times EBIT because the depreciation is a large component.

Is the EBIT multiple an arbitrary number? A rule of thumb is that if you buy a new machine for a factory, you should be able to pay for it in five years from the resulting labor savings. Likewise, a business should be able to pay for itself in three to five years, assuming that the earnings remain exactly the same for that period of time. To go one step further, a prudent person might expect a 20 percent return on an investment in a company with steady earnings. On that basis, the company could be paid for in five years at the same earnings level. Therefore, higher or lower multiples are affected by the corresponding difference in the rate of return. Historically, however, a five-year payback has been a de facto standard.

According to Joseph Myss, an intermediary from Wayzata, Minnesota, "The multiplier you select is market-driven, based on market conditions, comparables, and value in the eye of the beholder. The value the buyer sees in the company affects the market multiplier: Paying ten times earnings for a company provides the buyer with a

10 percent return on the invested capital based upon historical financial performance. Paying five times earnings results in a 20 percent return on invested capital; four times earnings results in a 25 percent return." Myss emphasizes that EBIT is most commonly used as the constant of the multiplier. "One needs, however, to separate the acquisition and financing features of the deal. Buyers will use their own capital structure as a model to finance the acquisition of the seller and will look at the company from that perspective."

VALUATION TECHNIQUE NUMBER TWO: BOOK VALUE

Book value, a multiple of book value, or a premium to book value is also a method used to value manufacturing or distribution companies. Book value is total assets minus total liabilities and is commonly known as net worth.

The book valuation technique is usually used as a method of cross-testing the more common technique of applying multiples to EBIT, cash flow, or net earnings. In the following situations, however, the use of book value as the primary method of valuation is prevalent:

When the company is losing money on an operating basis. In such cases, there are no earnings on which to apply the multiples previously discussed. Therefore, the reconstructed or fair market value of total assets less total liabilities is used for the valuation.

For small distribution companies with sales of less than $20 million. Distributors of this size are usually successful because of the departing owners' many close relationships with the company's suppliers and customers. These relationships are tenuous because they are usually noncontractual and nontransferable. Such companies usually sell at their book value plus a modest premium.

Book value is very common as a method of testing valuations for nonservice businesses for these reasons:

1. If the primary method of valuation is using a multiple of earnings, it is helpful to take the industry average of the book value multiples of other companies recently sold. Book value serves as a reference point. Some buyers will raise or lower their EBIT multiple for valuation purposes based on the relationship to the proposed selling price; some buyers will use only multiples of 4.5 to 5 times EBIT. If book value is higher than half the selling price, some buyers will use a 5 to 6 multiple.

2. By pegging the purchase price to a multiple of book value as of the date a purchase and sale agreement has been signed, the buyer is protected against a decline in the value of the business between the signing of the purchase and sale agreement and the completion date of due diligence.

When you use the book value technique, a seller will probably want you to consider an important variation. The assets may have a far greater value if the values are recast to reflect fair market value for machinery, equipment, buildings, and land. Also, the inventory might be adjusted to reflect current values and to pick up items that have been written off in order to minimize taxes. You must also determine that all the assets are actually earning money for the business. If they are not, you should request an adjustment in the purchase price to reflect this condition.

VALUATION TECHNIQUE NUMBER THREE: DISCOUNTED CASH FLOW

Discounted cash flow is what someone is willing to pay today in order to receive the anticipated cash flow in future years. It is the method most often used by large investment banks and consulting and accounting firms. The discount rate is based on the level of risk of the business and the opportunity cost of capital. In other words, it is the return you can earn by investing your money elsewhere.

In his book *Creating Shareholder Value*, Alfred Rappaport states:

The appropriate rate for discounting the company's cash flow stream is the weighted average of the costs of debt and equity capital. For example, if a company's after tax cost of debt is 6 percent and its estimated cost of equity is 16 percent and it plans to raise capital 20 percent by way of debt and 80 percent by way of equity, it computes the cost of capital at 14 percent as follows:

	Weight	Cost	Weighted Cost
Debt	20%	6%	1.2%
Equity	80%	16%	12.8%
Cost of Capital			14.0%

The use of discounted cash flow is a hotly debated subject among those in the M&A business, particularly in the middle market. Sales of larger companies that have predictable future earnings often use this approach, because it provides a rational economic framework for valuing acquisitions in that marketplace.

In the book *Mergers & Acquisitions: A Valuation Handbook*, Joseph H. Marren states:

One of the complexities with using the net present value method is that a target company's future cash flow depends on the method of acquisition and the purchase price. How? A target company's future cash flows are directly impacted by the taxes it will pay. The taxes it will pay depend on the company's taxable income. And the company's taxable income will depend, in part, on its taxable deductions for depreciation and the amortization of intangible assets. Such deductions depend on the target's tax basis for its assets, which in turn depend directly on the purchase price paid for the business.

Other opponents of the discounted cash flow method do not believe in paying for earnings that are not earned. Furthermore, the projections are speculative, and the selection of the discount rate is somewhat subjective. Nevertheless, I wanted to mention it, since it is one of the most popular methods of analyzing large companies. It is more appropriate for determining shareholder value than for valuing acquisitions.

VALUATION TECHNIQUE NUMBER FOUR: SERVICE COMPANIES

This section focuses on middle-market service companies with sales from $3 million to $50 million. The most important asset of a service company is its employees, from senior management to the most recent hiree. An equally important asset is its customers. The third major asset is the business systems utilized by the company.

Such service companies are very difficult to value, since they are highly dependent on the personal relationships of the management and its customers. In talking to the owner of a very profitable public relations firm who wanted to sell her company, I was stunned to hear that she not only got up for work every morning at 4:30 A.M. but was responsible for securing every new account in the agency. Even though she would stay on for a period after the business was sold, this superwoman was almost irreplaceable!

The company had $3 million of annual billings and reconstructed net before tax of about $300,000. Is this business worth $1.5 million? Possibly, but more important is the payout period and the extent to which the owner will remain in the business to retain the key accounts and teach the new CEO how to run the business. The most critical issue is the retention of the existing accounts, and for this reason the purchase agreement might be constructed as follows:

Payment at closing:	$1,000,000
Payment in 1 year:	$250,000
Payment in 2 years:	$250,000
Total:	$1,500,000

Conditions:

1. Owner works for two years at base salary or for one year plus two years as a consultant.
2. During the first year post-closing, any loss of an account existing at the time of closing will reduce payout by 50 percent of one year's billing of that account proportional to the total revenues.
3. A loss of an account in the second year will reduce the payout by 25 percent of one year's billing proportional to the total revenues.

Service businesses are varied, and that makes it very difficult to generalize valuation techniques. Business Brokerage Press (*www.bbpinc.com*) publishes the *Business Reference Guide*, now in its seventeenth edition, with 834 pages of business benchmarks. This book lists some of the advantages of using rules of thumb or formulas for small service businesses, such as:

1. They are market derived and provide market comparisons.
2. They provide a uniform guide and a range of values.
3. They are easy to use and can be preliminary value estimates.

The disadvantage of using rules of thumb is that they are general in nature and there is no single, all-purpose formula. The book *Guide to Business Valuations* by Fishman, Pratt, Griffith, and Wilson, states that "rules of thumb should not be used by themselves. They may, however, be useful in assessing the reasonableness of valuations based on other methods." A couple of examples of rules of thumb are:

Janitorial service: 4 times monthly gross billings plus equipment and inventory

Travel agency: 35 percent of annual gross sales plus furniture and fixtures

VALUATION TECHNIQUE NUMBER FIVE: USING BUSINESS APPRAISERS

I have seen many buyers spend a large portion of their personal net worth to buy a company without receiving expert opinion from professionals in the M&A field. Needless to say, some of these businesses failed, largely because the buyer overpaid when going into the deal. Yet getting advice does not have to be expensive—you do not have to hire an appraiser to put together a $7,500 to $10,000 "bulletproof" document that is defensible in court. You can hire an appraiser for $200 to $250 per hour to give you a verbal opinion. You might also want to consult on an hourly basis with a specialist such as appraisers who concentrate in providing values of machinery and equipment, inventories, or real estate and buildings.

Lesson Learned

One of the saddest M&A stories I've ever heard involved one of my closest and oldest friends. He had come from a broken home and had been unable to afford to continue at Andover Academy. He finished his last two years of high school in Texas but was able to earn a scholarship to Yale. After his freshman year playing on the hockey team, he had to give up the sport in order to earn tuition money. Following Yale, my friend had a thirty-year successful career at IBM. Upon reaching age fifty-five, he sought to fulfill his lifelong dream of owning a business. He bought a small distributorship in Pennsylvania that sold lockers, stadium seats, and warehouse storage racks. Like many marketing- and sales-oriented people, he drew a "hockey stick" type of sales projection and had grand designs for growth. But he made the fatal mistake of paying too much for the business. With dreams of success, he mortgaged his home, pooled his life savings, and left his secure job. The rest is history. The economy collapsed, the building business tumbled, and in two years he went to Chapter 11, and then to Chapter 7. The experience was almost life-shattering.

Many years later my friend stopped by my office seeking my advice on another business. I could not help but ask what lessons he had learned from his failed venture. Obviously he had thought about this question before, because he did not hesitate to rattle off the following:

1. Do not stray from the business field in which you have experience. (In his case, he had gone from a high-tech background to a low-tech business, from a white-collar to a blue-collar culture—a difficult transition to make.)
2. Do not acquire a company if you will be undercapitalized at the beginning of your ownership. (In his case, he had felt that the increased revenue he could generate from doubling his sales would cover the high debt load.)
3. Be sure you have highly competent people in the business.
4. Hire a business appraiser to assist you in determining how much you should pay for the business.

There are lessons everyone can learn, no matter our age or experience. One of my important business colleagues, Jim Tonra, has some very sage advice for business buyers. "Don't be afraid to consult your friends who have a sound business background in order to obtain their unbiased professional opinion on a deal you might be considering." I am sure that my friend could have avoided his unsuccessful purchase if he had followed Tonra's advice.

VALUATION TECHNIQUE NUMBER SIX: COMMON SENSE IN BUSINESS VALUATION

While I am not a professional business appraiser, I have been retained from time to time to value a company. I remember one episode where a plumbing supply distributor had to be valued because of the family owners' impending divorce. This distributor's sales had deteriorated from $8 million to $4.3 million in just a few years, and profits had gone from positive to negative. The company carried well-known OEM product lines, and at one time had had six branch outlets. It had been one of the leading plumbing supply houses in New England.

The divorce was headed for court, and yours truly was to be the key witness for placing a value on the couple's business. I was not a member of either the Institute of Business Appraisers or the

American Society of Appraisers. I was, however, a "somewhat seasoned" business intermediary who had sold three of his own businesses. I'm not telling you this story because this valuation was difficult, but because it shows how to approach a valuation when you do not have the appropriate experience as an appraiser.

The method I used in preparing my written valuation was so simple; it was just a matter of common sense. My client was well known in the plumbing supply business, having served on the board of the National Plumbing Supply Association. Working in conjunction with him, I called more than twenty owners of other plumbing supply distributors. I asked them if they had bought or sold any similar businesses, and if so, whether they would share with me their knowledge of their valuation. Plumbing supply distribution is similar to most other distributorships, so I discovered that 85 percent of the assets were in either inventory or receivables. Furthermore, it is a personal relationship business, with both vendors and customers having virtually no long-term exclusive contracts.

Based on those factors, I documented every conversation and came to the conclusion that my client's business was worth book value plus a 10 percent goodwill premium on the condition that the inventory and receivables were fairly current. Fortunately, like so many litigation cases, the divorce matter was settled out of court the day before the trial, so I never had to defend my appraisal. Nevertheless, I was prepared to base my valuation on the accepted wisdom of my client's peers.

OTHER VALUATION TECHNIQUES

Edmund Sears, a corporate valuation expert, lists the major approaches to valuation as follows:

1. Cost-based approaches
   A. Book value
   B. Adjusted book value
   C. Liquidation value

2. Market approaches using comparables
   A. Price to earnings
   B. Price to pretax earnings
   C. Price to cash flow
   D. Price to book value
3. Income approaches
   A. Capitalization of earnings
   B. Excess earnings methods
   C. Discounted future earnings
   D. Discounted future cash flow

Sears states that appraisals must be done with full knowledge of the facts, circumstances, and all relevant factors pertaining to the subject company. A particular valuation technique that is appropriate for one company at one point in time may not be appropriate for that company at another point of time or for another company at any time.

VALUATION ADJUSTMENTS

Recasting the financials is a major part of the valuation process. Such adjustments involve add-backs to the income statement and represent expenses that a new buyer would find unnecessary or discretionary, so that the recast EBIT would be higher for a new owner.

Let's assume that a company had $20 million in sales and had a reported EBIT of $1 million. The following adjustments will increase the EBIT:

Excess compensation:	$200,000
Condominium expense:	$50,000
Travel and entertainment:	$50,000
Above-market factory rental:	$50,000
Excess automobile expense:	$20,000
Pension plan contributions:	$80,000
Total:	$1,450,000
Adjusted EBIT:	$1,450,000

If the appraiser were using a multiple of 5 for income valuation purposes, the above adjustments would increase the value of the company from $5 million (EBIT of $1 million × 5) to $7.25 million (adjusted EBIT of $1.45 million × 5).

Just as adjustments are made to the income statement, you should also make adjustments to the balance sheet by appraising the assets at current market value:

ASSETS	BOOK VALUE	MARKET VALUE
Machinery and Equipment	$500,000	$2,000,000
Real estate	$500,000	$1,000,000
Automobiles	$50,000	$100,000
Goodwill	$350,000	—
TOTAL MARKET VALUE		$3,100,000
Stated book value	(1,400,000)	
Increase in book value	$1,700,000	

If you were using a multiple of 1.5 times book value for valuation purposes, these adjustments would increase the value of the company by $2,550,000 ($1.7 million × 1.5).

In this example, the company with revenue of $20 million, the *positive* adjustments increased earnings by $450,000. While the example above showed positive add-backs in order to normalize earnings to market conditions, the more challenging exercise is to identify *negative* adjustments which will decrease earnings, such as the following:

- Expenses that were capitalized rather than written off on current earnings
- Backlogs on orders priced sometime ago that are now unprofitable
- Under-reserved warranties
- Underfunded pension fund commitments
- Underaccrued liabilities for taxes, sales tax, and unused vacation and sick leave

- Unaccounted-for off-balance-sheet liabilities or contingent liabilities such as product liability suits
- Unrealistic depreciation on capital equipment
- Underinsured
- No allowance for bad debts

CASE STUDY: DEAL STRUCTURING FOR A SERVICE COMPANY

Several years ago, the two owners of a Massachusetts surveying company decided to sell the business. The previous year had been the height of the real estate boom in New England. The owners had each taken out $500,000 from the company, which was organized as a subchapter S corporation.

The potential buyers structured their offer as follows:

1. Acquirer to buy all the issued and outstanding stock of the company for $2 million plus a five-year noncompete agreement.
2. Acquirer to pay $1.5 million cash at closing, with the balance to be paid in the form of a five-year note with annual principal payments of $100,000 and interest on the balance at the prime rate plus 2 percent.
3. Owners to remain with the business for one year at annual compensation of $100,000 each. The purchase price, therefore, was 2.5 × adjusted EBIT ($1 million – $200,000 = $800,000 × 2.5 = $2 million).
4. After the one-year employment contract, the sellers agreed not to compete with the business for five years. They would be compensated for this assurance with a cash payment, beginning after each of the first five years of the contract, calculated as a percentage of the company's previous year's EBIT as follows:

INCREMENT	EBIT	PERCENT TO SELLERS
First	$400,000	0
Second	$400,000	30 percent
Over	$800,000	15 percent

5. During the first five years following the purchase, the sellers would be responsible for the payment of any contingent liability or claim that arose prior to the sale of the business.

The sellers refused this offer in lieu of a competing offer of $2 million cash at closing without notes or contingency payments. Ironically, the Massachusetts real estate market plunged and took this highly profitable surveying business into bankruptcy several years later, partly because of their business slowdown, but more importantly because the developers who used the surveyors ran out of cash to pay their debts.

The lesson here is that it is important to structure an acquisition to anticipate unexpected events, including competition from former employees and declines in the economy. The potential buyers who missed out on this deal were mighty glad that they did. Their safety net, ultimately, was the deal they structured.

VALUATION CASE STUDY: THE WOODCRAFT COMPANY

The Woodcraft Company Incorporated (WCI) was founded by Philip Davis, who was sixty years old in 2002. Phil and his wife ran the business but recently had tapered back to working three days per week. WCI's basic business was library shelving, preschool furniture, lockers, and easels. Its products were priced in the medium-high range. The company offered 125 separate items. And Davis believed they basically had five competitors.

Sales were $3 million annually. Peak sales three years before were just over $4 million. The company sold mainly through distributors, and sales efforts were mostly by telephone. Operating income, after officers' salaries of $400,000, were just under 5 percent. The company operated in a 40,000-square-foot multistory plant in Virginia. There were forty employees. Following is a review of the financials. What price would you place on this company and how would you structure your offer?

INCOME STATEMENT (IN THOUSANDS)

	2002	2001	2000
Sales	$3,200	$3,000	$4,000
Gross profit	$1,000	$1,100	$1,700
SG&A	(850)	(700)	(800)
Operating income	$150	$400	$900
Officers' salaries	$400	$350	$250
Owner replacements	(150)	(150)	(150)
Adjusted earnings	$400	$600	$1,000

BALANCE SHEET (IN THOUSANDS)

ASSETS		*LIABILITIES*	
Cash	$300	Payables	$50
Accounts receivable	$540	Notes	$10
Prepaid expenses	$100		
Inventory	$1,060		
Current assets	$2,000	Current liabilities	$60
Machinery	$600		
Automobiles	$50	Long-term debt	$10
Real estate	$150		
Total fixed assets	$800	Stock	$130
Depreciation	(500)	Retained earnings	$2,100
Total assets	$2,300	Total liabilities and equity	$2,300

The seller would not allow you to scrutinize the financial records until you had made a preliminary offer. A quick observation showed the following:

1. Sales were off 25 percent in the past two years, partly because of the post-9/11 business slowdown in the early 2000s, which affected library spending. Gross profit margins had gone from 42 percent in 2000 to 31 percent in 2002. Phil Davis explained that this is due to more distributor sales than direct sales to libraries. Also, the Davises were taking out $150,000 more in salaries; all of which resulted in a 50 percent decline in adjusted earnings.
2. The balance sheet was incredibly strong if you look at the working capital, plus the impressive retained earnings and very little long-term debt.
3. There was little risk of corporate liability if you bought stock instead of assets, a Phil Davis requirement.
4. You liked the company because it had a niche position with a long history of profitable operation and was presently being undermanaged.

In retrospect, what is your initial offer on both price and terms?

Answer: You offer $2.23 million based on a stock sale. You are thereby buying the entire balance sheet, including assets and liabilities. Your offer is a multiple of slightly more than 5.5 times the reconstructed operating income of $400,000, or 1 times the book value of $2.23 million.

Response: Phil Davis accepts your offer as long as it is all cash at closing. You agree subject to due diligence.

Due diligence: During your detailed examination of the financials of WCI, you find that one major customer accounts for 55 percent of total sales and receives extended ninety-day credit terms. You then revise your offer based on the same purchase price but with half cash at closing. The balance of $1,115,000 is payable in equal installments over five years, conditioned on your retaining this key customer's account.

Conclusion: Phil Davis turns down your offer, as the five-year payout period is beyond his comfort level. He takes the business off the market and plans to maximize his income from the company for as long as possible. Many negotiations end up this way, with companies becoming "cash cows" for their stockholders.

VALUATIONS: PRIVATE VS. PUBLIC COMPANIES

Edmund Sears states:

> *"Usually the stock market pricing of public company equities guides the valuation of private companies: IRS R4 Revenue Ruling 59-60 specifies that the market valuation of comparable public companies be one of the eight valuation factors specified for consideration. Even in the best of times, private companies are a long-term investment and an extremely illiquid one. It takes a long time to make a private company acquisition and often even longer to get out of it. Transaction costs are high and consequently private companies normally sell at substantially lower prices than those in a stock market which is highly liquid, is short-term in outlook, and has low transaction costs.*
>
> *Most private companies are substantially smaller than even the small capitalization public companies. Frequently, they operate locally or regionally rather than nationally and internationally. Further, they are likely to have fewer products or product lines and less diversified market segments. All these characteristics make private companies a much higher risk investment but risk for which the new owners are compensated for with higher rates of return derived from their owner initial investment. The market for private companies is not an extension of the market for public companies. It is a different market with different characteristics which have to be taken into account when looking at price."*

VALUATION TECHNIQUES: AN ASTUTE BUYER

George Berbeco is the owner of the Devon Group in Waltham, Massachusetts, a buyout company. The Devon Group has acquired numerous companies, and I consider George to be a very savvy and astute buyer. He has three questions that he addresses early in the valuation process:

1. Is the acquisition of the business worth the effort involved?
2. Are the reported earnings really there? For example, if the target company is a divestment, have all the overhead costs been included?
3. Are the earnings going to continue? Beware of "hockey stick" projections, with current sales representing the blade and projections the start of the stick, as sellers are almost always overly optimistic. For this reason, buyout companies place more emphasis on potential cost savings rather than on potential sales growth.

CONCLUSION

Numerous books have been written on the subject of valuing companies. Corporate valuations are an incredibly complex subject, because there are so many variables involved that affect the buyer's offer and therefore the net after-tax dollars received by the seller. As stated by Joseph E. Myss, "Sellers sell the future and buyers buy the past! Sellers are selling opportunity, whereas buyers are buying a track record." With this fundamental difference in approach, one can see why buyers and sellers have a different perception as to value.

CHAPTER 10

Valuation Considerations

Many people consider the sage of Omaha, Warren Buffet, to be the most astute investor/acquirer of businesses. His cardinal rule is not to overpay. Just as important is to recognize value in companies that others overlook. Just bidding lower than anyone else won't necessarily make you successful—you might find yourself unable to succeed in owning a business.

Some would-be buyers assume that given a complete set of financials including projections, it is possible to determine, fairly accurately, the value of the business. But it is not that simple. You have to peel back the onion further and ask questions such as the following:

What is the quality of earnings? Are the earnings strictly from operations or are some of the earnings one-time events such as the disposition of assets? Do the earnings contain substantial add-backs that puff up the actual reported income?

Are the earnings sustainable? How can you be sure the earnings will continue and/or can you believe the company's projections? This assessment is based on evaluating the market, the management, the products/services, etc.

Is the pertinent information verifiable? The valuation is based on hundreds, if not thousands, of numerical and non-numerical facts. To what extent is this information up to date and verifiable?

What does the SWOT analysis show? A key strategic tool in valuation analysis is SWOT—the acronym for strengths, weaknesses, opportunities, and threats—which encompasses the analytic process for the nonfinancial considerations.

Nonfinancial Factors

1. Industry status. A company is worth more when its industry is expanding and worth less when: a) its industry is constantly fighting technical obsolescence or, b) it's a commodity and is subject to continual price wars or, c) it's severely impacted by foreign competition.

2. Geographic location. A company is worth more if it is located in a state or country that has favorable infrastructure and tax rates, and provides an educated and competitive workforce.

3. Management. A company is worth more if it has a solid second-tier management team at different age levels with not much turnover.

4. Facilities. A company is worth more if it operates profitability at 70 percent capacity than a company that is near capacity now. Also, the equipment should be up to date and the leases renewable at reasonable rates.

5. Products or services. A company is worth more if its products or services sold to multiple industries are proprietary and diversified with some pricing power and preferable with a recognizable brand name. Also, the company should introduce new products or services regularly.

6. Customers. A company is worth more if there is recurring revenue from long-term, loyal customers along with new customers that are generated from a systematic sales process (i.e., the company does not have a high concentration of its sales from one customer).

7. Competition. A company is worth more if it does not go head to head with overpowering competitors like Microsoft or Home Depot.

8. Suppliers. A company is worth more if it's not dependent on one source for key items.

Other Nonfinancial Factors

1. Risk factors. All businesses have some degree of risk, but some businesses have considerably more risk than others—which will affect the valuation. Examples of risks would include a manufacturer that produces just one specific product, or has heavy customer concentration, or produces technology that has extreme seasonal or cyclical considerations. Let's assume a regional manufacturer makes just one product, snow shovels, which is highly seasonal, heavily dependent on the weather, and limited to local distribution. Without national distribution and a counter seasonal product, the company is vulnerable, resulting in a lower valuation.

2. Pricing power. If the company is capable of increasing the prices it charges for a product or service, it will somewhat affect the valuation of the company. Conversely, if a company sells a commodity or is squeezed so tightly by competition that there is no pricing flexibility, the company is less valuable. "Customers are willing to pay more for quality," states Lakshman Krishnamusthi. "Marketing is about product differentiation. Once you can establish a difference between your product and the competition's, you have a psychological edge with the buyer. Starbucks, for example, completely remade the perception of a commodity—coffee. What Starbucks did to the coffee model was to change the whole experience."

3. Workforce. Is the business labor intensive with little likelihood to automate? If so, this makes the company less valuable. There are various rules of thumb in this regard—some of which equate to certain industries, such as total sales per employee; or automobile manufacturers, which measure productivity to total "hours per car"; or service firms, which measure annual billable hours per employee. Other measures of the workforce are turnover statistics, whether

the employees have reasonable longevity, or whether the average employee age is the mid-fifties.

4. Customers and markets. Are the customers respectable Fortune 1000 type companies or are they marginal under-capitalized companies? Are the customers long-term steady users of the company's products and services, or are they one-shot users without repeat orders? Is the market new and uncertain and highly competitive with low barriers to entry? Does the company have national and international distribution or is the product or service only sold within a narrow area? Are the sales generated from a dedicated sales force or do orders come in willy-nilly? What are the intricacies for obtaining business either through special favors or family connections?

5. Manufacturing/production. Does the company evolve with new products and services from time to time or does it depend on the same item invented thirty years ago? Does the company devote any funds to research and development or does it make efforts to continually improve the product or service? Is the company dependent on old equipment, whether it is printing presses or computers and networking gear?

6. Value drivers. If the adhesive company, for example, has special formulations that competitors have not duplicated, that is considered a value driver. If a food company has a special recipe, that is considered a value driver. eBay and Amazon have capitalized on a marketing approach that has been copied but not really threatened—that is a value driver.

7. Value detractors. Operating in a very small market is a value detractor, as is having a product or service that is very price sensitive or has rapid obsolescence. Other items include high failure rate in that industry or high taxes for that area.

8. Corporate culture. This category is an intangible that is measurable, but often subjective. The effect of corporate culture on the company's profitability can be enormous, whether it

is Southwest Airlines versus United Airlines, or a small service firm that is ESOP owned versus a large family business where the owners take out millions of dollars.

IMPLEMENTATION OF NONFINANCIAL FACTORS IN VALUATION

Once a professional corporate appraiser thoroughly understands, evaluates, and determines the magnitude of the nonfinancial issues, he will adjust the company-specific risk premium that is one of the variables considered in what is known as the discount rate in the discounted cash flow (DCF) analysis. From here on, it gets a little complicated. For a solid middle-market company with dependable revenues and earnings, an investor normally will be satisfied with a 20 percent rate of return (that equates to a 5 multiple of cash flow, i.e., 1×20 percent = 5). Fast forward: let's assume the nonfinancial issues are troublesome to the extent that the appraiser determines that the risk factors have increased substantially. Based on the increased risks, the investor will want to receive a 30 percent rate of return, which affects the discount rate accordingly. (That equates to a 3.3 multiple of cash flow, i.e., 1×30 percent = 3.3.) The nonfinancial issues in a valuation are quantified and qualified, thus substantially affecting the final outcome of the valuation.

Corporate valuations are both a science and an art, some of which is objective and some of which is subjective. The financial issues of a valuation are considered the science while the nonfinancial issues are considered the art form. Obviously, the financial factors are extremely important, but the nonfinancial factors are equally important. In order for a corporate valuation to be comprehensive, the nonfinancial issues must be heavily weighed. You can never know too much about a business, but you can certainly know too little.

WHERE IS THE DIFFERENCE IN VALUE?

In a hypothetical case, but a totally possible situation, we have two different manufacturing companies. They are in the same industry, producing almost identical products, both operating in leased facilities with a nonunion workforce, and neither company has any bank debt ... but with significantly different valuations! How is this possible?

BASIC FINANCIALS

	COMPANY A	COMPANY B
Sales:	$10M	$10M
Compound Annual Growth Rate (CAGR):	10%	10%
Gross Profit:	$6M	$5M
SG&A:	$4M	$3M
EBITDA:	$2M	$2M
CAGR:	7%	7%
EBITDA Multiple:	6X	5X
Price:	$12M	$10M

PEEL BACK THE ONION

While the companies' financials are obviously extremely important in arriving at a valuation price for a possible acquisition, one must spend the time to dig deeper in evaluating the true worth of the company. The purpose of this analysis is to show how two seemingly similar manufacturers can be valued at a difference of 20 percent, when on the surface you might surmise that the two hypothetical companies might have near-equal enterprise values. Why the difference? While corporate valuations should be objective financially and operationally, you can't avoid a certain amount of subjective analysis, allowing for professional judgment based on experience. The following analysis on certain segments of the businesses is a determining factor in arriving at a price for Company A and Company B:

Balance Sheet

Company A: The book value of this C corporation is $4 million, mostly accumulation of retained earnings. The working capital ratio is a very healthy 5 to 1 supported by $2 million in cash. Most of the accounts receivables are current, with no credit problems, and they enjoy the benefit of sales principally to Fortune 500 companies. Inventory is also good and current, since the company relies extensively on contract manufacturers, thereby turning the inventory rapidly. The CFO uses very aggressive accounting procedures, expensing, not capitalizing, most capital expenditures, leasehold improvements, research and development, etc. The CFO also has generous reserves for accounts receivables, product recalls and warranties. There is a long-term triple-net lease on their modern plant with gradual lease increases for renewals based on the consumer index. There are no stock options outstanding, as bonuses are paid in cash, and there is no goodwill on the balance sheet. The financial statements are audited.

Company B: The book value of this subchapter S corporation is $2 million, or half that of its peer company, mostly because as an S corporation, it is customary to dividend-out most of the excess earnings. This company has constraints on its working capital and is at a 1 to 1 ratio with vendor invoices often running out ninety days. There are serious concerns about the validity for some of the accounts receivables and the usefulness for some of the inventory. The CFO has virtually no reserves for either of the previous two assets. All the capital expenditures have been capitalized. There is no lease renewal on the rather old plant facility. Most of the major machinery and equipment are leased and have substantial cancellation clauses. There are significant unexercised stock options outstanding and there is $1 million of goodwill listed on the balance sheet. The financial statements are not audited.

Income Statement

Company A: Its gross margins are 60 percent and invoices mostly to the end users and less to OEMs. Because of high gross margins, Company A has the flexibility to negotiate lower prices in order to win more OEM accounts, which would substantially increase revenues.

With $2 million in EBITDA, it is spending $1.5 million, or 15 percent of sales, on research and development. This high R&D budget indicates a greater probability of developing new products.

Company B: Its gross margins are 50 percent and it charges substantially lower prices for its products than Company A. And while it too has $2 million in EBITDA, it is only spending 5 percent of its sales on research and development. This choice hurts its chances at product innovation.

Products

Company A: It sells a branded product and does so directly to the end user. Its product line is broad and it uses new technology with some patents.

Company B: Working with a narrow product line, it uses old technology without the benefit of any patents. Also, its name is rather insignificant because it is sold to OEMs where it is incorporated into another product.

Sales and Marketing

Company A: With products sold nationally and internationally, it developed an extensive Web site which facilitated Internet sales, and registered more than 80 percent of its sales through that channel. It continually increased its market share in growing stable markets such as pharmaceuticals and the food industry, and had four territorial sales managers that covered all fifty states through the use of twenty-four sales representative firms—all of which had represented Company A for numerous years. Furthermore, it developed three marketing alliances with overseas companies to help them develop foreign sales.

Company A enjoyed a high degree of repeat business and none of their customers represented more than 10 percent of their total sales.

Company B: Choosing to only sell its products regionally, Company B still relied on orders via mail, fax, and telephone. These local and ancient strategies caused the company to struggle to sustain its market share in the textile and furniture industries which were not only flat, but cyclical. Company B's sales force was fragmented between a mixture of company principals and small sales representative firms that over the years had changed considerably. Therefore, the sales team had been unable to achieve similar success.

Management and Employees

Company A: Its management team ranged in age from thirty-five to fifty years old, and it had employment contracts with key people along with noncompete and confidentiality agreements. Company A created a culture of teamwork and employee empowerment, and instituted an employee training program which in part informed employees of the company's systems, procedures, and retirement plan.

Company B: The management team skewed significantly older, in the age range of fifty-five to seventy years old. It was also run by a CEO who was involved in all aspects of the business. Company B did not have any key employee agreements. And it had no key employee training programs in place.

Manufacturing

Company A: It used a plant that was fully computerized and tied into the sales and accounting departments. Their vendors were programmed into Just-In-Time (JIT) deliveries, and their plant shipped orders an average of ninety-eight hours after receiving them. They also averaged more than a 90 percent completion rate for their orders shipped. Company A was ISO9000 certified.

Company B: Its manufacturing operation had none of the above attributes.

Summary

These examples are obviously exaggerated to maximize the effect of the "operational" aspects of the business on the corporate valuation. But you simply can't effectively value companies based on the financials without significant consideration of the company's operations. In the process of articulating value, it is important to analyze the past, rationalize the present, and project the future.

What makes up value? Both tangibles and intangibles, but above all, it is understanding the company beyond just analyzing the financials. The real difference in value is best understood when we take the time to peel back the onion.

10 Mistakes in Valuation

1. Not verifying the quality of earnings. It is imperative that you understand the true earning power of the company. In a private company, it is not unusual for the owner to pay himself excess compensation. On the other hand, excess add-backs such as one-time events have to be scrutinized because all companies have some extraordinary expenses every year. Analytically, the appraiser of the business must separate the wheat from the chaff when it comes to establishing the true earnings of the company.

2. Not verifying the real value of the assets and liabilities of the balance sheet. The financial statements may be certified and accurate, but the real estate and machinery/equipment may be fully depreciated when in fact they are worth millions of dollars. On the other hand, there may be nontransferable leases on the real estate or onerous cancellation clauses for canceling undesirable leases on machines and equipment.

3. Not defining what earnings are being measured. Some people use EBIT, others use EBITDA. A multiple of six times EBIT can sometimes be equivalent to a five times EBITDA. Or maybe it is better to use EBITDA–CapX

(CapX stands for capital expenditures, which are above and beyond the amount allocated to normal depreciation). Furthermore, are the earnings a blend of the last three years, or last year, this year, and next year's projections? Or perhaps the earnings are the trailing twelve months regardless of the year-end. Are the earnings with or without add-backs and if so, what is the compensation for the incoming replacement CEO?

4. Not explaining why a certain multiple of earnings or why a particular discount rate is being used. The solution of multiples and discount rates can be objective based on comparables of other companies, subject to certain revisions. On the other hand, their selection of multiples and discount rates can be somewhat subjective, based on numerous factors such as company size, growth rate, industry, depth of management, proprietary business, etc.

5. Not defining what is really for sale. If you were buying a software company, find out where the value is. Does the sale include trademarks, patents, licenses, and contracts? Have the employees signed confidentiality and noncompete agreements? The definition of value for a software company is more difficult to define than a steel mill, for example.

6. Not considering the value detractors. Most companies, if not all, have some problems that detract from the business, such as: customer concentration, outdated machinery/ equipment, poor financial reporting, a messy plant, small market for product or service, price sensitive industry, technology threats, etc. Regardless of the magnitude of these deficiencies, the valuation must reflect their impact.

7. Not considering the effect of the current market. The external factors described by some as macroeconomics have a definite influence. For example, nowadays, middle-market manufacturers sell for four to six times EBIT, while in the years 1999 and 2000, the multiple would have been five to

seven times EBIT. In a company with a $2 million EBIT, the difference would be a $2 million valuation!

8. Not adhering to a process. Valuing a company is more than just reviewing the financials and coming up with a valuation. The process is threefold. Initially, analyze the financials. Secondly, interview the CEO, review the list of clients, observe the accounts receivable, learn about the market, note the number of locations, learn about the important aspects, etc. Thirdly, review the assumptions and adjustments with the CEO and then compare them to the industry ratios.

9. Not considering the intangibles. Some companies have an exceptional history—perhaps 100 years of doing business under a particular name. Other companies have recurring sales, such as magazine subscriptions, while others might only sell a product or service once to a customer in his or her lifetime.

10. Not considering favorable relationships. Some companies, such as a liquor store, may have the only available license in town. These favorable relationships would weigh heavily in the valuation.

CHAPTER 11

Use of Intermediaries

Executing an intelligent acquisition at a reasonable price is very difficult, even for the experts. For an individual buyer, successfully acquiring a middle-market company can be even more difficult, principally because of the individual buyer's lack of experience and the seller's perception that the individual buyer lacks sufficient capital. Frankly, individual buyers rarely are capable or willing to commit $1 million or more of their personal equity. However, far and away the biggest hurdle for the individual buyer is finding the deal in the first place.

Stephen Blum, former managing partner of KPMG Peat Marwick's corporate finance group in New York, states, "If you've decided to purchase a company, you face the question of whether and how to deal with intermediaries. Many buyers go it alone. Some mistrust intermediaries, some don't want to pay a transaction fee, and others assume that no intermediary would want to work with them . . . but deciding to do without intermediaries can be risky."

The intermediary can help you in numerous areas, such as ascertaining the criteria, assembling the information, determining the price, structuring the deal, and negotiating the transaction, but many buyers need intermediaries most of all to help them find the deal. Intermediaries are involved in about half of all deals.

WHAT TO LOOK FOR IN AN INTERMEDIARY

The basic difference for an intermediary buying a company, rather than selling one, is that he or she needs a more offensive mindset. The intermediary should be aggressive, imaginative, tenacious, and charming. Bear in mind that unlike real estate, most companies that are bought are originally not for sale. Therefore, you and your intermediary must be very proactive in approaching companies. Of course, there are many obstacles to overcome, such as the very simple one of just getting to talk to the target's owner. With barriers such as secretaries and voice mail, there is no assurance that you will be successful. There is even less assurance that the owner will be interested in talking about selling the company, much less meeting personally with you.

You must select an intermediary who represents buyers and is able to uncover *not-for-sale* companies whose owners will consider selling after all. The intermediary has to be skillful and experienced since there are a number of delicate letter-writing and telephone techniques that are critical for bringing buyer and seller together successfully. One of the critical issues to be aware of is how effectively your potential intermediary can package you to the seller. A good intermediary will also help you find a company with specific acquisition criteria that best matches your background.

A SUCCESS STORY

One example of a business buyer utilizing an intermediary to his advantage is Arnie Kovall, the former chief economist for Beatrice Foods. With the help of an intermediary, Kovall formed a company called Wellington Foods that specialized in buying snack food operations, initially in New England. Kovall brought together a board of directors that included the former chairman of Beatrice, a $13 billion conglomerate, and a well-known Harvard Business School professor. The only missing ingredient was sufficient capital, so Kovall went to the Boston office of a well-known brokerage firm. Kovall's concept was to replicate the early years of rapid growth at Beatrice Foods by acquiring relatively small regional food companies. The brokerage firm was anxious to back him.

Kovall had established a company with distinguished directors, focused on a specific industry that matched his background, involved an intermediary, and lined up a financial backer. Kovall's intermediary then telephoned numerous food companies and said, "I represent a group of former Beatrice executives who would like to talk to you about your company."

Invariably, Kovall was able to visit these companies because he had a believable story, he had credibility in the marketplace, and he knew the industry. And his intermediary packaged this story in such a way that even reluctant sellers were willing to consider selling.

HOW TO BEST USE AN INTERMEDIARY

You have three choices when it comes to intermediaries:

1. Work with them only if they represent the seller. However, most intermediaries do not have a large inventory of selling companies from which to choose. And in the case of investment bankers, they tend not to show selling companies to individual buyers.
2. Work with them on a nonexclusive basis, but sign an agreement stating that if a deal closes with his help, you are obligated to pay the intermediary an accomplishment fee. Most intermediaries have a standard agreement to this effect, but you can have a transaction lawyer draft your own agreement for the intermediary to sign. The process goes a lot faster if you use your own agreement.
3. Work with an intermediary on an exclusive basis. This arrangement usually is reinforced with a monetary retainer in order to solidify the relationship and motivate the intermediary on a daily basis. It is important to have a reasonable cancellation clause so that you are not locked in if you are not satisfied.

THE IMPORTANCE OF RETAINERS

Perhaps no other item causes as much consternation among intermediaries and their potential clients as retainers. Speaking as an intermediary myself, if a potential client cannot afford to pay a retainer, he or she, therefore, cannot afford to buy a business.

A retainer is a fee paid to a professional adviser for advice or services rendered. Commonly, retainers are paid monthly over the length of the assignment. Retainers could be for a period of six months to a year and could range from $3,000 to $10,000 per month. Additionally, retainers might be entirely or partly deducted from the Lehman-scale accomplishment fee. Another variation is a one-time retainer of approximately $25,000 to $30,000 paid all at once at the beginning of the assignment.

There are five basic reasons why retainers are usually required by intermediaries:

1. Intermediaries are not brokers. Unlike real estate, more time is often required to understand the business, to identify sellers, to maintain confidentiality, and to address the complexities regarding structuring, taxes, financing, security laws, etc.
2. Commitment. With many business buyers, it is necessary to separate the men from the boys—i.e., those who are very serious from those who are not. Many intermediaries believe that being selective is critical to their success. A retainer is a way to cement the relationship by committing the intermediary and the client so that the two parties are accountable to each other. A "best efforts" arrangement, where no retainer is paid, often results in failure even though a large accomplishment fee is involved.
3. Risk/reward ratio. Many intermediaries deduct part or all of the retainer from the accomplishment fee. You should select an intermediary in whom you have confidence that he or she will be able to complete the deal. Unlike Wall Street investment bankers, middle-market intermediaries do not make millions. In a $6 million transaction, the sliding scale of a modified Lehman formula works out to a 4 percent commission, which is small compared to

commercial real estate, where the commission is often 10 percent. For many clients, paying an upfront retainer with a reasonable accomplishment fee leads to better results than no retainer and a much higher accomplishment fee.

4. Incentive. It is important that the intermediary's confidence in the buyer's commitment be constantly reinforced. If an intermediary receives periodic monetary payments from one client and not from another, he or she will most likely spend more effort on the former. In many situations, the deal falls apart several times before closing. If you are not paying the intermediary, it appears that you may not be really interested or may not give the intermediary the attention and resources needed to complete the assignment.

5. Useful information. Executive search firms customarily charge their client one-third of one year's total compensation in three incremental payments during the search process, at the beginning, middle, and completion. The search firm's role is in many ways similar to the M&A intermediary's role in an acquisition search. In both instances, considerable consultation and input regarding the criteria, process, and evaluation techniques are most helpful to the client and should be compensated for accordingly.

WHAT TO EXPECT FROM THE INTERMEDIARY

There are a number of things you can expect your intermediary to do. They:

- Provide viable financing sources for the deal.
- Act as a mature sounding board and second opinion.
- Help negotiate the deal.
- Do not pressure you into closing.
- Introduce you to companies that are not being heavily shopped, and have not been on the block for some time.

- Screen out companies that do not meet your criteria.
- Provide an unbiased opinion on the deal—price, terms, etc.
- Offer alternatives as to how the deal can be structured.
- Give you a chance to respond to the potential acquisition before shopping it elsewhere.
- Leverage off his or her reputation.
- Act as buffer between you and the seller.
- Get the deal back on track if it is derailed.
- Know the seller's pricing expectations.
- Be reasonably sure that the target company is really a seller.
- Follow up on all pending matters.
- Focus on your project rather than juggling one or two other major projects.
- Have no conflict of interest or personal relationship with the seller.

WHAT TO EXPECT FROM THE INTERMEDIARY WHO REPRESENTS THE SELLER

You will also run into intermediaries on the other side of the table. Sellers also employ them to help facilitate the sale of their companies. You will have contact with the sellers' intermediaries, and within the months, or years, of sales negotiations, you can expect them to:

- Develop an in-depth relationship with you.
- Indicate commitment by the seller.
- Give the seller's range of valuations early on.
- Be aware of your chemistry with the seller and address any differences should they come up.
- Understand the issues so that he or she can help bridge the gap between the buyer and the seller.
- Present the company, the industry, the management, and the financials in absolute candor, so that any skeletons in the closet are flushed out. All representations should be absolutely true.

SELECTING AN INTERMEDIARY

The selection of the intermediary is critical in the success or failure of an impending transaction. The following ten points represents a due diligence checklist for your search.

1. Firm: General reputation, number of years in existence, number of principals and support staff, and other outward signs of competence are key. Of particular importance is the range of deal size the firm completes, because a small transaction for a large investment banker might not get their attention, and a big transaction for a small investment banker could be beyond their expertise.

2. The lead player: Often the intermediary will state that the project is a team effort. However, there inevitably is a lead person who understands the bulk of the project. Of the ten reasons in selecting an intermediary, this reason is probably the most important. It is no different than selecting an attorney at a law firm, for example. However, beware of an intermediary who customarily represents a selling company when you want to acquire a company. A deal is a deal, right? Wrong! Some intermediaries are better at selling companies than acquiring them and vice versa. The techniques on the buy side often take a more aggressive approach. The difference between buying and selling can be compared to offense and defense in football. Furthermore, a key question to ask the lead individual intermediary is how much of his or her time will be spent on your particular account, e.g., 10 percent, 30 percent, etc.

3. References: Do not be satisfied with just one or two references—almost everybody has at least a few good ones. Six to ten references on the individual would not be too many. Beware of references that may be for a transaction four or five years ago. Also, ask for names of clients who did not successfully close a deal so you can get their opinion as well. Ask questions about the individual's short-

comings as well as his or her strengths. Does the person communicate both often and well, does the person follow up and follow through, and does the person truly represent your best interest or is he or she so anxious to do a deal that in essence he or she represents the transaction?

4. Tombstones: The outward mark of a firm's success is the listing of tombstones. In the M&A business, tombstones is a jargon phrase for a drawn box with a simple listing of the buyers and sellers names involved in a transaction such as "XYZ Company of Boston sold to ABC Company of Chicago." Ideally, these tombstones will be listed both by the year and the type of business. If the firm can only produce a few tombstones for the past few years, beware that the best dealmakers may have left the firm. Which is more impressive, a firm of five that completed ten transactions last year or a firm of twenty that completed twenty transactions? Probably the former, which did more deals per person than the latter. However, the larger firm may utilize half their people for valuations, fairness opinions, and consulting assignments, all of which may not have been represented by tombstones.

5. Industry experience: Try to find a firm that specializes in your target industry. This industry knowledge includes the extensive database of likely buyers and sellers, the understanding of industry valuations, and the key relationships that have been sustained over the years. Notwithstanding these advantages, it could be a conflict of interest for the same firm to represent several buyers in the same industry unless their clients' criteria is substantially different.

6. Pricing, packaging, and processing: Whether you are a buyer or seller, you should review (on a no-name basis) recent transactions to assess the pricing the intermediary is able to achieve. Additionally, he or she should be prepared to show you how they will package your story in a most convincing way. You should also ask about the

process the intermediary uses to contact the numerous target companies. Ask him or her to show you examples of how the target referrals are reported, logged, and contacted.

7. Contract: Most firms have a number of elements of the engagement agreement that are easily comparable to others in the industry, e.g., the amount of the retainer, whether it is deductible, the amount of the accomplishment fee, the minimum compensation, exclusivity, exclusions if any, and cancellation period. Intermediaries' terms and conditions vary and their willingness to compromise also varies. Beware of those who are too compromising on their compensation, because it might be reflective of their services. On the other hand, higher compensation does not necessarily guarantee superior performance.

8. Intermediary style: Intermediaries must monitor a transaction's progress and be prepared to intervene when necessary. Clients often value those who allow them to meet independently with the other party. The intermediary must be able to sustain the momentum, put the deal back on the tracks when derailed, never give up, and have grace under fire.

9. Location: In most cases, you'll want an intermediary located near you for the obvious necessary interaction; however, the advantage of selecting an industry specialist can offset the advantage of being close to him or her.

10. Chemistry: All the other reasons for selecting an intermediary are objective. But you also need to trust your gut feeling as well. Just because it's a subjective feeling doesn't mean it's not an important part of the decision-making process.

The chances of completing a successful transaction are obviously increased by selecting the best intermediary for your particular situation, so take your time.

TEN QUALITIES BUYERS SHOULD HAVE WITH INTERMEDIARIES

The relationship between the intermediary and the client is obviously a two-way street. The following are observations that can improve your relationship with intermediaries:

1. Pay retainers. We've already talked a lot about retainers, and that's because they're important. Almost all executive search firms require a retainer partly because of the scope of their assignment. Very few of the most successful intermediaries do an acquisition search out of pure speculation—they wait until they have a buyer in mind. Just as the buyer wants a hardworking, committed intermediary, the intermediary wants the client to demonstrate the same commitment.

2. Be patient. Acquisitions are not easy. The process can take a year—in some cases, longer. If you rush the process, you may make some hasty decisions that you later regret. Additionally, many deals falter once or twice before closing, and it takes time to get back on track. (Although you should be patient with the process, an intermediary's key responsibility is to maintain the momentum once it is apparent that there is serious interest by both parties.)

3. Give direction. The buyer often does not provide the precise focus to the intermediary, feeling that it is up to the intermediary to decide. A good intermediary should be helpful in recommending certain strategic directions, but the ultimate leadership must come from the buyer. It is very important that both the buyer and the intermediary spend sufficient time up front to decide what types of target companies they should pursue.

4. Make sure financing is in place. Some buyers have high aspirations for a successful acquisition, only to realize that they haven't secured the cooperation from their board of directors and/or major stockholders. Is the necessary financing for such an acquisition really available? One of my former clients was an executive from a Fortune 500 company who

assembled an impressive board of directors. Both the buyer and I thought he had sufficient equity to close the deal, but we were wrong. He was missing one of the most important components of a transaction—equity.

5. Provide buyer's documentation. An intermediary needs to present the client as a reputable, credible, and financially capable buyer. Writing a short buyer's business plan that can be presented to the targeted potential sellers demonstrates professionalism, thoroughness, and commitment to the acquisition process.

6. Know your competitive advantage. You need to be able to identify your strengths and be forthcoming about them to your intermediary, so he or she can use them to your advantage. The intermediary needs to know your strong suit, just as a bridge player must know his or her partner's strength. The intermediary is your advocate and needs to promote you as best as possible.

7. Define the intermediary's role. There is no right or wrong way for an intermediary and a buyer to work with each other, but you should establish a crystal-clear understanding of what you expect from the intermediary. For example, do you want the intermediary to communicate often or seldom? Will you treat the acquisition search as a priority and take all telephone calls, even if they interrupt something else? Do you want the intermediary to make the first visit to the target company alone? Do you want the intermediary to do the negotiating and/or some of the due diligence?

8. Listen to the seller. One of the keys to understanding the workings of the target company is to ask the right questions and to listen very carefully. If you are talking most of the time, you cannot do much listening. Therefore, listen to the seller—what the seller is saying, what he or she is not saying, and what is in between the lines.

9. Recognize and accept the need for hand-holding with the seller. A good intermediary is aware that many sellers

have an emotional attachment to their business, and so listen to the intermediary when he or she advises the buyer to be sensitive to the seller's concerns about employees, customers, and the business in general.

10. Display quickness. In conjunction with the intermediary, you often have to react quickly to a situation to sustain the momentum, or to prevent the buyer from going to the auction process, or to be a step or two ahead of other potential buyers. Quickness means that you might have to drop everything and jump on a plane the next day to visit the target company.

THE QUESTION OF FEES FOR INTERMEDIARIES

While the Lehman formula historically was the standard compensation methodology for the middle-market M&A business, there are now numerous variations on it and interpretations of its use. In today's market, the standard Lehman formula has been replaced by a variation known as the modified Lehman formula.

The intermediary's commission from the Lehman formula is a sliding scale of 5-4-3-2-1 percent—5 percent of the first $1 million, 4 percent of the second $1 million, etc. Either you or the seller pays the commission, depending on which intermediary initiated the transaction (the one representing you—the buyer—or the one representing the seller). In some cases, both you and the seller are represented by intermediaries, which can result in a double commission. While some people might feel that two commissions are exorbitant, buyers and sellers should primarily focus on the big picture, i.e., the viability of the deal, the overall price, the terms, and the credibility of the other party. If both intermediaries contribute significant value to the transaction, then two commissions may not be onerous. Alternatively, the two intermediaries may agree to split their fees, either on a 50/50 basis or on a 60/40 basis. In the latter case, 60 percent would be paid to the intermediary who has the fee agreement under contract with the principal. Splitting fees, however, can be a disincentive to intermediaries.

Modified Lehman Formulas

In talking with an intermediary, clarify whether he or she uses the "standard" or "modified" Lehman formula. The two most common variations are the double Lehman, 10-8-6-4-2 percent, and the stuttering Lehman, 5-5-4-4-3-3 percent. Based on a $5 million transaction, the following example shows the difference.

TYPE	COMMISSION	OVERALL PERCENTAGE
Double	$300,000	6.0
Stuttering	$210,000	4.2
Standard	$150,000	3.0

Perhaps the most important aspect of the fee agreement is the *minimum fee*. Simply stated, regardless of the purchase price, the minimum fee might be $150,000, $200,000, $250,000, etc., which discourages buyers from making really small transactions. From the intermediary's perspective, it takes just as long to do a small deal as a large one.

Example #1

The commission is based on the value of the transaction. Let's assume that a target company is losing money, has a negative net worth, and has $2 million of interest-bearing debt. You negotiate to acquire the company for $1 plus the assumption of the debt. Your fee agreement with the intermediary states that the intermediary will receive a minimum commission, no matter what the sale price, of $150,000. What does the intermediary receive as an accomplishment fee? The answer is whatever the minimum fee, not a percentage of the $1 purchase price. Assumption of interest-bearing debt, usually bank debt, is part of the company's capitalization. In this case, you acquire the company's "stock," which includes all the assets and all the liabilities.

Example #2

Let's look at a second example. This is an "asset" transaction in which you acquire certain assets and assume some liabilities of the following balance sheet.

Cash	$10,000	Accounts payable	$100,000
Accounts receivable	$100,000	Notes payable	$200,000
Inventory	$50,000	Long-term debt	$300,000
Machinery and equipment	$240,000	Book value	$400,000
Real estate	$600,000		
Total Assets	$1,000,000	Total Liabilities/Equity	$1,000,000

Let's assume that you buy the company for $300,000 and you take over the receivables, the inventory, and the payables. The seller keeps all the other items and leases you machinery and equipment and rents you the real estate. What is the intermediary's fee? Would it be the $150,000 minimum as stated in the intermediary's fee agreement?

The answer is no, not if the intermediary has properly included a commission, like a broker, for equipment leased and/or real estate rented instead of acquired. If the seller rented the real estate for five years at $50,000 per year, the commission would be based on the $250,000 value, normally paid at closing and not spaced out over the entire period. Commercial realtors utilize the following commission schedule:

RATE	YEAR
5.0%	1
4.0%	2
4.0%	3
3.0%	4
2.0%	5
1.5%	Over 5 years

If the corporate M&A intermediary does not have a real estate license, he or she should work with a colleague who does.

Example #3

In a third example of fee calculation, the buyer has identified the target company and is ready to make an offer. However, the buyer lacks the knowledge, expertise, and confidence to value, negotiate, and close the deal. Therefore, the buyer hires an experienced intermediary and pays a nonrefundable retainer (let's say $20,000 plus a 1 percent commission on the transaction price as an incentive). If the target company is acquired for $5 million, then the intermediary would receive another $50,000. The intermediary could be well worth this expense!

Ancillary Conditions of Fee Agreements to Negotiate

- If there is a retainer, whether it is deducted in part or entirely from the accomplishment fee
- Whether the agreement is cancelable after thirty days' notice, or perhaps after a three-month grace period
- Whether the agreement is an exclusive with the intermediary
- Whether there is a minimum commission to the intermediary (such as $150,000) and a possible cap on the upside (such as $500,000)
- Whether there is a time period (such as two or three years) in which the intermediary's contract will be honored.
- If the buyer, as an individual, takes a job with the target company, whether the intermediary will be compensated as if it were an executive search firm, i.e., one-third of the annual salary

Value Received

The real question is not whether the intermediary receives a 3.0 percent commission, a 4.2 percent commission, or even a 6.0 percent commission for a $5 million transaction. What matters is the service you receive. Will the intermediary spend a considerable amount of time on your behalf, identifying target companies, analyzing these opportunities, valuing and structuring the deal, and negotiating the closing? Is the intermediary capable of getting a deal back on track if it is derailed? If so, is he worth his compensation?

CHAPTER 12

Your Acquisition Team

Acquiring companies in the middle market can be very competitive. While the selling company may be too small to attract an auction sale, invariably the owner of the selling company talks to several potential buyers. Often the most experienced and best prepared buyers succeed in acquiring the target companies.

Why are some buyers vastly more successful than others? Do these buyers pay significantly more than their counterparts? Not necessarily. However, many successful buyers, whether they be manufacturers, buyout groups, or individuals, often have preassembled an acquisition team. The team members are usually consultants, advisers, and other professionals, who usually work outside the buyer's entity and occasionally have a vested interest in the project. Some team members may receive reduced compensation until the transaction closes or until the buyer becomes a regular client of their firm. Successful acquisition teams have a high degree of commitment. They could have the following members:

- Intermediary
- Transaction lawyer
- Transaction CPA
- Financiers
- Corporate valuation expert
- Machinery and equipment appraiser
- Real estate appraiser
- Due diligence consultant(s)

BUSINESS INTERMEDIARY

We've already talked about the importance of an experienced intermediary, who will often serve as your team quarterback through the entire process and will involve other team members as required and necessary.

Joseph E. Myss, former president of the Institute of Merger & Acquisition Professionals and an intermediary from Wayzata, Minnesota, says, "You should consider a team of qualified professional advisers from the beginning. The team provides experience and insight in completing a sale. Your team members are all-important, but not all members are required all the time. Team involvement must be coordinated. A team quarterback promotes efficiency and enhances communication. Transaction attorney Dave Broadwin of the Boston law firm of Foley, Hoag & Eliot, has the following suggestions for those seeking a transaction lawyer:

- Always seek recommendations from reliable sources about attorneys who specialize in mergers and acquisitions. It is extremely important that the particular lawyer have extensive experience in this field of expertise.
- Your attorney should not just focus on the deal, but should be cognizant of your personal affairs, your tolerance for risk, and your financial limitations. By being sensitive to these issues, your lawyer will know how stringently to negotiate the representation and warranties or whether it is advisable for you to personally guarantee the notes to the seller.

If the debt load in the acquisition is heavy for you as an individual, then your attorney should help you negotiate alternative structures to mitigate that problem. For example, if there is real estate included in the conveyance of assets, then there might be a possibility of renting instead of buying the real estate. Also, the seller might be willing to lease the machinery and equipment instead of including these assets in the purchase price.

- Evaluate the size and complexity of the transaction to determine whether you need the extra services and resources of a large law firm. If the target company has some lingering unresolved issues such as environmental problems, litigation, the employee benefits plan, foreign subsidiaries, etc., a small law firm may not be equipped to handle these matters successfully. Such shortcomings could ultimately cause a breakdown of communications and result in a failure to close the transaction, or the purchase and sale agreement could be unfavorably written from your standpoint. Generally speaking, the larger, well-known, long-established law firms charge more for their services. For larger transactions, sometimes it is psychologically better to use a law firm with a better image.
- Your attorney should give you up front his hourly rate and an estimate for the entire transaction. Ask to receive monthly invoices from the law firm and let the attorney know that keeping legal fees within the estimate is important. Otherwise, you may end up with a legal bill twice what you originally expected.
- Obviously, the selection of your attorney will be in large part a result of the personal chemistry between the two of you.

Another transaction attorney, Dennis White of McDermott, Will & Emory in Boston, emphasized the importance of having extensive knowledge about the number and generic nature of the law firm's transactions. For example, if you want to buy a software company, there are so many intricacies in that particular industry that you probably would be best served by a firm that specializes in that business. The attorney should be practical and pragmatic and certainly a dealmaker who will not be adversarial with the other side.

Lou Katz of Boston's Ruberto, Israel & Weiner urges buyers to be sure that they choose a firm with easy access to such standard items as letters of intent, purchase and sale agreements (asset or stock), noncompete agreements, employment contracts, and other important documents. You certainly do not want your attorney to reinvent the wheel by writing an original document for each legal process in the transaction—the firm should have boilerplates in place already. Katz also emphasizes the ability of some excellent transaction lawyers to identify additional sources of debt or equity to help finance the acquisition.

TRANSACTION CPA

In selecting a transaction CPA, you might start by getting recommendations from your banker or lawyer or your business peers.The size of the firm may be indicative of the attention you will receive and/or the range of services provided. For example, if you select one of the "Big Four" accounting firms (PricewaterhouseCoopers, Deloitte Touche, Ernst & Young, or KPMG), your account might be relegated to junior members of the firm. On the other hand, if you select a small accounting firm, its resources may be limited and its reputation may not be established. Typically, you will retain the firm you use for the acquisition after the transaction is completed. During the acquisition process, the accounting firm should provide the following services:

- Analyze the target company's financial statements
- Value the company
- Conduct due diligence
- Structure the deal, with attention to the tax consequences
- Review the letter of intent
- Audit the seller's financial status to verify such items as accrued employee vacation time, valuation of inventory, and that the company is current on all federal, state, and local taxes, including payroll taxes

The firm's fees are important, but not as important as the quality of work or services rendered. Obviously, you have to use your best judgment in this regard. In most cases, you will be charged a blended rate of anywhere between $200 and $400 per hour, depending on whether the person doing the work is a junior accountant or a senior project manager. If you are anticipating a stock purchase rather than an asset purchase, you should expect to pay more in accounting, legal, and overall due diligence fees. For example, an audit could cost from $30,000 to $60,000. These higher fees are usually acceptable because the purchase price of a stock deal is normally less expensive. The reason is that an asset sale for a C corporation is taxed twice, once to the corporation and again when the assets are distributed to the stockholders.

Advice on Choosing the Correct Firm

Accounting firms often find themselves with a reputation for having numerous clients in a particular industry. Each industry has idiosyncrasies and knowledge that are only gained from experience. So if you are buying a software or biotech company, do not expect that all accounting firms will be up to speed on these industries. If you are acquiring a publishing company, will your accountant know how to place a value on its "backlist"? Or if you are acquiring a distributor that services copiers, does your accountant have enough experience in that industry to book the unexpired service contracts as a liability? Recommendations from the chief financial officers in a certain industry are helpful.

Services Offered

Not all firms offer their clients a broad range of services. Let us assume you want to install an inventory control system adhering to the "just-in-time" (JIT) method. Can your accounting firm provide this service? If you are a small retail chain, you should have a point-of-sale cash register inventory system. Will your accounting firm be able to orchestrate the implementation of this computerized system? If you intend to take your new acquisition public in five years, you should probably start with a "Big Four" firm, which has the necessary experience and credibility in that regard. Does your firm have the capacity and inclination to achieve tax savings not only for your company but for you as the CEO and owner of that company?

Response Time

It is quite possible to have the partner of the firm who is soliciting your account be very responsive, but to have the account manager who is assigned to your company be very slow. To properly evaluate the firm's response time, you need to have an understanding of its culture, whether the account manager is overly committed, and how important your business is to the firm.

Reputation

Almost every company has three or four good references, so beware of the names that are volunteered by the firm. There are other ways to check a firm's reputation. Your banker would be a good place to start. Another way is to review the manufacturer's directory for the particular state in which the company is located. Most, but not all, directories list the companies' accounting firms. If you do receive references, especially from clients in the same or similar industry, also ask for names of a few of the firm's former clients.

Chemistry

As important as this ingredient is in the selection process, chemistry is the only subjective one. You must rely on your intuition to confirm your positive reactions or to red flag your concerns. Are the principals of the accounting firm overinflating their capabilities and interest in helping your company? After you have done your own due diligence on the firm, it boils down to whether you personally like the people in the firm and, of course, whether you implicitly trust them.

Direction of the Firm

Service companies like accounting firms have their problems, just like other businesses. Hopefully, you will select a firm that does not have internal problems of its own, with constant turnover or layoffs. The large accounting firm Laventhol & Horwath went out of business some years ago. There were two midsize firms in the Boston area that merged and then a year later split apart again. Is there a positive corporate culture in the firm of your choice? Are the senior partners in accord on how to operate and grow their business? Is there a succession plan in place for the junior partners or is there a chance the firm will lose its corporate leadership when the senior partners retire? In any event, the internal viability of the firm is an important consideration.

Relationships

Above and beyond the logistical ways in which an accounting firm helps its clients, a final factor in your consideration should be whether the firm has strong influential relationships with third parties. For example, would the accounting firm's reputation greatly enhance your ability to obtain your bank loan? If you need to raise equity for your company, does the firm have sources with which to connect you? And if you plan to acquire other companies, certain accounting firms can be more helpful than others in introducing you to the right situations.

FINANCIERS

Many individuals do not line up their financial sources before identifying their target acquisition. This is a big mistake.

Your banker can be the heartbeat of the business. Selecting the right banker can be crucial not only to providing the acquisition financing but to the future success of the company. Receive recommendations from your business peers, your lawyer, and/or your accountant. Not only do your advisers have specific knowledge of the individual loan officers, but they should be more comfortable in working on your behalf with a banker they already know.

Just as you will be analyzing various loan officers and their banks, they will be analyzing you. In fact, according to most bankers, the borrower's character accounts for half of the criteria of analyzing a loan.

It will take the banker some time to evaluate you as well. One way for each of you to get to know the other is to show the banker a few potential acquisitions to determine how he or she might finance the deal. Naturally, until you have a letter of intent, the banker will not conduct any due diligence on the target company.

Select the Correct Bank

If you are involved in a transaction requiring several millions of dollars of debt financing, you may also need to know asset-based lenders, mezzanine lenders, and bridge lenders. When a deal is hot, you have to work very quickly to keep the momentum going. Furthermore, you may be competing on the same deal with another party that already has financing in place. In addition to debt financing, you may need more equity to do the deal, in which case there are individuals and institutions that will take minority positions.

Some banks have a reputation for specializing in certain industries, such as Silicon Valley Bank in technology. Small banks have limitations on the size of individual loans, and large banks may not be interested in small loans. Take the time to match the characteristics of your loan with the most appropriate bank and banker.

While you may have the ability to obtain a loan when necessary, most borrowers are unprepared for loan negotiations. Of course, before you sign the loan documents, you should have your legal counsel not only review these papers, but perhaps assist you in the negotiations. Again, this is an example of your acquisition group working as a team.

CORPORATE VALUATION EXPERT

Although your intermediary and accountant should be well versed in valuing target companies, valuations can be extremely complex and difficult nonetheless. Before I spent several millions of dollars purchasing a company, I would certainly want a second or third opinion, especially from an expert in that field. There are so many advantageous ways to structure a transaction that it is essential that you know your alternatives.

Your corporate appraiser should have the capability to help you in the negotiating process. Appraisers can charge you by the hour, and if they do not have to submit bulletproof testimony in court, they can spend a lot less time in preparing their conclusions. Appraisers can be enormously helpful, especially if they are willing to be on call.

MACHINERY AND EQUIPMENT APPRAISERS AND REAL ESTATE APPRAISERS

After the letter of intent and during the bank negotiations, you will need appraisals to help verify the purchase price and to secure the bank note. Having these experts on tap will help you round out your acquisition team.

DUE DILIGENCE CONSULTANTS

Many acquisitions fail principally because due diligence was inept. The majority of the work takes place after the letter of intent is signed. This consultant provides hard-to-get details on target companies, usually prior to the letter of intent stage. The results of this firm's findings are used by its clients in a variety of ways:

- To negotiate from a more favorable position
- To screen possible acquisition targets more effectively
- To verify suspicions
- To obtain unbiased perceptions and impressions about the target company and its managers

The due diligence after the letter of intent is to determine whether you are going forward with the deal. You want to be sure that you will be receiving the assets you expect and that there will not be any unexpected liabilities postacquisition. Your accounting firm should be able to handle most, if not all, of your due diligence post–letter of intent.

CONCLUSION

As Joseph Myss states: "The purchase of a business is a time-consuming and very detailed process. In order to maximize your efforts, it requires an experienced professional team from several disciplines resolving a variety of transaction-related issues."

CHAPTER 13

Finding the Deal

There are six distinct steps in buying a business:

1. Assess your strategy.
2. Find the right company.
3. Price the business.
4. Structure the transaction.
5. Finance the purchase.
6. Close the deal.

Unless you are lucky, finding the right company to buy is by far the most difficult of the six steps. Most individual buyers who spend all available time seeking a middle-market business to buy will take six months to two years to complete a deal. By comparison, most well-organized corporate buyers take three to six months to find an acquisition and three to six months to close the deal, or a year on the outside. I've found that a less experienced and less qualified individual will generally take twice as long as a corporate buyer to purchase a business. However, there are certain areas to focus on that will make your business buying easier.

INTENSITY

In the Harvard Business School case study 9-385-330 copyrighted in 1985, "Buying an Existing Business: The Search Process," the authors make the distinction between casual and serious search.

A serious and realistic search will significantly increase the probability of identifying and negotiating opportunities of interest to you. Therefore, it is imperative to evaluate your motives, expectations, and risk profile. This self-assessment will probably place you in one of three broad search categories: serious and realistic; casual and realistic; and unrealistic.

The serious and realistic search involves:

- *High level of commitment to the search*
- *Expectations consistent with the degree of effort*
- *Willingness to:*

  - *Risk at least some personal wealth/security*
  - *Deeply research the target industry*
  - *Be patient and wait for the right opportunity*
  - *Move quickly and decisively as needed*
  - *Pursue the search full-time if needed*

The casual and realistic search involves:

- *Expectations consistent with degree of effort, but*
- *Not a high level of commitment to the search*
- *Less willingness to move quickly or decisively on opportunities*
- *No specified time horizon for search*
- *Not being overly hungry to control one's own firm*

The unrealistic search involves:

- *Objectives inconsistent with level of commitment*
- *Waiting for a great deal to fall in place*
- *Looking for bargains and shortcuts*

While there is nothing wrong with being a casual shopper (many have found excellent deals), the number and quality of the deals available often reflect the quality and intensity of the search. For example, almost everyone you meet in your search will size you up at your initial encounter, because intermediaries and sellers are usually reluctant to invest time unless they feel there is a reasonable chance you will follow through with your plans. Thus, the better you have assessed yourself, the easier it will be to convince others of the realism of your intentions and get them to work productively for or with you.

WORK TOOLS

In an article by the former Franklin Wyman, chairman of O'Conor, Wright Wyman, Inc. a Boston intermediary, he cited the following:

Detailed acquisition criteria against which you will screen acquisition possibilities.

Knowledge of the sources of business information, such as state manufacturing and service directories, trade publications, trade show listings, chamber of commerce membership directories, the Dun & Bradstreet Million Dollar Directory, Wards Business Directory, and the Corporate Technology Directory, to name just a few.

Contribution to your search efforts by your banker, lawyer, and accountant.

A professional adviser such as an intermediary who will assist in the search process as well as act in an advisory role in valuation, structuring, and negotiation.

A search technique that will disqualify sellers with unreasonable asking prices or owners looking for a free valuation of their company.

Negotiating skills to convince hesitant sellers that they should sell to you.

Creativity to structure the transaction in order to obtain the greatest tax advantage to the seller and to minimize the drain on your personal resources. Professional help is usually necessary in this case.

If you add a persistent attitude to the above seven work tools, you should have a winning combination.

TURNING OVER STONES

In today's fast-moving mergers and acquisitions market, good middle-market manufacturing companies that are officially for sale will probably be presented first to synergistic buyers and established private equity groups. Historically, synergistic buyers who are interested in entering into a particular line of business are usually willing to pay more than competitors. Private equity groups, with their vast sources of capital, will frequently pay up as well. Therefore, individual buyers are initially not apt to get a chance at buying these good middle-market manufacturers.

If you do get a chance to make an offer on such a company, presumably after the business was shown to synergistic buyers and private equity groups, you have to ask yourself why those groups passed. Is the business overpriced? Are there inherent problems with the business?

By now, you have probably begun to realize how difficult it is to buy a good middle-market company. Luckily, you can improve your chances by positioning yourself differently from your competition. Your competition includes both corporate buyers and other individual buyers. The market for buying and selling businesses is not efficient like the real estate market, where properties are listed, advertised, and priced on full knowledge of previous comparable sales. Information is difficult to obtain, there are few listings, prices of private sales are not published, etc.

What can you do about that inefficient market? Turn over stones—seek companies that are not officially for sale. This category has the greatest potential for individual buyers.

First, when you uncover these gems, there is a good chance that you will not be competing with other buyers.

Second, if you are lucky enough to approach the buyer at the right time (perhaps when he or she is burned out and ready to sell), you just might have the right chemistry and offer enough money to do the deal.

Third, you have an excellent chance to arouse the owner's interest if you have a respectable background in a similar industry. A former CEO of Ginn & Company, a $75 million textbook division of Xerox, had no problem visiting smaller regional publishers and/or specialty printers because his reputation preceded him.

CONSULTING LEADS TO PROSPECTIVE SELLERS

Numerous corporate refugees from the executive level of Fortune 1000 companies become consultants for relatively small firms. Many who do this really want to own their own company.

What better way is there for a prospective business buyer to see deal flow than to work for a mergers and acquisitions firm? Ethically, the buyer needs to be clear about his intentions up front. If he does buy a company through this exposure, he or she will pay a commission to the firm almost as if he or she were a regular client.

In Chapter 27, "Case Studies of Buyers," you'll find a story about John Ela, who started his own consulting practice while searching for his own business to acquire. This strategy ultimately proved successful.

The Johnny Appleseed Approach

Johnny Appleseed, a pioneer who was a legendary figure in American history, spread apple seeds from Massachusetts to Ohio by freely casting them from side to side as he walked.

The Johnny Appleseed approach describes an individual buyer who sets out to buy a business, equipping himself with business cards, a resume, and a criteria sheet. Initially, he has lots of energy. He visits lawyers, bankers, accountants, brokers, intermediaries, investment bankers, and friends. He attends breakfasts and luncheons at the Association for Corporate Growth, the Planning Forum, venture groups, the Turnaround Management Association, etc. He writes letters to friends, companies, and all his contacts—then waits for a response.

If he is lucky, he will receive some positive responses after six months of effort, particularly if he diligently follows up with all his contacts. My experience, however, is that this approach generally does not work. It is not focused, it is not targeted, and it is too broad. Occasionally the Johnny Appleseed approach is successful, but generally it is considered unprofessional and ineffective.

OPPORTUNITIES THROUGH NETWORKING

Using networking might actually land you a target company to buy, but at the very least it will also get the word out that you are seeking a business to buy. For you to succeed in networking, you should be ready to reciprocate someone's assistance. If the flow of helpful information is not give and take, chances are that such a relationship will fade away.

I once read that when Ben Franklin wanted to have a friendship with someone, he first loaned that person a book. He gave a favor first so that he could ask for one when the occasion arose. If you play the networking game seriously, there are some unwritten rules to follow, one of which is that eventually the chips will be called. In other words, if you are a recipient of some business, you are under moral obligation to some day respond in kind. Don't seek businesses by networking unless you can return the favor someday. Successful networking is a long-term endeavor. The more you give, the more you will receive. Networking is an effective marketing tool that encompasses trust. Here are a few recommendations.

Networking needs a two-way relationship. Basically, people feel appreciated when approached for assistance or ideas, but as I have gotten older, I value my time more than ever—and expect something in return. If you plan on using a contact to advance your purchasing of a company, see if they want anything in return. In other words, don't ask a favor unless you intend to return the favor.

Effectively pursue leads. If you are following a lead supplied by a friend or business contact, be sure to use the third-party introduction: "Your friend, John Smith, suggested I call you." In this case, how can he turn down his friend, John Smith, the third-party referral? You could also have your friend or business contact make the introductory call for you.

Leverage your association relationships. Most business people belong to at least one industry association. The Association of Corporate Growth has approximately 11,000 members in fifty chapters throughout the United States, Canada, and abroad. As a member, I have always been able to reach other members and receive their full cooperation by merely prefacing my introduction by saying: "We are both members of ACG." The organization is like a fraternity and creates a bond with individuals who have never met. There are other peer groups, such as the Young Presidents Organization (YPO) that will be helpful in networking.

Respond quickly and report back. In order to handle the business lead most effectively, follow through expeditiously and most importantly, report back to the person that gave you the referral with a status report.

Select professional firms carefully. If you ask for referrals from employees at a law firm, an accounting firm, or even a bank, they will be helpful if they are confident that there is a good chance you will engage them to do the deal when and if you buy a company. Try to create a meaningful relationship with them.

Continually solidify your relationship. Rather than wait for people to remember you, go right up to them and reintroduce yourself. Put people at ease by announcing your name. If you are at a scheduled meeting with the person, it is fine to exchange business cards, but if you are meeting for the first time at a function, it is very tacky to exchange cards until a certain rapport has been established following your conversation. Be discreet. It is better to politely ask for the other person's card before you foist your card on them.

Schedule right then and there. How many times have you seen an important networking business contact at a meeting and he or she says: "Let's get together for lunch sometime." Carpe diem! Seize the day! Pull out your schedule and set a date right then and there.

DEAL FLOW

Developing a strong positive deal flow is the key to finding the deal—the more options you see, the more likely you'll find one that's right for you. The secret is to increase the number and quality of the deals for you to analyze. Bear in mind that if you receive a number of leads from an intermediary who is not on retainer with you, he or she will eventually become discouraged and lose interest unless you pursue these leads vigorously.

Let's say that two individual buyers in Boston, Mike Stevens and Phil Harris, each have $2 million to invest in a business. That's a lot of money even in this day and age! Both of them are totally reluctant to pay an intermediary a retainer to speed up the search process; yet they have spent over two and four years, respectively, looking for a business to buy. Fundamentally, these two buyers are penny wise and pound foolish.

Cornelius Vanderbilt once commented that if you are concerned about the financial upkeep of a sailboat, which in his day was made of wood, don't buy one. On a similar rationale, my feeling is that if you can't afford to retain an intermediary, you can't afford to buy a business. If you save all your money for a closing, you may not have one!

Mr. Stevens's and Mr. Harris's experiences certainly emphasize the importance of having a steady source of deals.

TABULATION OF DEAL FLOW OVER TWO YEARS

	MIKE STEVENS	PHIL HARRIS
COMPANIES LOOKED AT:	428	250
COMPANIES LIKED:	34	20
OFFERS:	6	10
NEGOTIATED:	3	4
BOUGHT:	1	1

Because of the enormous number of opportunities to consider, both Stevens and Harris became very proficient in analyzing the deals and moving the acquisition process forward. If Stevens and Harris had engaged an intermediary, the latter would have screened out many of the poor opportunities, thus saving them substantial time and effort.

CONSOLIDATING SMALL BUSINESSES

If you can't find one big company to buy, you could try to buy smaller mom and pop operations in fragmented businesses and consolidate them into one company.

Here are a few examples. All Seasons Services Inc. in Braintree, Massachusetts, has $75 million in sales, mostly in the vending machine business. Every year All Seasons buys small mom and pop vending companies that are struggling financially and/or whose owner wants to retire. Since the vending machine business is very much relationship-driven, it is often easier to buy accounts through acquisition than to hope that your sales force will eventually win the business.

Mindis International Recycling, a metal recycling company headquartered in Atlanta, has grown to over $100 million in sales mostly by buying local scrapyards.

The *Fortune* 500 companies Blockbuster and General Cinema started their original growth by buying individual video stores and movie theaters and/or small chains.

Buying and consolidating mom and pop companies is a viable way to grow through acquisition.

VENTURE CAPITAL COMPANIES

Traditionally, venture capital funds have a ten-year life cycle, at which time the venture capital partnership terminates. The goal, therefore, is for these funds to resolve their investments either by having the companies go public, selling out, or liquidating the companies.

More specifically, according to Gordon Baty, formerly of Zero Stage Capital of Cambridge, Massachusetts, the disasters usually pop up within two years of the venture capitalists' initial investment. The winning companies are apparent within four years. The rest of most venture capital holdings are the underperforming companies, commonly known as the living dead. It is these latter companies that require the venture capitalists' money, time, and energy, with their best hope being to just get their original investment back.

Baty goes on to say that these underperforming investments are one of the biggest problems for venture capitalists. By nature, venture capitalists are eternal optimists and reluctant to admit defeat. However, they have limited options with these underperforming investments. They can give their stock back to the company's owners as a total write-off, sell their shares at a low price, liquidate the company, or convert their general partnership to a limited partnership. Or, they could sell the business, which is where you come in.

Unlike many family businesses, whose owners often have second thoughts about selling when the negotiations begin, venture capitalists are decisive about selling and usually have placed a realistic valuation on the company. Venture capitalists' portfolio companies will have audited financials, a clean set of books, a limited number of shareholders, and no suspect "side deals" with vendors.

With thousands of venture capital firms across the United States, you could also try to buy underperforming businesses where the company may have turned the corner but the stockholders have lost patience. To do so, you need to qualify yourself as a viable buyer, both financially and operationally.

DIVESTMENTS

The annual statistics of the M&As of public companies are readily available. Historically, between 40 and 50 percent of the transactions in this marketplace are divestments. With both public and private companies, there are opportunities to acquire small divisions that do not fit the parent company's core business, are too small for the parent company, and/or are appendages from other acquisitions made by the parent company.

If you are capable of raising a significant amount of equity either from your own resources or in partnership with others, you are in a position to approach directors of corporate development of companies that own numerous divisions. Depending on the target's size, the target's leverageability, and your negotiating skills, anywhere from $1 million to $5 million of equity will put you in the game.

Corporate spinoffs are desirable candidates because once the directors decide to sell a division, they usually follow through with it. Unlike the owners of many family-owned businesses, they do not get seller's remorse and change their mind. Also, divestments have a fair chance of being valued reasonably because the parent company knows what other comparable companies sell for. If the spinoff is from a public company, you will have the advantage of receiving audited financials instead of the loose and sloppy recordkeeping and unaudited statements usually provided by family businesses. You will, however, have to recast the financials to adjust for the parent company's overhead allocations to the division.

Also, for a spinoff from a public company, you probably will be referred to the company's investment banker, who will determine whether you are a qualified buyer. Since the selling process is in the hands of professionals, you will be presented with a thorough selling memorandum, machinery, equipment, and real estate appraisals; a list of assets that will be sold or retained; and maybe a predocumentation of warranties and representations. You will be required to submit your offer quickly, and so if you are inexperienced in the M&A process, be sure the others on your acquisition team are not rookies too.

Spinoffs are almost always put out to bid, and so you will be competing with other potential buyers. The parent company will rarely accept buyer's notes unless the buyer is a formidable company, so be prepared to offer all cash. You are more likely to get the director of corporate development's attention if you present yourself as a buyout group rather than as an individual. Another possibility is to collaborate with the existing management team of the divesting company. The existing management team usually has credibility because of their specific experience and knowledge. However, they are often risk-averse and lack sufficient capital to complete a transaction on their own. If you joined forces with the existing management team, and you were willing to give up some ownership, you could approach an asset-based lender to help finance the deal. Such an acquisition plan could be very attractive.

Another way to track down companies with divisions is to ask your nearby library if it carries annual reports of various local companies. If it does not, you can refer to the manufacturers' directory for your particular state. If you skim through the directory, it will usually indicate if a listed company is a subsidiary of some parent company. Or, seek out large holding companies that have sales from $500 million to $3 billion and own a few subsidiaries with sales in the $5 to $10 million range. Occasionally, these holding companies will reassess their corporate strategy and divest numerous small subsidiaries or divisions at the same time.

Let's look at an example of divestment. One small medical device manufacturer in Massachusetts was running out of capital. It had two product lines; one had FDA approval and one was pending FDA approval. Since the company had spent most of its capital on developing its products, it had virtually no money left to properly market and promote the FDA-approved product.

Since the product with the biggest potential was the one with FDA approval pending, the company was forced to sell the product line that was already generating sales. The most interesting aspect of this deal was its structure. The company decided to sell the product line for $3 million but retain the right to manufacture the product at cost plus 15 percent for a period of time. The buyer was able to acquire an excellent line of medical products with very high gross margins. With an additional investment for marketing, the buyer could concentrate on selling, since the manufacturing was to remain with the seller for a period of time. The seller received the cash it desperately needed for its potentially greater product, but it also received a profitable manufacturing contract until its new product was up and running.

TURNAROUNDS

Turnarounds can be a growth industry for investors. The best targets are companies that have not yet filed for Chapter 11 bankruptcy. According to John Whitney, professor at the Columbia University School of Business, "the heart of the matter is fixing problems and understanding operations."

Paul Hunn, senior vice president of Manufacturer's Hanover Trust, uses the following four questions as his initial screen before advancing additional debt to a troubled company:

1. Is the company intrinsically viable?
2. Is good management now in place?
3. Can the company return to positive cash flow in six months?
4. Can it return to solid, honest profitability within two years?

Among the assets to look for in a turnaround, according to John Whitney, are the following:

- Excellent product line or service
- Sound distribution network and customer base
- Proprietary technology
- Manufacturing know-how
- Skilled workforce
- Licenses, patents, or distribution agreements

Whitney goes on to say: "Buyers should not delude themselves into buying a 'bargain' when the only hope is for short-term improvement through balance sheet management. On-the-job training for new owners is risky and expensive, especially for an enterprise as fragile as a turnaround." Relationships with bankers, vendors, customers, and employees are tenuous at best. The balance sheet should be restructured before the deal is consummated in such ways as:

- Swapping some of the debt for equity.
- Lowering interest rates for a period of time and extending maturities.
- Negotiating accounts payable downward.

Even though the turnaround company is troubled, it should have a core activity generating positive cash flow from operations. Many troubled companies find themselves in a precarious position because their noncore businesses have substantially diverted their resources, such as their management, sales force, plant, and, of course, cash. According to Carl Youngman, a turnaround specialist:

> Unless the business has a reason to exist and is worth perpetuating, even to start the turnaround effort is a futile exercise. Once identified, the viable core business must be protected from the rest of the activities in the turnaround company. This protection often means a different set of rules (i.e., financing policies, capital budgets, and human resource issues) than for all other parts of the business.

Unless you are experienced in turnarounds, I certainly do not recommend that you buy a company in this position. You may have identified a few problem areas, such as an inadequate sales organization or inferior financial controls; however, there may be many other problems on the factory floor or with quality control that you have overlooked.

GENERAL OBSERVATIONS FROM BRIAN KNIGHT (KNOWN AS CBI)

Brian Knight is the president of Country Business Inc., a thirteen-office business brokerage firm that specializes in the purchase and sale of small and mid-size companies. While Country Business sells mostly businesses with sales of less than $3 million, they are considered an excellent resource for individual buyers seeking to acquire companies in the lower end of the middle market, especially in Maine, New Hampshire, and Vermont.

Knight wrote the book *Buy the Right Business—At the Right Price*; however, the following information was delivered to the New York Venture Group during Knight's speech on "How to Find a Business to Buy."

The demand for small businesses far exceeds the supply. Screening telephone calls from Knight's Manchester Center, Vermont office, most inquirers are looking for small medium-tech manufacturers with a proprietary product and a proven record of increasing revenues and profits. The buyers would like to move to the Stratton, Vermont area and have a relatively short commute to the target manufacturing company. The only problem is that there are very few manufacturers in Vermont, particularly in the Stratton area. What is available as businesses to buy in Vermont are hospitality and retail companies. The first lesson to be learned as a buyer is not to have unrealistic expectations.

Concurrent with the first lesson is deciding whether you should buy a company at all! Buying a company, much less finding a company to buy, does not suit everyone, nor does it assure financial success. Buyers can and will succeed if they buy an excellent book on this subject, seek professional advice, and take their time (maybe two years).

Knight emphasizes that buyers should:

- Be self-analytical of their capabilities.
- Write down their acquisition criteria.
- Carefully interview and select a buying intermediary.
- Work on interpersonal skills with the potential seller.

Country Business' mission is to find good and profitable businesses, not to represent unprofitable businesses. Knight believes that the key to success in finding the right business to buy is your ability to commit to the above items. If you can do so, success in finding the deal will be more likely.

The following section was written by Stephen B. Blum, former managing partner of KPMG Peat Marwick's Corporate Finance Group in New York, and reproduced from M&A with permission.

Finding desirable and profitable privately held companies whose owners will sell for reasonable prices constitutes a tough middle-market M&A hurdle.

Either owners fail to adjust to today's more modest selling prices, and therefore don't sell the company, or a controlled auction escalates the price beyond reason for many suitors. Most attractive businesses aren't on the block for precisely the same reasons that they're attractive; the trick is finding, contacting, and wooing the private business owners who haven't previously thought of selling.

Properly orchestrated acquisition searches allow purchasers to sidestep auctions, so that the courtship can develop at a pace that both sides can live with. Finding the right seller almost always demands the same patience and ingenuity as finding the right purchaser.

Once you have narrowed the criteria for the acquisition and identified various target companies, the time comes to contact these companies directly and to measure the owners' willingness to talk. Remember, most owners haven't decided to sell their businesses. They may, in fact, have a powerful emotional attachment to their businesses.

Contact Tactics

Use an intermediary to perform an acquisition search.

1. Look at the manufacturers' directory or the industry directory in which each target is listed. You may find a list of officers, bankers, accountants, law firms, and directors. In some cases, you may have a personal connection with one of these people. For example, you may know the corporate lawyer or a director. If so, that person may be your starting point.
2. Carefully compose a letter to your contact, or to the apparent controlling shareholder. This letter can, for example, explain that the intermediary has been retained by XYZ Company, and that XYZ has reason to believe that a joint venture between the two companies could make sense. The intermediary might even enclose his or her client's brochure—if your client is ready to reveal its identity to the

target. Using the words "joint venture" (or "strategic alliance") instead of "merger" or "acquisition" can put the target more at ease—but these phrases shouldn't be used if they are misleading.

3. Follow up by telephone within a few days at most. We all know that most companies have well-trained secretaries who often are your initial roadblock in reaching the CEO. Naturally, the secretary will immediately ask the nature of the call, "Does the president know you?" etc. The response might be, "I'm calling Mr._____ in connection with my letter dated _____." If you do not get through or get a return call, then perhaps one more call will help—preferably prior to 9:00 A.M., before the controlling shareholder's secretary arrives and before his or her day gets plugged with meetings. If you are unable to make progress by telephone, then you may have to attack differently—either by fax, Federal Express, or e-mail. The more specific you can be in the communication, the better, but be aware that the more you find it necessary to refer to M&A, the more intimidating this may be to the owner.

4. Once you have established a dialogue with the target's owner, you should supplement telephone information with a direct meeting involving the owner and the potential buyer. You should push for this early, while there is momentum. Generally speaking, the immediate goal is to build chemistry between the two parties and agree on the best next step (an exchange of financial data, a lunchtime chat, a visit to the target's headquarters, etc.).

The best acquisition opportunities can be the least predictable, especially if the owners viewed them initially as not for sale.

GATHERING INFORMATION ON THE COMPANY FOR SALE

Let's say that you are visiting the owner and president of a manufacturing company for the first time and you have allocated two to three hours to ask questions and to tour the plant. Do your best to gather the following information.

Business Overview

To break the ice, ask the owner to give you a quick historical overview of the company—when it was started, major changes and developments, etc. Ask the owner to track a typical order from point of entry—checking credit, entry into the system, schedule for manufacturing or stock item—in order to get a sense of how efficiently and thoroughly the company executes. Also, ask what the core business is, whether it is a niche business, what makes the business unique, and whether the business is seasonal or cyclical. Is the company a C or an S corporation?

About the Products

Ask for a description of the products, their price points, their market share, the rate at which new products are developed, the number of SKUs in the product line, and whether 20 percent of the products equal 80 percent of the sales and, conversely, whether 80 percent of the sales are to 20 percent of the customers. How are the products priced, i.e., mostly to market prices, or to costs plus profit, or both?

Market Overview

How big is the market? Is this a commodity business (price-driven)? Is it fragmented among lots of small companies, or is it affected by large *Fortune* 500 companies or by foreign competition? How fast is the market growing? What affects growth, e.g., the economy, the weather, military spending, etc.?

Sales History

What are the sales for the past few years, and what are projected sales? Describe the average sales cycle from original sales call to receipt of order. What is the channel of distribution—direct sales, sales reps, distributors, catalog, telemarketing, online, direct mail, trade shows, etc.? What are the sales costs? Do you export or import, or have you considered strategic alliances or joint ventures? Tell me about the sales manager and the sales team. What is your return policy, and how large a factor are product returns on total sales?

Who's the Competition?

Have the owner identify and describe the major competitors, i.e., their size, location, breadth of product line, and pricing. Does his company have a competitive advantage, and if so, what is it (financial resources, automation, sales coverage, dealer network, longevity)? Is the competition national, international, regional, or all of the above? To what extent is this a relationship business, or will customers exhibit little loyalty? Are the customers apt to single-source, double-source, or more?

Plant/Manufacturing Capabilities

How large is the plant? Is it leased or owned? What is the plant capacity? Could production be increased 50 percent in the same facility? How many production people and how many people altogether are there in the company? What are the sales per employee and how does that compare to the industry average (which you can find from Robert Morris Associates' industry analysis)? Is the manufacturing fully integrated, or is it subassembly? Who are the largest vendors, and what terms does the company receive on their invoicing? Does the company use just-in-time (JIT) inventory, and how much of the inventory is work in process (WIP)? What are the bottlenecks? Describe the quality control (QC). What is the reject rate? What are the labor rate, bonuses, benefits, and average age of the workforce (if it is fifty-five, this could be a problem)? What are the capital equipment needs in the next few years?

Management's Function

Ask the owner to describe the management team's roles, i.e., CEO, CFO, COO, etc. As CEO, how do you allocate your time? What are your major problems and concerns? Who do you use for advisers, such as consultants, lawyers, accountants, etc.? As CEO, what are your strengths and shortcomings? What contractual arrangements or incentive plans do you have with the management team? Do you have a management chart?

R&D Initiative

How much time, effort, and money does the compay devote to new product development or new manufacturing process innovations? Does the company have any patents or licenses?

Financials Summary

Are the financials certified? Does the company provide monthly financials? What key benchmarks does the company use to monitor progress, e.g., gross margin, inventory, inventory turnover, working capital, sales per employee? What percentage of receivables are over ninety days? How does the company handle collections? Does the company take 2 percent net ten days on your payables? When and how are price changes implemented? Are all major accounting functions computerized—purchases, sales, inventory, etc.? What sort of insurance liability does the company carry for potential customer claims? What are the financial projections, and how did the team figure them out? Go over the financials line by line to be sure you understand each item and also to see if there is some possible restructuring of the balance sheet that will help you make a more realistic offer.

- Consider removing the real estate if included.
- Remove shareholders' receivables or payables.
- Remove owners' assets, e.g., automobiles.
- Disclose owners' perks.
- Review reserves and accruals.

Selling the Business

Why is the company for sale? How long has the business been for sale? Are there other stockholders, and if so, what is the ownership breakdown? Does the owner have the authority to sell, or is it the decision of the board of directors? Are there other offers for the business? Who will be doing the negotiating? What is the rationale or methodology for determining the price of the business? Are there any add-backs or reconstructed earnings? What is the owner's total compensation? Is there any pending litigation or prior litigation? Are there any contractual obligations—to employees, vendors, customers, landlords, intermediaries; noncompete agreements; buy/sell agreements? Are there any "soft assets," such as uncollectible receivables? Would the owner stay on for a transition period? Would the seller take a note as partial payment, subordinated to the bank or unsecured? Is there anything in the offer that is not negotiable, such as an asset versus a stock sale? Are there any violations with OSHA, EPA, unions (if any), etc.?

Final Questions for the Owner

- If you miraculously received $1 million in the company, how would you use it?
- How do you grow the business?
- What differentiates this company from its competitors?
- What is the culture of the company?
- What is the company's most important resource?
- What haven't we talked about that I should know or what have I overlooked?

OBTAIN ANOTHER BUYER'S TARGET LIST

If you are networking to buy a business, invariably you will meet others trying to do the same thing at one of your various business group meetings.

One person I know spent two years canvassing, identifying potential companies for sale, and building a database of 300 active accounts. This buyer visited a majority of these companies and kept an ongoing history of his findings. When he finally acquired a company, a small two-man buyout firm was so impressed with the work he had done over the two years that they bought the search list. The deal was structured with a certain amount of money up front for the list, plus more money if the buyout group closed on a company included on the list. Additionally, the buyout group agreed to give him 5 percent of the stock of the acquired company.

This unusual win-win scenario will work, but obviously the two parties have to have a high level of confidence and faith in each other. This situation is just another example of what can be achieved with innovative ideas.

FINDING THE DEAL TAKES BRAINS, BUCKS, AND BRAVADO

Jim Thomas of Dynamic Development Capital Partners (*www.dynamicdevelopmentcapital.com*), wrote an article in the Association for Corporate Growth's May 2007 monthly publication. After having been part of two successful private company sales, he went out on his own to buy a business and shared with me the context of his article. After eight months of searching, Thomas had looked at 100 deals, drafted five term sheets, and was negotiating two letters of intent.

When Thomas began his endeavor, he asked himself five essential questions:

1. What type of company do I want to buy?
2. How much capital will it require?
3. How much time will it take?
4. How will I find the right company?
5. Who can help me?

Next, Thomas set a goal for himself: "I decided to target a low/medium technology manufacturer/distributor with less than $20 million in sales and no succession plan. Having spoken with successful independent sponsors, I learned that I was going to have to look at many buyout candidates, or 'kiss a lot of frogs to find my prince.' The interviewees did not find 'their deal' until looking at a minimum of 110 prospects. The gestation period to find, negotiate, and consummate a purchase agreement was twelve to twenty-four months. So I set a personal goal of one year to review 200 qualified prospective acquisitions."

Thirdly, Thomas formulated his strategy on extensive networking with his objective to meet face-to-face with nine different categories of contacts. His previous experience helped him to compute the math as follows:

20 percent of contacts lead to an opportunity
50 percent of the people return your calls within one week
80 percent respond to you eventually

Originating four deals per week (a deal equaling a signed nondisclosure agreement) equates to 200 potential acquisitions in one year.

Fourth, Thomas targeted eight different contact groups to cultivate relationships and deal flow.

1. Business brokers/intermediaries/investment bankers
2. Accountants/valuation firms
3. Private equity groups
4. Banks (commercial/mezzanine)
5. Attorneys
6. Executive search firms/recruiters
7. Turnaround consultants
8. His own networks (corporate executives/friends)

Fifth, not surprisingly, 50 percent of Thomas' deals came from business brokers, intermediaries, and/or investment bankers who are in the business of providing deal flow. Thomas found that he was most successful in surfacing deals when he provided:

- A target description, e.g., size, industry, location
- A personal financial statement
- Prompt returns to telephone calls
- Details as to why a deal did not materialize
- His deal status
- Monthly contact for new deals and updates

Sixth, Thomas enjoyed the most productive relationships with his deal sources when they:

- Analyzed the buyer/seller fit and communicated potential trouble spots
- Ensured that their pricing was within his financing range
- Qualified his financing sources
- Remained involved in every step of each negotiation to ensure that the deal stayed on track (most important)

Thomas learned the following lessons:

- The big deal-quality source came from contacts within his personal and professional network.
- The "perfect deal" does not exist at a reasonable price, therefore a prospective buyer must make meaningful changes to improve the existing company.
- The process of buying a business is one where the more calls you make, the greater your results.
- To be presented a good business opportunity, you must realize that the process is a two-way street . . . so constantly communicate, be professional, market yourself authentically, and be respectful of others' time.

CHAPTER 14

Raising Cash

T he amount of cash you are willing to invest or are capable of investing in an acquisition will in large part determine the size of the companies you should target. The following is a very simplistic rule of thumb for ascertaining the size of the manufacturing company you can afford to acquire. Most manufacturing companies with "average" profits sell for 50 percent of sales. Furthermore, most acquisitions require one-third of the purchase price to be cash at closing. Therefore, let's assume that you want to acquire a company with at least $3 million in sales. While the formula below is very general, it gives you a general understanding of how much cash you'll need:

Sales of company:	$3,000,000
Probable purchase price:	$1,500,000
Cash at closing:	$500,000

I know someone who acquired 51 percent of a printing company for $25,000. The company had unprofitable sales of $3 million and was just then breaking even. This was an anomaly. However, companies that are losing money or breaking even can be acquired with very little cash, especially if the buyer is willing to assume the seller's debt.

Many buyers underestimate the importance of raising sufficient cash early on. Let's assume that our buyer has only $200,000 in cash but still wants to acquire a profitable company with $3 million in sales. One alternative is to elicit other stockholders and raise another $300,000. You would not have to lose ownership control even though your investment is only 40 percent of the invested capital ($200,000 divided by $500,000 = 40 percent) because you consummated the transaction from beginning to end. Let's assume that you want to capitalize your acquisition company with $500,000, of which $200,000 will be your own capital. The ownership allocation could be as follows:

NONMONETARY:		
Consideration for putting the deal together		40%
MONETARY:		
Your investment	$200,000	
Other investors	$300,000	
		60%
TOTAL	*$500,000*	*100%*

Therefore, the ownership of the acquisition team would be as follows based on the above scenario:

Your nonmonetary portion	40%	
Your monetary contribution	24%	
Your ownership ($200,000 invested)		64%
Other investors ($300,000 invested)		36%
		100%

OVERVIEW OF CORPORATE FINANCING SOURCES

Larry Nathan, president of L.R. Nathan Associates (Larry. Nathan@lrnltd.com), offers the following advice.

The most fundamental contrast between funding sources is the distinction between lenders and investors. Very briefly, lenders just want to be paid back with an appropriate return on their money. They are only interested in protecting against downside risk—which they try to do through some combination of credit assessment and collateral. When you pay off a lender, they go away. They do not share in upside potential. They are *not* your partner.

Senior Lenders

The purest kind of lender is the senior lender, which I define as one who feels that your first priority in life should be to pay him back before anyone else. I will give you a quick overview of who these senior lenders are, what their money looks like, and how to deal with them.

Banks are the most prevalent senior lenders. Despite all the bank mergers you hear about, there are plenty of banks out there and, these days, they're killing each other for business. Because banks get their money mostly through deposits, they are short-term lenders by nature. They are most comfortable providing demand lines of credit for working capital, but also will do some term lending, usually not beyond five years. Banks like to be secured when lending to small and middle-market businesses, and usually require a personal guaranty of the owner and they avoid lending to companies that do not have a track record for generating sufficient cash flow to pay them back. As regulated institutions, banks also are concerned about the "cosmetics" of the balance sheet—i.e., the degree of leverage, a positive net worth, etc.

Most companies borrow from banks. There are regulatory limits within which banks have to operate and, therefore, it's hard to get any bank to do things that banks can't do. For example, even if you have lots of collateral, it's hard to get a bank to lend to a business with sustained losses—or, even if a turnaround has materialized and there's plenty of collateral, banks have difficulty coping with a negative net worth. Or finally, even if everything is wonderful, it's unlikely that your bank will make a ten- to fifteen-year fixed rate unsecured loan to your company. It's just not what banks do. However, for companies in any of these situations, there are alternatives—in the form of nonbank senior lenders.

Asset-Based Lenders

The first two circumstances mentioned—plenty of collateral with sustained losses; some evidence of a turnaround but a negative net worth—would likely make a financing unbankable, but not necessarily unfinanceable. This brings us to the world of asset-based lending, which describes borrowing in which the lender's primary focus is the liquidation value of his collateral. He is always asking the question, "If everything goes to hell in a handbasket, how can I get my money back?" Asset-based lenders evaluate their collateral carefully before lending and then monitor it closely after closing. The most attractive collateral to these lenders is accounts receivable (A/R), followed by certain kinds of inventory and production equipment. These deals are structured as revolving credit loans, where borrowings go up and down depending upon the level of eligible accounts receivable and inventory—perfect mechanism for dealing with working capital fluctuations. These nonbank asset-based lenders usually will also provide a five- to seven-year term loan against the liquidation value of machinery and equipment, known as M&E.

Many banks do asset-based lending, but still are constrained by the credit considerations I mentioned earlier. There are numerous alternatives among finance companies—some of the better known names include Congress Financial, CIT, Finova, Foothill, Norwest Business Credit, and Fremont. Their money generally is more expensive than banks, but not too much more these days. We currently are in an extremely competitive lending environment.

The nice thing about nonbank asset-based lenders is, while they do care about your credit—nobody wants to lend into a certain liquidation—they have much more tolerance for a "story" credit. A story credit is when the company has invented the next best widget that will revolutionize the world. While this is not a "hard" asset, the potential is perceived to be so doable that there is value in the concept, or "story." They often can maximize funding levels because they're not really concerned about debt/equity ratios—just good, eligible collateral—and usually have minimal, if any, covenants.

Factoring

Are form of asset-based lending, which isn't technically lending, is factoring. Instead of lending against the value of accounts receivable, the factor actually purchases them outright in exchange for 80 to 90 percent of their value. The balance of the face amount typically is advanced when the A/R is collected. Factoring can be a flexible, effective way to achieve maximum funding of working capital needs in a troubled situation because the factor doesn't care one wit about the borrower's credit story—only about the genuineness of the A/R and the credit of the account debtors (the business customers that owe the money). Personal guaranties usually can be avoided also. The bad news is that factoring is quite expensive—typically ranging in percentages from the high teens to mid-twenties, or even higher, when all costs are taken into account.

Capital Leases

Machinery and equipment also can be financed on a stand-alone basis outside of banks. Nonbank financial institutions such as GE Capital, Textron, Heller, and others will make term loans against your existing equipment and are even more eager to provide high advances against new equipment purchases. These loans often are called capital leases but really are installment loans at varying rates and terms, depending upon credit and the type of equipment. Generally speaking, though, terms tend to be longer and advance rates are higher than banks will provide. Early prepayment usually is impossible or very expensive. There usually are no covenants. These transactions can close very quickly, because the documents are carved in stone; totally inhospitable to changes—just sign here and close!

Having said that, this kind of financing can be particularly beneficial when done with captive finance companies of equipment manufacturers. This "vendor financing" is designed to facilitate the purchase of new equipment. For example, if you are buying a Mitsubishi printing press, Mitsubishi Acceptance Corporation may provide more than 90 percent of the new purchase price—sometimes including installation costs—for a longer term at below market rates than would other lenders.

True leasing, of course, is another option where the equipment literally is owned by and rented from the lessor, who usually retains tax advantages and will pass these benefits along in the form of a rent schedule that is lower than comparable loan payments. This can be most attractive from a cash flow standpoint.

Mortgage Financing

The financing of owner-occupied real estate involves special issues. Traditional commercial real estate lenders who provide mortgages on so-called "income" properties such as apartments, office buildings, shopping centers, hotels, etc., are uncomfortable lending on real estate that is occupied by a manufacturing or distribution business. This is because the cash flow generated to repay the mortgage loan does not come from multiple tenants, but instead from a single business. The soundness of the cash flow, therefore, is dependent upon the creditworthiness of the company using the building, the failure of which results in an empty building. Traditional commercial real estate lenders simply do not relate to the kind of financial analysis involved in this determination. For this reason, most owner-occupied real estate is financed as part of an overall loan package to the business which occupies the facility, where the mortgage is only a portion of the total financing. There are some limited opportunities today to secure stand-alone mortgage financing through nonbank credit companies, or as securitized transactions where the mortgage is bundled with others, guaranteed by an insurance company and then sold off in the public markets as a rated security. Finally, for smaller fundings, the SBA 7(a) program provides attractive terms for owner-occupied real estate up to $1 million.

Insurance Company Private Placement

One other kind of senior lender is worthy of note, however, and that is the insurance company private placement lender, who really will make that ten- to fifteen-year fixed rate unsecured loan. Insurance companies are purely credit-driven lenders. In fact, if you offer them collateral, they assume it must be a bad deal and will reject the opportunity. The catch, of course, is that these loans are made only to very creditworthy companies whose debt is—or would be—rated roughly BAA or better. These private placements are structured as unsecured senior notes with terms typically of ten years and often long periods of interest-only, sometimes for the full term. Pricing is fixed for the full term of the note at some spread above the U.S. treasury note, whose term equals the average life of the loan. For example, a private placement of ten years, with the first five years at interest-only would have an average life of about eight years. The rate would be fixed at some spread—say, 1 percent to 1½ percent—above the eight-year treasury note. The amount of the spread is a function of creditworthiness.

Finally, insurance companies do not engage in relationship lending like banks do. They prefer to put their loans on the shelf and do not have frequent contact with their borrowers. However, they monitor their credits through extensive, sometimes ridiculously complex, sets of covenants relating to the financial health of their borrowers.

This completes the cursory survey of senior lenders—both secured and unsecured—and leads into a whole different realm of corporate financing . . . the role of the investor, as opposed to the lender.

Mezzanine Financing

In this context, the term mezzanine refers to the middle position in the balance sheet, with senior debt on the above and pure equity below, in terms of the right of repayment. It applies to nonsenior debt and many forms of quasi-equity instruments—from highrate, long-term subordinated debt, sort of a private junk bond, to preferred stock. In all cases, mezzanine funds are subordinated to the senior lender, thereby providing something of a capital cushion for the least expensive money.

The purpose of mezzanine financing is not to replace bank debt, but to supplement it in some way. It's intended to fill a gap created by some need that is not appropriate for senior debt. For example, a business may need more capital to support new product or market development, which may be beyond the bank's appetite for more senior debt. Or, there may be a succession issue—very common today—that needs to be funded, but there's just no room for more senior debt. Or finally, your company may have a terrific opportunity to acquire a competitor for $10 million in cash. Let's say the deal makes great sense in every respect, but your company has only minimal cash equity to invest in the buyout and your bank can't lend more than a $6 million portion of the buyout price. That leaves upward of a $4 million shortfall, yet the synergy of the acquisition is compelling! What to do? Well, you might consider raising more equity capital, but that could be highly dilutive of your ownership position because private equity investors typically seek 30 to 50 percent annual returns on their money. Mezzanine financing may provide a more attractive option under certain circumstances.

The exact structure of the transaction will vary from deal to deal and also depends upon the needs of the particular investment fund providing the financing. A common structure is a long-term subordinated note with a term in the range of five to eight years and about five years of interest-only. Pricing is a fixed rate—typically 12 percent nowadays—plus warrants (options to purchase common stock at a nominal price) for some minority interest in the company. The mezzanine investor hopes that the value of his warrants will appreciate over a five-year holding period by an amount which, when combined with the interest rate, will yield his total return objectives. For example, if the total return objective is 25 percent per year and the interest rate is 12 percent, then the mezzanine investor will want to perceive an additional thirteen points from appreciation in the value of the warrants. The amount of equity play required will be backed into analytically, based on the company's five-year business plan. So, unlike senior lenders, mezzanine funding sources are very much interested in sharing the upside that their money helps to create. They *are* your partner, at least for awhile.

THE SEARCH FUND CONCEPT

The search fund concept is not very common, but I have seen it executed successfully. One success story is Andrew Cousins of Amersham Corporation of Santa Monica, California. In his investment proposal, Cousins states:

The financing for the acquisition will be accomplished through a two-step process. Amersham will first raise the funds to meet search expenses. The company is seeking equity investors to capitalize the company with $200,000. The search fund will be raised in ten units of $20,000. For each unit purchased, investors will receive: (1) an equity position in the acquired company equal to 200 percent of the dollar value of their search fund investment and (2) the right of first refusal, but not the obligation, to invest additional equity in the acquisition.

Andrew Cousins's investment proposal goes on to say:

Search fund proceeds will finance the expenses incurred in the identification of an acquisition on behalf of the company and its investors. The fund enables Cousins to conduct a full-time search for a period of up to twenty-four months. The search fund also establishes an investor group capable of making a significant equity investment. Such a group provides Amersham with greater financial credibility in approaching prospective sellers and lenders, and may facilitate the closing of a time sensitive transaction. Operating expenses are estimated to be approximately $100,000 annually.

CATEGORY OF EXPENSE	ANNUAL EXPENSE
Salary	$50,000
Travel	$15,000
Office rent	$8,400
Legal and accounting	$7,000
Administrative	$6,600
Telephone	$6,000
Prefunding expense	$5,000
Office equipment	$2,000
Total Expense	$100,000

Other buyers have used the search fund concept, of course. The technique is extensively described in Harvard Business School Case 9-387-009 regarding Jim Southern, which is available at cost by calling the institution at (617) 495-6117.

OBTAINING A BANK LOAN

Let's assume that you are in the process of buying a company. Along with presenting an essential business plan, in your meeting with the bank, you'll want to tell them the following things about the company you want to purchase:

1. Describe how you run the business. It is important for the banker to fully understand the financial nature of the business, such as whether sales are seasonal, special customer or vendor payment terms, how you check your customers' credit, whether you allow production overruns, how you treat overdue accounts, whether you require deposits for special orders, and what financial controls you incorporate in the business.

2. Describe how you market your product/service. What is the customer base, by industry and key accounts, as well as by product/service? Also, how do you market your business and what are your competitive advantages? Specifically, who are your competitors and how does your product/service compare?

3. Describe your company's management. As well as providing the individual backgrounds of important management personnel, it is important to relate how their backgrounds pertain to this particular company. Perhaps no other factor is as important as the ability of management in achieving the company's objectives, both strategically and financially.

4. Financial considerations. The bank is particularly interested in managing its risk and seeing that your company

has the resources to match planned growth. The banker will want to know how you intend to spend its money and how and when you will pay it back.

5. Preparation for financing presentation. A professional presentation showing the following critical considerations is considered essential by most debtors:

- Estimated sales and expenses by month for at least a year's period of time—showing how the bank debt is to be paid down and what is the proper debt covered.
- A balance sheet showing leverage not to exceed a debt to equity ratio of approximately 3 to 1, along with the borrowing power based on 75 percent of receivables and 30 percent inventory.
- A clear-cut analysis of how the company expects to make money.

And finally, depending on the size of the company and previous relationships, most owners of small businesses must submit their personal financial statements and be prepared to personally sign for the company notes.

PERSONAL GUARANTEES

Personal guarantees are usually a sticky wicket for owners of middle-market companies. For some, the personal guarantee defeats the purpose of incorporating. While some loan officers might say that a personal guarantee for small companies is standard procedure, the fact is that every item on the loan agreement is negotiable.

When I asked Warren Morrison, former senior vice president of U.S. Trust in Boston, what the rule of thumb is for obtaining personal guarantees, he responded: "The rule of thumb is, always get them." Naturally, the banker's objective is different from the borrower's. Basically, the borrower has the following alternatives:

1. Shop around in the hopes of finding a bank that will not require a personal guarantee because of the company's

strong financial position and your personal reputation. While this may be unlikely at the outset, the bank may waive your guarantee and counter by reducing the borrowing base from 75 percent on receivables to 50 percent.

2. Establish at the outset that the personal guarantee will be a pivotal issue. If you sign the loan agreement with the guarantee, it will be your objective to eventually have the bank release you from that obligation.

3. Sign the personal guarantee but place restrictions on the extent and limits to which the bank can collect from the personal guarantor, such as $200,000. One does not want to sign a joint and several guarantee, which allows the bank to simultaneously collect the bank note from both the business and the individual signer. An indemnification guarantee restricts the bank from suing the individual guarantor until the business fails to pay its obligations.

4. Arrange a scenario that will trigger when the guarantee will go into effect, e.g., the personal guarantee will go into effect if you are late on more than three consecutive loan payments or if working capital falls below a specified amount.

5. Alter the loan provision so that the grace period to cure the issue in default is extended, for example, from a week to fifteen days.

6. Share the personal guarantee liability with other major stockholders, e.g., a 20 percent owner of the company would be responsible for 20 percent of the guarantee liability.

7. Write an agreement stating that the bank will let you off the personal guarantee when the note is, say, 70 percent paid off. The banker will use certain benchmarks that must be obtained based on either the income statement or the balance sheet.

In spite of the above recommendations, let's assume that you flatly will not sign a personal guarantee. If your company is financially strong, you can always threaten to take your business to another bank.

Or, in lieu of a personal guarantee that might be open-ended, you could counter with another piece of collateral, such as your summer house. A real power play is to ask your board, early on in its development, to vote on a resolution that officers and shareholders will not be allowed to sign personally for any debt. Another suggestion is to not fill out the bank's preprinted financial statement, which implies that you will not sign such a form. Instead, substitute a signed and notarized financial form of your own that in essence provides the same information. Also, remember that the days of automatic signing of personal loan guarantees by the spouse are over.

YOUR BANKER

Pick a banker rather than selecting a bank. You should get a referral from a respected business friend and/or entrepreneur. An excellent banker can be invaluable to your company and tremendously important to the success of your business.

Well-respected bankers measure and evaluate the desirability of a new loan based on a number of key factors:

- The reputation and character of the principal is paramount. The recommendation of a credible third party such as a lawyer, accountant, or other businessperson carries a lot of influence. Regardless of a recommendation, however, the banker either will feel intuitively comfortable with you or he won't.
- Bankers will critique the business plan defining the purpose, need, and repayment schedule. "The numbers have to work," states an experienced banker.
- Lenders feel more comfortable if the creditor has carved out a niche in its industry and is not just producing a commodity product that wins or fails on price alone.
- Lenders become more motivated when the potential loan is within a certain size range. For example, a mid-sized bank generally makes corporate loans from anywhere between $750,000 and $10 million; however, its bread-and-butter loan is between $2 mil-

lion and $5 million. If a potential corporate borrower is seeking a $200,000 loan, he or she is less likely to get the loan officer's full attention at a mid-size bank, because it takes the same amount of effort, if not more, to process this as to process a $2 million loan.

- Lenders are concerned about the leverage of the balance sheet. If the company is highly leveraged, then bankers would like the principal to be personally fully committed also by investing a significant sum of his or her own equity, say, $500,000 to $750,000. The purpose of the guarantee is as much psychological as collateral. One of the banker's worst fears is that the owner will throw the factory keys on the table and walk away from a business that has had a downturn.
- Lenders' concerns are numerous, but since the bank is borrowing principally against accounts receivable, inventory, and machinery and equipment, it will want to closely monitor accounts receivable and inventory either by computer systems and/or by having certified statements for verifications. If the borrower has more than 50 percent of its business with one customer, the bank may want the borrower to carry accounts receivable insurance. Bankers often hedge themselves by structuring the loan so that they will lend at 80 percent of receivables and 50 percent of inventory or, more conservatively, 70 percent of receivables and 40 percent of inventory.

Your banker wants to know the following items regarding the loan:

- How much money do you need? The answer to this question places a frame around your discussion.
- For how long? The longer the loan, the more the unknown and the greater the risk for the bank.
- For what use? Fundamentally, is the loan for working capital, a marketing program, to buy out a partner, or what?
- How will you repay it? Your repayment schedule is essential.

Because the banker relies on two items for repayment, collateral and cash flow, your strategy should be as follows: When your banker talks about inadequate collateral, you should talk about cash flow. And conversely, when your banker talks about inadequate cash flow, you should talk about collateral. This strategy is simply negotiating or posturing yourself to counter the banker's position, otherwise you may not receive the loan from the banker. It is also important for the banker to know how the additional money will improve your business. You should be able to show that you can lower your costs, improve sales, or expand your capabilities.

As Joseph R. Mancuso states: "It is imperative that you know what your credit history looks like before your banker runs a credit check on the company. It's very simple—sometimes credit agencies make mistakes, and it's your responsibility to correct those mistakes before your banker sees them."

In interviewing your potential banker, find out what are the secured and unsecured lending limits. Also, determine the size of the loan the banker can execute without going before the loan committee and/or receiving a second signature.

Your accountant can be the critical link between you and the banker by properly presenting the financial posture of the company. In some cases, you should ask your banker to recommend a good accountant. Additionally, you need a lawyer who specializes in banking to scrutinize the loan agreement, preferably one who represents clients who have negotiated loans from competing banks. It is important that you know the extent to which you can negotiate with your banker based on the knowledge of your advisers, who are in the marketplace on a routine basis.

BANK LOAN SUMMARY

In summary, the critical issues in obtaining a bank loan are the following:

- Prepare a formal written business plan within which you propose to operate. Additionally, make a verbal presentation that is crisp and makes sense.
- State exactly how much money you need, why you need it, and how you will repay the loan.
- The key factor for the banker is to be convinced that your company has the ability to service the debt and repay it. A detailed cash flow analysis month by month is critical.
- In bankers' jargon, the 6 Cs of credit are:
  Character: The key to a long-term relationship
  Cash flow: Ensures repayment
  Capital: Necessary to run the business
  Collateral: To cover any shortfall in the debt to equity
  Condition: Lender's tolerance of risk
  Capacity: Ability to earn more money
- Do your research up front by knowing what bank is most apt to be interested in your industry and/or your company. For example, the Silicon Valley Bank, with twenty-seven U.S. offices in fourteen states and three international subsidiaries, specializes in emerging and rapidly growing technology and life science companies. Unlike most conventional banks, which shy away from black-box products or software companies, this billion-dollar bank embraces these companies. Over the last twenty years, the Silicon Valley Bank has loaned money to 30,000 companies including former startups such as Cisco Systems, Electronic Arts, Infinity, IDS Uniphase, etc.

RAISING CASH FROM THE BALANCE SHEET

Most traditional lenders will base their loans on the cash flow of the borrower. Depending on the stability of the business and the risk tolerance of the bank, your banker will expect debt coverage between 1.2 to 1.8 times. The following is an example of an acquirer's pro forma analysis of the EBIT debt coverage.

Operating income	$600,000
Add back interest	$200,000
Add back taxes	$200,000
REORGANIZATION ADD BACKS	
Excess compensation	$100,000
Vehicles, travel, etc.	$100,000
Total	$1,200,000
Less: Bank interest	$300,000
Shareholder return	$200,000
Noncompete agreement	$100,000
Bank repayment	$200,000
Total	$800,000

Debt coverage ($1.2 million divided by $800,000) = 1.5

In spite of this analysis, your banker will ultimately look to the balance sheet for collateral. You might expect to raise the cash as follows:

		ALLOWABLE AMOUNT
Accounts receivable	$1,000,000 × 75% =	$750,000
Inventory	$2,000,000 × 25% =	$500,000
Fixed assets	$3,000,000 × 75% =	$2,250,000
Loan Availability		$3,500,000

The preceding analysis was principally based on cash flow and debt coverage; the following analysis is an asset-based analysis.

Developing a Financing Package Based on Company Assets

The following example is printed with permission by PricewaterhouseCoopers from its book *The Buying and Selling a Company Handbook*.

Background

A target company has had a history of strong, steady cash flow with the current year at $7.5 million. A $25 million purchase price has been agreed upon by the buyer and seller. Appraisals indicate that the land and buildings have a market value of $4 million and the liquidation value of machinery and equipment is $3 million. Standard ratios by senior lenders are applied herewith.

1. BALANCE SHEET (000S)

ASSETS		LIABILITIES & EQUITY	
Accounts Receivable	$6,000	Accounts Payable	$3,000
Inventory	$8,000		
Land and Buildings	$2,000		
Machinery and Equipment	$4,000	Equity	$17,000
	$20,000		$20,000

2. SENIOR DEBT FINANCING (000S)

A. REVOLVING LINE OF CREDIT:

Accounts Receivable	$6,000 × 80% =	$4,800
Inventory	$8,000 × 40% =	$3,200
		$8,000

B. TERM DEBT: SECURED

Land and Buildings (market)	$4,000 × 80% =	$3,200
Machinery and Equipment (liquidation)	$3,000 × 60% =	$1,800
		$5,000

C. TERM DEBT: UNSECURED

Cash Flow	$7,500

3. SOURCE OF ACQUISITION FUNDS (000S)

Buyer's cash (equity investment) $4,500

SENIOR DEBT:
Revolving line of credit $8,000
Term debt: secured $5,000
Term debt: cash flow loan $7,500
                                                    $25,000

Balance Sheet Summary

PricewaterhouseCoopers advises clients on how to structure acquisitions. In this case, PricewaterhouseCoopers reminds us that a lender will not necessarily lend funds based on the result of applying standard percentages to recorded values. Lenders will also evaluate your ability to service the debt through an analysis of proper debt coverage.

CHAPTER 15

Picking Apart the Financials

In analyzing a company to acquire, one scrutinizes the financials for a number of different reasons. First, the current balance sheet and income statement give you a quick snapshot of how well the company is performing. Second, taking a minimum of three years' statements, and ideally five years', will show you how well management has run the business. Third, the recent financials will indicate to what extent you can leverage the balance sheet in order to finance the potential acquisition.

In this chapter, we will be analyzing the financials principally to assess management's ability, which is different from analyzing the numbers for the purposes of a valuation. For example, it is very possible to have a second- or third-generation family business with a well-known product that the company has manufactured for 100 years, a strong balance sheet, and an income statement that shows healthy gross margins but minimal profits. In this situation, you might determine that the target company is mismanaged and could indeed be very profitable. There are four basic conclusions, as follows:

1. As a buyer, you should not pay a full price for what the company could earn if properly managed.
2. If you buy the company, you should be confident that you can implement moderate price increases over time without adversely affecting sales; you can reduce operating and overhead costs; and you can improve sales over time.
3. If you buy the company, you probably should be reluctant to keep management in place based on the company's underperformance.
4. All things considered—the economy, the industry of the target company, its products, its reputation, its facilities,

and its general financial condition—this could be a good acquisition at the right price, notwithstanding its current undermanagement.

It is therefore important to pick apart the financials to understand if and how the operations of the company can be improved. The following techniques are recommended.

DISCLOSE TRENDS

Using three years of past financials or two years plus the projected current year, arrange each item in vertical columns by percentages of the total.

SAMPLE BALANCE SHEET

ITEM	YEAR 1	YEAR 2	YEAR 3
Assets			
Cash	8%	6%	4%
Accounts receivable	37%	40%	45%
Notes receivable	3%	2%	0%
Inventory	20%	25%	30%
Prepaid expenses	2%	2%	1%
Total Current Assets	70%	75%	80%
Land and buildings	20%	17%	15%
Machinery and equipment	10%	8%	7%
Less depreciation	(2)	(2)	(2)
Goodwill	2%	2%	2%
Total Assets	100%	100%	100%
Liabilities			
Notes payable	5%	3%	1%
Accounts payable	20%	28%	35%

Taxes payable	4%	3%	2%
Accruals	1%	2%	2%
Total Current Liabilities	30%	34%	40%
Capital			
Long-term debt	10%	12%	13%
Stock	40%	36%	32%
Paid-in surplus	20%	18%	15%
Total Capital	70%	66%	60%
Total Liabilities and Capital	100%	100%	100%

PROFIT AND LOSS STATEMENT

	YEAR 1	YEAR 2	YEAR 3
Gross sales	100%	100%	100%
Less: Returns and allowances	2%	3%	4%
Net sales	98%	97%	96%
Cost of goods sold:			
Materials	(40%)	(41%)	(42%)
Labor	(20%)	(21%)	(22%)
Gross profit	38%	35%	32%
General and administrative expense	(20%)	(20%)	(20%)
Selling expenses	(10%)	(10%)	(10%)
Total Expenses	(30%)	(30%)	(30%)
Operating profit	8%	5%	2%
Interest	(2%)	(3%)	(4%)
Taxes	(3%)	(2%)	(1%)
Net profit after tax	3%	0%	(3%)

Analysis

In this case the sales were rising. However, in a period of three years the company went from making money to losing money. By looking first at the profit and loss statement and then at the balance sheet, we can determine what happened.

Returns and allowances. Any number over 2 percent should be of real concern. Either the quality of the product is poor or the company has a far too liberal return policy, or both.

Selling, general, and administrative expense (SG&A). This is commonly known as overhead. Many companies faced with severe price competition, making it unwise to increase prices, have the alternative of cutting their overhead in order to remain profitable. In this case, management did not select this alternative.

Gross profit. This is the second most important item, other than net after tax. One can afford to operate at a reduced gross margin if sales increase dramatically and SG&A expenses do not materially increase. In this case, management should have been able to either increase prices to offset the higher material and labor costs or find alternative ways to keep these costs from increasing.

Accounts receivable. Along with inventory, this requires careful scrutiny because it should be turned into cash in a relatively short period of time. Former I.T.T. CEO and business icon Harold Geneen once said, "The company can lose money indefinitely, but once it runs out of cash, the game is over."

Inventory. Managing inventory is one of the most important functions of modern-day management. Just-in-time delivery, inventory turnover, order completion, etc., are the benchmarks for success. A number of years ago it was common to build cars, computers, and other goods, for stock. Nowadays, customers' orders are specifically matched to production schedules, which reduces unnecessary inventory, thus allowing management to utilize its cash most effectively. The major problem with this hypothetical company is the rapid increase in both accounts receivable and inventory, which is a result of management not properly managing its assets.

In order to finance these two items, the company has increased its accounts payable and long-term debt.

Long-term debt. Usually long-term debt is incurred to finance the plant and equipment. However, in this case one can see that it was used to finance working capital, or more specifically the increased accounts receivable and inventory. In other words, the company is using more permanent capital to finance short-term obligations. This method of financing is not considered sound.

In summary, by going through every item and converting the numbers to percentages, one can quickly understand how the company is performing and why. A well-managed company makes adjustments quickly, assuming there are accounting systems in place to flag the various indicators. If the selling price of the product must be cut to meet the competition, then the lower gross margin must be offset by cutting the overhead (SG&A). If sales are faltering, then perhaps management needs to increase its sales expense but offset this increase by reducing some other expense. The point of this analysis is to evaluate management's ability to manage the business and to determine whether there are systems in place that will give management timely information in order to make these decisions.

Benchmarking

Numerous books and various consulting firms concentrate on benchmarking, which is basically comparing a company against certain industry standards. For financial benchmarking, Robert Morris Associates has compiled the most comprehensive figures not only for every industry and/or type of business but for various business sizes within these groups. Robert Morris Associates is located in the Philadelphia National Bank Building in Philadelphia, PA.

The purpose of benchmarking is to compare the target company with its peers in its particular industry. If we look at the retail business, for example, there are basically four major variables:

1. Volume
2. Overhead as percentage of sales
3. Inventory turnover
4. Cost of capital

It would not make sense to compare the financial ratios of a small office products retailer with those of a large chain of office superstores such as Staples. The ratios would not be meaningful. However, you might want to think twice about buying a small office products retailer if there is any possibility that you might be competing with a nearby Staples, Office Max, or Office Depot sometime in the near future, as they could drive you out of business.

Based on the four major variables mentioned above, let us observe the different gross margins on which the following types of retailers operate successfully.

TYPE OF RETAILER	GROSS MARGIN
Warehouse clubs	10–12%
Superstores	25%
Small retailers	40–45%
Department stores, high-end retailers	50% or more

Ratios

There are basically three types of ratios:

1. Balance sheet ratios: Various balance sheet items compared.
2. Operating ratios: Expense account items compared to income.
3. Operating items: Compared to balance sheet items and vice versa.

Within those types, there are a number of possible ratios; some of the basic ones are as follows:

Current Ratio (arbitrary numbers)

$$\frac{\text{Current assets}}{\text{Current liabilities}} = \frac{\$125,000}{\$75,000} = 1.67$$

Short-term obligations ($75,000 in this case) should have a cushion of liquid assets such that the current ratio is a minimum of 1.5 to 2.0.

Average Collection Time for Accounts Receivable

$$\frac{\text{Sales per year}}{365 \text{ days}} = \frac{\$1,000,000}{365} = \$2,740 \text{ average sales per day}$$

For some businesses, the acceptable average is 45 days. If we multiply $2,740 × 45 days, the accounts receivable would be $123,300. If accounts receivable in this case are substantially larger than $123,300 for a nonseasonal business, corrective action should be implemented.

Inventory Turnover (figures from balance sheet)

$$\frac{\text{Cost of goods sold}}{\text{Inventory}} = \frac{\$400,000}{\$100,000} = 4 \text{ turns}$$

While every business has different norms for turnover, one rule of thumb that I like to use is the following formula:

GROSS MARGIN	TURNOVER	NORM
50 percent	2	100
25 percent	4	100
10 percent	10	100

The norm of 100 is somewhat of an arbitrary figure. The rationale is that as a business you can justify a low gross margin if you are turning over your inventory four times a year. Conversely, if you only turn your inventory twice a year, you better have a gross margin of 50 percent or more to make economic sense.

Return on Investment (ROI)

$$\frac{\text{Net after tax}}{\text{Invested capital}} = \frac{\$100,000}{\$500,000} = 20 \text{ percent}$$

No single ratio is as important as ROI, and there is no one acceptable number for all investors. The principal variable is the amount of risk associated with the investment, known as the risk/reward factor. A venture capital investment usually requires a ROI of 30 percent or more. A very solid company should return 18 to 20 percent. These ROI numbers ultimately compare to the safest investment, Treasuries, with an approximately 8 percent return.

PRICING IS THE KEY INGREDIENT

When you are picking apart the financials in your analysis of whether you should buy a particular company, and if so, at what price, be sure to assess the pricing issues of the company's products or services. If for example, you determine that there is no way the company can successfully increase its selling price over the next year—beware. Also beware if you determine that there is no way you can reduce the company's cost of goods sold over the next year.

Let's assume you acquired your target company and that over the next two years you successfully increased your overall selling prices for the product or services by 3 percent and you reduced the cost of goods (COG) sold by 3 percent while keeping the SG&A the same. The following would be the result.

	AT ACQUISITION	TWO YEARS LATER	
Sales	$100	$103.0	(3 percent price increase)
COG	70	67.9	(3 percent cost reduction)
Gross Profit	30	35.1	
SG&A	(25)	(25.0)	
EBIT	$5	$10.1	

In the above example, by increasing prices by 3 percent and decreasing costs of goods sold by 3 percent, you *doubled* the EBIT, or profit.

Beware of acquiring a company in which it is doubtful that you can successfully increase prices or reduce costs over a reasonable time period of a year or so. In the above example, the $5 (or 5 percent) is too low of an EBIT and is not a viable level of profitability for long-term survival. The minimum benchmark for growing companies is a 10 percent EBIT. Alternatively, you could reduce the SG&A expenses to arrive at 10 percent EBIT, but many pundits would frown upon the cut of such expenses as research and development, advertising, or bonuses, as they are important factors for your company's future growth.

Simplify the Financials

It is somewhat confusing when you are presented with the financials of a company with 30-plus line items. For purposes of a quick analysis, spread out several years of historical condensed results plus one year of projections as follows:

BALANCE SHEET

CURRENT ASSETS	CURRENT LIABILITIES
Net Plant & Equipment	Long-Term Debt
Other Assets	Equity
Total Assets	Total Liabilities/Stockholders Equity

INCOME STATEMENT

	2005	2006	2007
Sales			
Gross Profit			
SG&A			
EBIT or EBITDA			

The above abbreviated version will quickly show the financial trend of the company.

CONCLUSION

It is important to pick apart the financials to determine how well the company is managed. The decision about the strength of management will affect the ultimate valuation of the company.

There are obviously many factors to consider in analyzing the financials. One company may have a higher profit as a percentage of sales, but upon closer observation it may appear that more capital is invested in the company than is actually required. Therefore, scrutinizing the financials in great detail is imperative before acquiring a company.

CHAPTER 16

Looking Beyond the Numbers

L et us assume that you have spent a year seeking a company to acquire; you have spent considerable time negotiating the deal and an equal amount of time securing the necessary financing, and now all you have to do is some due diligence. You have retained a prestigious accounting firm to verify the inventory, accounts receivable, accounts payable, etc. However, you have charged yourself with the responsibility of evaluating the status of the company to be sure there are no skeletons in the closet and that you won't buy a pig in a poke.

You have outlined the four most important areas of concern: finance, management, manufacturing, and marketing. Specifically, you have segmented these areas of concern as follows.

Finance

Cash. If the target company is not taking trade discounts or is not able to buy at the quantity price or is late in trade payments, you might assume that there is poor cash management.

Lack of profitability. One might consider that the company lacks controls, has too much overhead, or underprices in order to make the sale. A comparison of the gross margins from year to year is a quick indicator of whether the manufacturing efficiencies are slipping or whether there is a price erosion.

Bank problems. One might find that the company's financial ratios are out of compliance, that it is under particular scrutiny from the bank, that it has used its complete credit line, or that it has suspect relations with its bank.

Outdated financials. One might discover that the company does not have monthly financial statements or detailed cash flow projections. Furthermore, one might discover that the company's annual financial statements are three to four months after year end and that the statements are not audited, all of which mean that they lack credibility.

Management

Continual crisis. Every time you meet with the owner, he or she is constantly interrupted by emergency telephone calls and secretarial demands for immediate decisions.

Substantial changes in key personnel. A review of the last three years shows an unusual turnover in key management positions, including CFO, sales manager, and vice president of manufacturing.

No changes in senior management for many years. This may indicate a stagnant business, not up with the times, and dominated by the CEO.

Lack of pride. While pride is somewhat subjective, one can often sense the tempo and spirit of the personnel by the tone of their voice and the bounce in their stride.

Manufacturing

Dying market. The company is in a dying market and has no capability to shift gears.

Rejects. Determine the rate, the reason, and what quality controls are in place. What do the records show, and how does management address this important issue?

Just-in-time (JIT). What the inventory turnover is and whether there are too many vendors would be part of the JIT analysis.

Sales per employee. Many industries are different, but a fully integrated manufacturer should have at least $150,000 in sales per employee, and a distributor should have $300,000 in sales per employee.

Marketing

Loss of market share. The key in evaluating market share is to be able to compare the increase or decrease in unit volume with that of the direct competition. Sometimes specific price increases will increase dollar sales, but the true measure is unit sales.

Trade shows. During due diligence, one should observe the interest and activity in the company's booth at trade shows compared to its competitors.

New products. The rate and success of new products is partially related to the extent of the company's R&D. Part of 3M's success is due to the fact that 30 percent of its products are introduced in every five-year cycle.

The above is a quick overview of items that you should look into beyond the analysis of the financial statements. Almost all companies have warts. Prospective buyers tend to focus on these problems. It is more important to focus on the company's strengths, and in particular, what the company is doing well. The following is an example of a company that can be analyzed both ways, analogous to the expression that the glass is half full or half empty.

A third-generation family business with $20 million in sales has a management team of four. Three members of the team are from the family. The business is growing at 15 to 20 percent annually, has an operating income equivalent to 10 percent of sales, and has no long-term debt. Its products are office partitions of excellent quality. Manufacturing is low-tech but very efficient in a favorable labor market. Sales are somewhat seasonal, and the workforce fluctuates between 150 and 200. The sales breakdown is as follows:

Home Depot	50%
Distributors	40%
Government	10%
Total	100%

The company depends on Home Depot for half its business; however, this manufacturer won the supplier of the year award from Home Depot based on service, quality, merchandising, and customer support.

Based on this limited information, would you buy this business and, if so, would you heavily discount the value because of the dependence on one customer? There is no clear-cut answer. If you have a tolerance for a certain amount of risk, you might buy the company with the full intention of broadening the sales base. Bear in mind that the new wave in business is for the customer-vendor relationship to be equivalent to a partnership. Many companies in the automotive parts business are heavily dependent on a major customer or two.

ADDITIONAL RISK FACTORS

Ideally, your target company will have very few warts. In addition to the obvious problem of heavy dependence on a single large customer, other risk factors include the following:

Industry

Many times we have heard people talk about a company being in the proverbial "buggy whip" industry, implying that the industry has passed its prime. Many issues concerning the target company involve external forces that are beyond your control. In the book *How to Buy a Business* which is currently out of print, by Richard A. Joseph, Anna M. Nekoranec, and Carl H. Steffens, the authors state:

By thinking about these competitive and industry issues, you may be able to expose the strengths or weaknesses of the business and its competitors. If a weakness is discovered, try to determine if it is temporary or a permanent part of doing business. External forces are often the most difficult to manage, so caution should be exercised in planning the ongoing business on the assumption that these forces can be modified or mitigated.

This is true, but there are other industry considerations, such as possible product obsolescence in the high-tech industry or fad changes in the fashion industry. In order to have meaningful growth in the food industry, manufacturers must pay "slotting fees" to get their products on supermarket shelves. Almost every industry has its peculiarities, and it is up to you, the buyer, to thoroughly familiarize yourself with them.

Products and Services

Back in the 1960s a friend of mine, Leif Nashe, decided to sell the Dovre Ski Binding Company. Although under $1 million in sales, it was one of the premier companies in its industry. A number of entities wanted to buy Dovre, including United Shoe Machinery, a well-known New England manufacturing company. Leif turned down United Shoe's generous offer because he insisted that the buyer be willing to keep the business in West Concord, Massachusetts, for the sake of his employees.

Leif was born in Norway and naturally grew up on the ski slopes, particularly the jumping hills. He started the company in the 1930s, just as downhill skiing caught on in the United States. His cable bindings were well-known and at one time had the highest industry rating worldwide for quality, price, service, and reliability. During World War II, Dovre received a windfall of orders from the U.S. Army. After the war, recreational skiing really started to catch on, and Leif capitalized on the industry's growth. Dovre rarely advertised and had no sales force. Marketing consisted of Leif calling on his ski dealers once a year, buying them a drink, and giving each dealer a special box of custom-made chocolates.

In the mid-1960s, Leif sold the business to two smart young Harvard MBAs on the condition that they not move the company. By then, the ski industry was changing rapidly: The wooden ski was replaced by the Head metal ski and cable bindings by the modern "popout" safety bindings. Dovre had just started to produce the new bindings and was undaunted by the invasion of new high-tech German bindings.

The two buyers were aware that Dovre was no longer on the leading edge of product innovation, but what they didn't realize was how much money it would take to rebuild the company. No longer could they sell the old-style cable bindings, and no longer could they successfully solicit orders by handing out a box of chocolates to their dealers once a year.

Giant companies from Europe, like Salomon, had invaded the U.S. ski industry overnight; they were able to offer huge quantity discounts and off-season deals that allowed the dealer to withhold payment for six to eight months.

Without going into further details, the new owners decided to vastly expand their product lines, including ski and boat racks, imported cross country ski equipment, and finally, opened a factory outlet operation. By the early 1980s, the business was bankrupt.

Clearly a multitude of mistakes were made in the example above. Not only should the two young entrepreneurs have turned down the opportunity to buy the business, but having bought the company, they wandered too far away from their core business. If Peter F. Drucker had been the key adviser for the two buyers when they were considering the acquisition, he probably would have asked them three of his stock analytical questions.

1. Is the company's market standing going up or down, and is its industry being negatively affected by alternative products or services?
2. Is the company's achievement as a successful innovator in its market equal to its market standing, or does it lag behind it?
3. Is the company concentrating on improving its productivity in order to gain a competitive advantage?

Customers

Earlier in this chapter, I discussed the risks of being dependent on a few key customers, so I will not repeat that aspect. In addition to the mix of customers, it is important to understand the quality of customers, their financial stability, and their likelihood to grow. Naturally, if your customer base grows rapidly, it will increase your chances of growing also.

Back in the 1960s, I owned a fiberglass boat manufacturing company. Most of our dealers struggled to make a living. Inevitably we would extend thirty-day billing terms, which in turn led to shipping product to them in the fall with spring payment terms, commonly known as "dating"—ship now and collect later (*hopefully*).

Our manufacturing company was not financially strong itself. Luckily we operated without too many losses, but we were fortunate that there was no industry downturn or recession.

So when you are checking up on a possible acquisition, look at the target company's customer list. Ideally, many of the customers are from the *Fortune* 1000. Also track each customer's volume of business over the past three years. And finally, understand the characteristics of the industry payment terms. For example, some segments of the retail business, especially discount chains, continually dispute manufacturers' invoices. They may continually return so-called faulty merchandise, claim shortages in shipments, take 2 percent discounts beyond the specified ten-day period, and so forth.

Analyze the customers. Are they the type of companies and the type of people to whom you want to sell? If not, think twice about pursuing the target company.

Suppliers

Obviously, vendor relationships are important and should be transferable to the new owner(s). This should be of particular concern in the purchase of a distributor. Many relationships between the distributor and its suppliers are personal, and those that are contractual are for a very limited time period. If you are contemplating the acquisition of a distributor, be sure the retention of key suppliers is linked to the payout period for the purchase of the business.

Management

In looking beyond the numbers, it is imperative that you assess the management team early in the process. In the book *How to Buy a Business*, the authors write: "Understanding the strengths and weaknesses of current management will help determine what changes are possible. The most important issue you need to consider is whether the owner is the reason for the success of the business. If so, the company is extremely vulnerable to management changes. If he or she leaves, can you fill this role?"

Most companies with sales under $5 million to $10 million are heavily dependent on the chief executive officer. In many cases, a full management team is not in place. I know of one public company with sales just under $20 million that has no chief operating officer and only a part-time chief financial officer. A company's strength is often its management team.

DETERMINE THE COMPETITIVE ADVANTAGE

In looking beyond the numbers, you should be seeking characteristics that make the company special, separate it from its competitors, and in essence give the company a competitive advantage. The well-known Harvard Business School professor Michael Porter popularized the theory of competitive advantage in his bestselling book on that subject.

To determine the competitive advantage, I like to ask the president of a selling company three basic questions:

1. What differentiates your company?
2. How do you grow the company?
3. What would you do if the company received a sizable windfall in cash?

Surprisingly, many company presidents will not have a definitive answer to these simple questions, which merely dampens my interest in their business. Specific examples of competitive advantage would include:

Investment in capital equipment. A $7 million distribution company sells coffee and citrus juices to institutions, e.g., universities, hospitals, hotels, etc. It charges a higher price than its competitors, but it has loaned (not leased) over $1 million of dispensing machines to its customers, guaranteeing twenty-four-hour service. Unless this distributor's competitor is willing to invest sizable amounts of money in capital equipment, there is little chance that the distributor will lose its competitive edge.

Price elasticity. An adhesive company with sales of $3 million was showing operating profit and owner's compensation of $500,000 because it was able to raise prices considerably without loss of business. Since adhesives are often custom produced, the adhesive company is able to retain the formula as proprietary information. The actual cost of the adhesive in a customer's product, e.g., boat, camper, etc., is such a small component of the total cost that the risks of the customer's switching to another vendor are slight.

Low-cost producer/response time. A $15 million manufacturer in the office supply business is located in a modern plant in a rural area where occupancy and labor costs are relatively low compared to those faced by other industry players. Because the company services only a few, but large, accounts, orders are shipped in truckload quantities. The direct sales results in a very low selling expense, and the general and administrative staff is kept to a minimum. This company's competitive advantage is that it executes the basics very well. The company's response time is quick, whether it is developing a new product for a customer or shipping within two days of receipt of order. If a customer has a surge of orders as a result of the seasonal factor of "back to school" business, this company will ramp up production by going to three shifts.

Uniqueness. Most of us know that location is one of the critical elements in the retail business. For most major retailers, it is desirable to be located in the primary malls as opposed to the secondary malls. Most malls have a restriction of one of each type of store per mall, e.g., one bookstore, one men's shoe store, etc. Therefore, if you own a chain of bookstores or men's shoe stores, you could be prohibited from renting space in the primary malls. When The Nature Company developed an exclusive product line of merchandise, there was virtually no retail competition. As a result, the company had almost no barriers to entry when it applied for space in a primary mall, except of course, if there was no vacancy.

Other examples of competitive advantage include license agreements, franchises, brand recognition, patent protection, like that of the exercise machines of NordicTrack.

QUICK RATING SYSTEM

Tom Ellis of The Ellis Company is a successful individual acquirer of companies assembling a group of investors mostly from his personal network of friends. Part of his ability to rapidly assess whether he should seriously pursue the purchase of a company is his quick rating system for target companies.

The following scoring system of fifteen items are ranked between a low risk of five descending to a high risk of one. Since Tom's objective is only to acquire "low risk" companies, the total score should be 60 points or higher (average of four or higher per item).

FACTORS	LOW RISK	HIGH RISK
1. History	Long/Profitable	Short/Unprofitable
2. Industry	Stable/Growing	Unstable/Declining
3. Special Skills	Not Specialized	Specialized
4. Location	Near Ft. Wayne	Distant Ft. Wayne
5. Labor Source	Plentiful	Scarce

6. Management	Qualified/Staying	Unqualified/Leaving
7. Gross Margins	High	Low
8. Return on Investment	High Return	Low Return
9. Return of Investment	Easy Liquidation at Cost	Not Liquidated
10. Vendor Dependency	Modest	Very
11. Reputation	High	Poor
12. Products	High Quality/Niche	Low Quality/Commodity
13. Special Requirements (licenses, insurance, bonds)	No	Yes
14. Competition	Limited	Intense
15. Technology	Not Vulnerable	Extremely Vulnerable

Total Score

THE ROLE OF A DEVIL'S ADVOCATE

When looking at companies, it is important to look at the downside as well as the upside. The seller has the advantage over the buyer in that he or she will know more about the industry and the company than the buyer. The stated reason for selling the company may not be the real reason. Undisclosed reasons might include such things as the following: the industry may be quickly changing, the competition might be increasing, customers might be having financial difficulties, and capital spending requirements might be escalating.

Maybe the owner realizes that middle management is weak and there is no strong successor, or that there are no new products in the pipeline. Perhaps his or her gut feeling is that now is the time to sell. Many consumer product companies, whether they be sailboat or wood stove manufacturers, have gone from boom to bust in a short period of time. The consumer market can be fickle, while the industrial market is more stable.

If you have some apprehension about buying your prospective acquisition, particularly as it applies to items beyond the numbers, then I suggest you take the following advice of Andre Laus, principal of The Recovery Group, a Boston consulting firm.

It is usually desirable for a founder to remain temporarily in place. Additionally, the best deal for buyers is one in which seller paper can be used as subordinated debt. Consequently, as long as former owners are owed money, then they have a right to view themselves as quasi-partners, and I would suggest that the insightful buyer consider structuring a share of future earnings improvement to the former owner's benefit—as long as he's in place. Of course, it is desirable for the seller to have some sort of security on the notes, and there should be a reasonable risk rate on the coupon. The fact that the seller continues for a short time as a quasi-partner, albeit as a debt holder, certainly creates value in the deal. The seller as your quasi-partner in the transaction has a vested interest in helping you foresee problems and keeping you out of trouble.

ANALYZING THE DEAL

As a potential buyer, the major challenges are to uncover the serious problems with the business and to ascertain the company's real value drivers. Almost all companies have the previously mentioned "warts," in various degrees, so the challenge is to determine what the seller has done in the last few years to dress up the company in order to maximize earnings, e.g., frozen expenditures on capital equipment, cut back on research or marketing, withheld introduction of new products, etc.

For a financial buyer, like a private equity group, the challenge is to understand the new industry and whether they can be sufficiently educated in a short period of time. Let's suppose the financial buyer was presented with an acquisition opportunity in which the industry and the particular company's problems were not addressed—the challenge for you, the financial buyer, is to uncover these shortfalls. Your due diligence, therefore, may require the need to retain an industry expert to guide you through the discovery process.

As an industry buyer, your problems often dwell around verification of the synergies since you are up-to-speed on the nuances of the industry unlike many of the financial buyers. One very fine investment bank, which specializes in a certain industry, makes a major effort to identify and quantify financially the synergies of the buyer and seller. This approach can make a very compelling argument, but you have to be able to determine the time and investment required to achieve these synergies, and whether in fact these synergies are truly achievable.

What often appear to be achievable synergies frequently do not materialize. Acquirers are not just combining the target companies balance sheet with the profit and loss statements, but they are acquiring management and employee capabilities and special skills and know-how. While you, the acquirer, factor in certain synergies, you should also factor in certain erosions, like key people leaving, loss of key accounts, or delay of new product launches which are placed "on hold" until the integration process is complete.

To Buy or Not to Buy

In the article published in the April 2004 *Harvard Business Review,* "When to Walk Away from a Deal," the authors state that "the momentum of the transaction is hard to resist once senior management has the target in sight. Of 250 CEOs interviewed, fully a third admitted they had not walked from deals they had nagging doubts about."

The secret is not just to use due diligence to verify the target company's financial statements, but to use due diligence as an analysis of the deal's logic and whether the acquisition will prove substantial enough to justify the decision to buy or not buy a company based on the diligence.

Let's assume you are in the equine business and your company manufactures a complete line of tack for the growing recreational market. You have an opportunity to acquire a small but very profitable buggy-whip product line at a reasonable price which would contribute accretive earnings within the first year. As part of the due diligence you inquire whether you can "scale up" the business. Can you achieve sufficient overseas sales by exporting? Can you gain significant economics of scale by doubling or tripling the volume? Can you increase prices or are the products' prices competitive? After further due diligence, you decide to walk away from the deal, because while you determine that while this buggy-whip company is a cash cow, it would be too difficult to grow. Ultimately you have to ask yourself, what are you really buying? A cash cow or a growing business?

Surprise, Surprise

The mere fact that you must conduct extensive due diligence implies that you might identify sufficient business practices that will kill the deal. On the other hand, you might be so impressed with your investigation that you conclude the business is actually worth more than your bid for the company.

Here are some of the most obvious areas to examine in the due diligence process:

- Stuffing products in the distribution channel
- Overly optimistic projections
- Recurring events listed as extraordinary costs
- Underfunding capital expenditures
- Offering free service to boost short-term sales
- Exaggerating their Web site potential

INTUITION COUNTS

Often the best decisions in the M&A business are the decisions not to acquire a company—some of which are determined by thorough evaluation, some by instinct, and some by luck.

Lesson Learned

In the late 1980s, my two partners and I almost acquired a very profitable surveying company with $3 million in revenues and $1 million in cash flow. Literally on the way to present our final offer, we changed our proposal so there was less cash up front. That final adjustment was just enough difference that we lost the bid and another company acquired the business. A year later, the real estate business turned south. Not only did the surveying jobs dry up, but many of the company's customers did not pay their invoices. Fast forward two years from the date the company was sold, it went bankrupt. In retrospect, I can't say we were so smart we walked away from the deal, but our intuition must have influenced us to be more cautious in our offer. As they say in poker: "Know when to hold and when to fold."

CHAPTER 17

Negotiating

Negotiating the purchase of a business is the most dramatic segment of the transaction. Just as the last act of a Shakespeare play is the climax, the negotiation is the climax of an acquisition. Inevitably, the buyer ends up paying more for the company than he or she originally planned and the seller ends up receiving less than he or she expected.

Throughout the book I have mentioned this axiom: The seller sets the price and the buyer sets the terms. With an individual buyer, the seller will probably be somewhat reluctant to accept unsecured notes and/or significant consulting and noncompete agreements, which are also unsecured because of the perceived risk of selling to an individual rather than to selling to an established business.

Usually a seller will receive the best deal from a synergistic buyer who will gain additional complementary products or services and/or distribution with marginal increase in overall overhead. In other words, the modus operandi for the synergistic buyer is to make an acquisition whose result is $1 + 1 = 3$. Therefore, a synergistic buyer can afford to somewhat overpay for an acquisition because he or she can make up the difference by increased efficiencies and sales when the two entities are combined. On the other hand, an individual buyer is acquiring the company as a stand-alone without any synergies and is concerned about return on his or her investment (ROI). I have a friend who is a very successful businessman and who has several million dollars to put toward buying a company. After four years he still has not bought a company. My characterization of this fellow is that he always offers 5 times earnings before interest and taxes (EBIT). For good companies, that formula is at the bottom of the scale; however, very anxious corporate buyers will simply pay considerably more.

M&A NEGOTIATING

Before I explain the different styles, techniques, and nuances of negotiating, it is important that you understand the negotiating process commonly undertaken in the M&A business. When the selling company is represented by an intermediary, you are usually faced with the following auction process:

1. You qualify yourself operationally and financially.
2. You sign a confidentiality agreement.
3. You receive an offering memorandum.
4. You decide to submit a letter of interest, not to be confused with the letter of intent, which is a price range and deal structure.
5. If your initial offer is perceived to be satisfactory, you are requested to submit a formal letter of intent.
6. If your letter of intent's offer is of sufficient interest to the seller, then you become one of three or five finalists and the intermediary invites you and your support team to a half-day management meeting with the owner or CEO and receive a tour of the facility.
7. You will be asked to sweeten your offer and submit your very best price and terms.
8. If the seller's intermediary states that you are the preferred buyer, you can now expect to really negotiate. That means you will meet again with the seller to hammer out the details. As we all know, the devil is in the details, such as the security for the notes, how the earnout will be measured, employment contracts, etc. Here is where the real negotiating takes place.

Obviously, if as a buyer you try to acquire a company *not* represented by an intermediary, the process is different and apt to unfold as follows:

1. You meet with the CEO/owner of the company.
2. You express interest in buying the company and offer to sign a Confidentiality Agreement in order to obtain the financials.
3. You make an offer, probably without competitive bids.
4. Without counsel at this point, the seller either walks away from further discussion, tries to negotiate a better price and/or terms, or accepts your offer with minor alterations.

Ways to Negotiate

From prior surveys, I know that negotiating is one of the most popular topics in the M&A business. The following section highlights advice from professional negotiators.

Susan Pravda and Gabor Garai are partners from the law firm Foley & Lardner in Boston. I've summarized their comments here:

There are three aspects of negotiating, the first of which is information gathering. It is important to understand what kind of person is on the other side of the negotiating table. It may take a number of telephone calls to find out about the principal negotiator (who is usually an attorney), but this knowledge is invaluable. Does the counterpart bluster, bluff, sue over "reps and warranty" issues, and is he or she honest, straightforward and willing to compromise on some issues to complete a transaction?

The second aspect of negotiating is to offer an incentive to complete the transaction. For example, as a buyer, you might offer all cash at closing, or that you will close within forty-five days of the letter of intent, or you will include an additional piece of technology, or you could offer the selling owner a very generous consulting agreement. In the latter case, the owner is flattered that the buyer deems him or her as being so important, but in reality the former owner is hardly even called upon after the deal closes.

The third aspect of negotiating is the initiative to keep the flow going in the transaction. Concede the minor points (with some pain for effect) but concentrate on the important points which you have prioritized and predetermined at the outset.

Creativity is the hallmark of great dealmakers. For example, in one case, Garai's selling client was faced with a deal in which one-third of the purchase price was exposed to an onerous list of "reps and warranties" which gave the buyer a contractual right to sue over areas in question. By alternatively offering the buyer an escrow account equivalent to 25 percent of the purchase price, Garai lowered the exposure for the seller while assuring the buyer that a portion of the purchase price was readily available in case a claim arose.

Other initiatives are, for example, poignant statements or questions that crystallize the issues such as the following:

- My client is hung up on this issue.
- What are your goals?
- Here is the problem with the $9 million purchase price.
- We do not know how to get to that price.
- This is how we arrived at this price.
- We want to pay a fair price, show us how you got to $7 million.
- What is your position here?
- What would you like to see happen?

Besides those outlined by Pravda and Garai, other techniques for negotiating include the following:

Take it or leave it. Regardless of the seller's price and terms, you make an offer, perhaps your only and best offer, and let the chips fall where they may. This is obviously a disciplined approach. Unlike corporate buyers, you do not have to buy the company to prevent your competitors from acquiring it. Nothing is forcing you to buy the company, so you can easily walk away from the deal.

The problem with the "take it or leave it" approach, however, is that it is apt to sever the communication with the seller in case you want to get the discussions back on track. Furthermore, if your offer is made before other offers, your price will be used as a stalking horse to extract a higher price from others.

Split the difference. Assuming that you purposely underbid, leaving yourself some latitude to increase your offer, an oversimplified approach to negotiation is to split the difference between your price and the seller's price. For example, if you offer $3 million for the business and the seller wants $4 million, then $3.5 million is a reasonable compromise.

This for that. It is really important, if not imperative, that the buyer find out what the seller really wants as well as what are the seller's "hot buttons." It is very helpful if you take the time to break bread with the seller in order to determine his or her psyche. You should find out the nonmonetary items that are important to the seller such as the following:

The seller would like to stay involved with the business in some small way and/or would like to maintain an office there.

The seller would like to have one of his or her children remain in the business.

The seller would like to see contracts for key personnel.

The seller does not want the factory to be closed down and the business moved.

The seller may have spent a lifetime building up a dealer network of small retailers and does not want the new owner to change the distribution system to mass discount chains.

The seller may have subcontracted much of the piecework to various handicapped associations and does not want the new owner to terminate those relationships.

Knowing the nonmonetary issues will help you understand what concessions you can give up to achieve your monetary goal. You also have to assess how close or far apart you are in the negotiation.

Negotiations in Action

Let us assume that you have determined that the seller's price is based on a fixation on receiving the magical figure of $1 million after taxes. He has dreamed and worked all his life to become a millionaire; any other approach to valuing the business is not meaningful to him. There are ways to structure the transaction to mitigate some of the taxes. For example, if a C corporation sells its company stock instead of selling its assets, the company will avoid the double taxation, i.e., one tax to the corporation and another tax to distribute the money out of the corporation into the owner's personal account. One of your concessions could be to buy the stock of the corporation, even though this disadvantages you since assets cannot be written up to provide a higher basis for depreciation, and you must assume contingent liabilities from the previous management. But it may be worth doing to get the deal done.

It is not unusual for a verbal offer to be discussed as soon as the third meeting. It is better to get some cards on the table fairly early on. My experience is that many owners do not want to name a price before and until the potential buyer goes first. If a seller has retained an intermediary, there is often a better chance that the seller will discuss a price range or a methodology of pricing the company. Assuming that this is not the case, then it is up to the buyer to initiate the conversation regarding the pricing and terms of the deal.

In this conversation, you, the buyer, should be cordial, polite, businesslike, firm, patient, candid, and open. While you should show some humility, you should be confident and self-assured, and take the lead in the meeting. As an introduction to the conversation, you should be complimentary about the seller's business, emphasize your capabilities to finance the acquisition, and continually remind the seller of the need to treat this matter as totally confidential.

The next facet of the conversation should be a general description of how you determine valuations of companies in general and how that relates to the seller's industry, followed with a brief analysis of how you went about valuing the seller's business. Having gotten this far, I would then say: "After considerable analysis, I am willing to pay you $2.5 million for your business." Watch very carefully to sense any and all reactions from the seller. It is highly unlikely that the seller will immediately accept your offer. It is more probable that he or she will respond by saying, "No way."

At this point, the seller should reveal his or her price and how he or she arrived at that number. Let's assume the seller responds with a price of $3.5 million. Then you should respond by saying, "We should figure out how we can structure the deal so that I can get closer to your price." You should ask if the seller is willing to help you finance the transaction, which of course means seller's notes (secured or unsecured). You should not discuss the financial aspects any further at this meeting. However, you should find out, if you haven't already, about all the nonfinancial issues discussed earlier in this chapter. It is better to wait until the next meeting to discuss the details of the structure of the transaction—unless you feel that you and the seller are fairly close on the pricing.

As a buyer, it is important that you assess your advantages and disadvantages before you begin to negotiate. For example, if the owner has decided to sell the company, he or she usually has made the mental decision to complete the transaction even if the buyer's offering price is lower than what was originally expected. Your advantage is that the seller is somewhat committed to sell, but you are not necessarily committed to buy. On the other hand, if you really want to buy this business, there will undoubtedly be other buyers whom you have to compete against. Having numerous potential buyers gives the seller some leverage over you.

If you approach a company that is not on the market, you have even less leverage because the owner is probably not motivated to sell. In this case, the owner would not have a need for a well-documented selling memorandum. Additionally, the owner always has better information on the company and probably has better knowledge of the industry than you do. The power of information should not be underestimated. It is believed that one-third of all acquisitions are failures and another one-third fail to live up to their buyers' expectations. Part of the reason is that buyers do not have sufficient information to properly evaluate the situation. Many buyers look for information to confirm or corroborate their hunches. Therefore, the first order of business in negotiating is to be well prepared with careful analysis—not just number crunching, but an alertness to the business and its industry.

Going forward, you should assess what are the real issues and how important each is to you and the seller, which items are negotiable and which are not negotiable. It is best to start with the negotiable items and see if a compromise can be reached. You should think of the possible tradeoffs and possible alternatives before you begin the negotiation. For example, if the seller wants the buyer's note secured, then the buyer can negotiate a lower interest rate on the note. You should predetermine your best price, only to be used in the last hour, and you should assess your bargaining zone ahead of time. And of course, you should anticipate the seller's reaction to your offer.

TIPS IN NEGOTIATING FROM A BUYER'S PERSPECTIVE

"Negotiation is a basic means of getting what you want from others," according to the authors of *Getting to Yes—Negotiating Agreement without Giving In*. Of course, you have to negotiate with substance, knowledge, and skill, but negotiating to buy a business requires a greater understanding of the dynamics of the deal than, let's say, buying an automobile. With that statement in mind, let us proceed with some additional negotiating tips.

Style

Often we have heard the expression that a lawyer who represents himself has a fool for a client. This statement is not limited to lawyers and courtrooms. In the book *Smart Negotiating*, James Freund states:

Anyone approaching a significant negotiation should consider whether to go it alone or use an agent. There are many good reasons to conduct negotiations through an agent:

- *The agent's technical expertise or negotiation skills.*
- *The principal's emotional involvement in a high-stakes deal, which hampers his ability to negotiate effectively.*
- *The principal's desire to avoid having to answer certain questions or to react to a new proposal on the spot.*
- *The agent's ability to float a trial balloon without implicating his principal.*
- *The principal's reluctance to cross swords directly with a counterpart who will be working closely with the principal once the relationship is established.*
- *The possible advantages obtainable through limiting the agent's authority.*

The use of an agent isn't an unmixed blessing, however. It can involve such potential risks as:

- *Faulty communication between principal and agent that harms the principal's cause.*
- *An agent with his own agenda or bias who doesn't faithfully represent his principal.*
- *A principal who won't level with his agent and thus impairs their dealings with the other side.*
- *A nitpicking agent who misses the big picture and thereby undermines the deal.*
- *The inability, due to interposed agents, of one principal to reach the other agent's principal directly in order to be able to persuade, to pressure, or to extract a decision.*

The obvious answer to the above two scenarios is for the principal and the intermediary to work as a team. Of course, the first decision to be made is who should be the lead spokesman. If the intermediary is to be the spokesman, then the principal can play the "good guy" and the former can be the "bad guy." The good guy/bad guy routine is a form of psychological manipulation. In other words, the intermediary takes the forceful position and, when necessary, the principal can step in with statements such as, "In the interest of moving the deal ahead, we will concede that issue." On the other hand, if the principal is the spokesman, one approach is for him to be a little bit like Lieutenant Columbo. As we know, Columbo asks blunt and naive questions that result in candid answers by the other party. Taking the "Columbo approach" will help you extract information from the seller that he may not have originally intended on providing.

Information

You can never obtain enough information on the industry, the company, the owner/employees, the products/services, etc. But unless you have reason to trust someone, don't. When an owner tells you why he or she is selling the company, be sure that the reason can be confirmed and that the sale is not due to some hidden fact. The seller has the advantage of knowing more about the situation than you do. Perhaps a casual visit with the owner away from the company will enable you to understand more of the key issues.

Leverage

This works both ways. As a buyer, you should be able to sense under what constraints, if any, the owner has to sell, i.e., financial, time, emotional, etc. The seller has leverage over the buyer if there are numerous other buyers negotiating or about to negotiate with him or her.

Brainstorming

Before entering into negotiations, spend several hours with a corporate valuation expert to determine a rational price range and deal structure. If possible, bring a group of your peers together to obtain various opinions and ideas as to how you might present your position.

Anticipate

One of the most important skills a negotiator can possess is the ability to see the situation from the other side. A buyer should go into the meeting with several options and with an open mind. If you cannot agree on a substantive issue such as the price of the business, then agree on a procedure in an attempt to bridge the gap. One buyer actually suggested that both the buyer and the seller retain a mutually agreed-upon valuation firm to arrive at a price. If the firm determined a price that was mutually acceptable, then the buyer would pay for the valuation. If the seller refused to accept the firm's valuation, then the buyer and seller would split the cost of the report.

Presentation

It is very important for you to present a plausible case for how and why the price was determined. You should express interest in the company, give the reasoning behind the proposal, and then deliver the proposal. The offer should be supported by objective criteria and relevant precedent.

Control the Price Issue

Traditionally most buyers prefer that the seller initially state a desired price. However, if you initiate the price you are willing to pay, this figure is considered the anchor price—the price that is the basis for further discussion.

As a buyer, you want to take control of the price. You want the seller negotiating off your opening number, not off his or her number. However, under no circumstances should you mention the price until you have made a plausible case for your opening bid and gone through an objective process. Part of the reasoning behind this is that once the seller hears your proposed price, his or her attention level wanes.

Nonprice Issues

You will hear over and over again the expression, "The seller sets the price; the buyer sets the terms." Or you might hear the statement, "Terms are more important than price." When we think of terms, naturally our initial focus is on the payment structure of the deal. Actually though, as previously mentioned, there are many other nonprice issues, such as key employment contracts, a commitment not to move the factory, an obligation for the company to maintain a commitment to the town, or the retention of the owner's son in the business. Many deals that were about to crater, have been resuscitated by such issues. Inventing an idea, any idea, that can be decided on later shows your initiative to break the logjam.

Concessions

According to Marc Diener, an expert negotiator and author of *Deal Power—Six Foolproof Steps to Making Deals*: "When it comes to creative negotiation, dealmakers must master two tools: The concession and the condition. Simply put, a concession is what you give, and a condition is what you get."

Regarding the above advice:

- Refuse to make any concessions until you know all the demands.
- Keep your concessions small and infrequent, and do not be too quick to make a concession.
- Negotiate how you'll negotiate. Condition your very participation on the time, place, number of participants, agenda, and so on.
- Condition all your concessions on each other. This is sometimes called a package deal, and it gives your opponent a strong incentive to close.
- Offer your concessions in reverse order with the least important ones first.

- Make every concession contingent on getting something in return from the other side.
- Behave as though every concession is a loss of something vitally important to your side in the negotiations.
- Don't concede something until you ask your counterpart to justify his or her request.
- Be careful not to become swept up by equal-dollar concessions. If the seller reduces the asking price from $4 million to $3.6 million, the seller has come down ten percent and you have gone up thirteen percent.

Part of finding a good deal (with or without concessions) is to recognize bad deals, or red flags, early on, such as:

- Any deal you don't fully understand
- Any deal you're asked to do in a hurry
- Any deal involving a company whose accountants, bankers, or lawyers have quit
- Any deal in which you're being harangued, manipulated, or schmoozed
- Any deal that sounds too good to be true

Another expert negotiator, Dr. James Hennig, Ph.D., produced the CD-ROM, *Crash Course for Everyday Negotiation*, and submitted the following guidelines for concessions.

Give yourself room to make concessions. As you begin a negotiation, remember the extreme importance of your opening offer. It must be as low as it can possibly be without being perceived as unrealistic. The experienced negotiator positions the initial offer in a way that concessions can be made without going above their goal position.

An unrealistically low offer can often be made realistic by backing it up with sound, logical reasoning or facts. The initial offer, which at first appeared to be unrealistically low, when backed up with sound logic and facts, made some sense and gave the party room to make some concessions.

In thousands of simulated negotiations in hundreds of my seminars, I can report a very direct correlation between opening offer and finally agreed upon price. Remember this important fact: The opening offer usually correlates directly with the final agreement. The higher the opening position, the higher the final agreement: The lower the opening offer, the lower the final agreement.

Don't make the first concession on a major item. Most expert negotiators will use the strategy of "forbearance" on the major items in their negotiation. They simply hold fast to those important items, making no offer to compromise. This presumes of course, that they may make concessions on other less important items. They may, incidentally, use those concessions on some of their lesser items as reasons they cannot compromise on their "more important" items. The psychology of concession-making becomes very important and leads us to the third guideline.

The best time to get a concession is when you give one. Stated another way: Don't give a concession without getting one in return, even if the concession is just a brownie point for one you will use at a later time. The law of reciprocity comes into play here: People expect value for value. Capitalize on that basic human nature. "If I do that for you what will you do for me?" is an excellent question when asked for a concession. Not only might you get something of value you hadn't bargained for, but it will discourage the other party from asking for additional concessions.

Rarely accept the first offer. With practically every negotiator, some concessions are possible. Begin every negotiation by saying to yourself, "Every negotiator will concede something." About 99 percent of the time this will be true. By not accepting the first offer and by creatively probing for areas where concessions may be made, you open your mind, and hopefully the mind of the other party, to every possibility.

Make people work for their concessions. Let's assume you just placed a classified ad online to sell a car. A party responded an hour after the ad was posted and after a quick look at the car, offered to buy it immediately for the price you were asking. You complete the deal and have the cash in your hand as she drives away with the car. You're happy, right? . . . . Wrong. You are saying to yourself, "I didn't ask for enough!"

Now analyze this situation. When you do, you realize that if the negotiators don't have to work for the concessions they get, they will not be happy. If you want to keep the other party happy, make them work for their concessions.

Avoid a pattern in concession-making. Skilled negotiators watch carefully for patterns in the concession making of their opponents. Be aware of this fact and avoid patterns because of habit or convenience.

Don't assume you know what concession the other party wants. So many times we give more than is necessary. Probe before giving concessions. Find out what the other party is really looking for.

Try to determine all demands before you make a concession. Defend against the use of "a piece of the pie" strategy by the other party. Ask, "In addition to this, are there any other requests that you have?" Where possible, try to get the other party to lay out their entire agendas before making any concessions.

Don't make a counteroffer to an unrealistic offer. Many negotiators simply refuse to negotiate until the negotiating range falls within a reasonable level. The philosophy here is that there is no reason to make a concession of any kind when we are so far from agreement. Refusal to move forward with the negotiation in this way is risky, but often very powerful. It saves time. Either the other party concedes and the negotiation moves forward, or it is terminated.

Remember relative value or give things that don't give something away. The skilled negotiator remembers the concept of relative value—what can I concede that costs me little in time or money, but has very high value to the other side.

The art of getting or giving concessions is a very important one in the negotiation process. Review these guidelines often and they'll become second nature to you. And remember, as a buyer, you have two other negotiating tools during the concession phase. One is dead silence, which you purposely let pervade a room when you are at an impasse. Invariably, your counterpart will become so uncomfortable that he or she may retract the previous statement. Another tool is the use of time, e.g., "We have to resolve this deal by tomorrow because I am flying to Europe on Wednesday."

Bluffing

Before you start bluffing, you should have full knowledge of your "reserve" price—the limit at which you will do the deal. Again, I draw on the concise advice from the author of *Smart Negotiating*:

- Save your bluff for a significant issue.
- Bluff at the end of the process.
- Make your offer appear consistent with something you have been saying all along.
- Try to come up with a plausible explanation for why there's no give in your position.
- If possible, couple your bluff with a show of flexibility on some other issue.
- If you're forced to back down, have a "changed circumstances" ready to go in order to mitigate any harm to your credibility.

Minimize Risk

Deal-making is about taking risks as well as minimizing risks. There is a wonderful statement by Fredrick Wilcox: "Progress always involves risks. You can't steal second base while keeping your foot on first."

There are a number of tradeoffs that can be made during the negotiation process. For example, less money up front usually means a heftier purchase price down the road, and vice versa.

Normally, the seller wants all cash at closing, and the buyer wants to pay the least amount of upfront cash at closing. Therefore, there are often a number of instruments used in a deal in order to protect you, the buyer, such as:

Offset: Savvy purchasers know not to pay everything at closing because if a problem comes up later, they'll have little leverage against the seller. Instead they insist on a right of offset, or the right to reduce the money owed by the amount of any liability.

Escrow: This is like having someone referee the deal. Along with formal escrow instructions, a buyer deposits money with an escrow agent. Upon the completion of the various filings, title insurance, inspections, financing, apportioning of taxes, returns, deposits, etc., that lead to a final closing the escrow is released when the buyer takes title and the seller gets the money.

Option: This gives you the right to buy or sell something for a set price at some later date. For example, a buyer might buy 40 percent or 60 percent of a company with an option to buy the balance in five years at some sort of agreed formula.

Representations and warranties: In M&A transactions, these are often the most heavily negotiated aspects of the deal and will include everything under the sun: accuracy of financial statements, payment of taxes, title to assets, inventory, patents, accounts receivables, lawsuits, trademarks, and so on. It is important that the principals of the deal become involved and not just leave these important details to their attorneys.

Collateral: From a seller's point of view, not only getting collateral for promissory notes is important, but also whether the collateral is primary or secondary (after the bank), and whether it has personal guarantees.

In the final analysis, while minimizing risk is important, one should remember Jawaharla Nehru's statement: "The policy of being too cautious is the greatest risk of all."

Negotiating Guidelines

- **Preparation**
  - Assemble your documentation and go through the sequence of events of your presentation.
- **Presentation**
  - Face to face, deliver your proposal backed with your reasoning. Realize that the seller may need time to digest the information from this initial meeting concerning the deal.
- **Demeanor**
  - If your counterpart becomes very excitable and disagrees vehemently with your offer, remain absolutely calm and unflappable. Find out where you agree and where you disagree, and start resolving the easy issues first, leaving the most difficult issues until the end.
- **Options**
  - Think of alternative ways to resolve your differences so that there is a win-win situation; however, always get something in return for a concession. Focus on the needs of both parties.
- **Preserve the relationship**
  - Keep the mutual respect intact and remain cordial and professional at all times. If you are at an impasse, break off and reconvene some other day in the near future.

Remember, perseverance is the key to successful negotiations. In order to prevail, you must persevere. Also, never commit yourself to a material point unless everything is on the table. If it is a substantial issue, you need to know what else is to be discussed and settled.

LESSONS FROM OUTSIDE THE M&A FIELD

Bob Woolf is not known for negotiating M&A deals, and I doubt he actually ever negotiated one. He is known, however, for negotiating more than 2,000 contracts for some of the biggest names in sports and entertainment. Often we can learn from others who are in a similar but slightly different profession.

In reading his book, *Friendly Persuasion*, it becomes apparent that Woolf's style can be summarized by his own words: "I never think of negotiating against anyone. I work with people to come to an agreement! Deals are put together."

Of the 101 proven tactics, techniques, and strategies that Woolf cites, the following ten particularly caught my attention and can be applied to your business buying negotiations:

1. As basic as it sounds, your first mission in negotiating is to present your views as reasonable expectations and to secure the other side's full understanding of exactly what you want.

2. It doesn't hurt to ask. Salespeople are often reminded to ask for the order. In negotiating, you must ask for everything you want.

3. Your style should not be demanding or filled with ultimatums, and never let a counterpart's ultimatum intimidate you.

4. Silence is one of the most important tools. Either it is the things you don't say or it is a deliberate method of not committing yourself at that time.

5. You should assess both your leverage and your counterpart's leverage. You should convey that you want to do a deal, but you do not have to do the deal. It is "do or don't, but not do or die."

6. Be prepared with alternatives. Since there are a number of components to the deal (price, terms, collateral, intangibles), there are a variety of alternatives.

7. Take notes on everything relevant to the price, terms, and conditions during the meeting so that there is less chance of misunderstanding. Upon agreement on the deal, send your memorandum of understanding to your counterpart.

8. Come up or go down slowly on your concessions; otherwise you will imply that your previous position was probably out of line. Also, try to make minor concessions in return for your counterpart's major concession.

9. Do not give tit for tat. Just because your counterpart comes down $100,000, you do not have to go up the same amount. Also a drawn-out negotiation makes your counterpart feel that he or she "earned" the deal even if it was less than originally planned. If you pounce on an offer, you reveal your position too easily.

10. Perhaps the best advice from Bob Woolf is that "some of the best moves are the ones you don't make"—i.e., know when to hold and know when to fold.

And the final thought to take away about negotiations is one Woolf emphasizes in his book *Friendly Persuasion*: Fair play is always the winning strategy. Appropriately, he quotes the broadcaster Edward R. Murrow:

To be persuasive, we must be believable.
To be believable, we must be credible.
To be credible, we must be truthful.

CHAPTER 18

Letter of Intent

The letter of intent (LOI) is a precontractual written instrument from the buyer to the seller that usually covers the preliminary understanding of both parties. Other names used for the LOI are memorandum of understanding and agreement in principle. The LOI precedes the acquisition agreement, better known as the purchase and sale agreement. In order for the LOI to be nonbinding, it must state that this is the case. The LOI is the centerpiece of the transaction. It both eliminates the less serious buyers and/or sellers and uncovers key issues early on in the process.

Letters of intent are written after the two parties have had a serious discussion concerning the price, terms, conditions, and time period of the proposed transaction. Commonly, in my experience, buyers submit an LOI after they think they understand the parameters of what the seller will accept. In many cases, the buyer uses the LOI as the initial basis of negotiating. If there is reason to believe that the two parties are fairly close to agreement, the buyer will draft a second LOI. If the buyer is experienced or is working with an experienced intermediary, it may not be necessary to involve a lawyer at this time. However, it should be noted that lawyers resent being pulled into the deal after the LOI, and if it is necessary to make a material change in the future, it becomes very difficult to do so.

As you prepare the letter of intent, the more knowledge you have about the company and its financials, the stronger the case you will be able to build. I urge you to solicit a second or third opinion from a competent intermediary and corporate appraiser. A few hours spent with these professionals at approximately $200 per hour would be well worth the expense. However, although you should take their advice seriously, ultimately you have to make the decisions.

THE CONTENTS OF THE LOI

1. The price
2. The form of purchase: Stock or asset sale (assumption of what assets and liabilities, and exactly what is being purchased and what is not)
3. The payment structure: Cash, notes, stock, noncompete and/or consulting agreements, contingencies
4. Management contracts: For whom, duration, and incentives
5. Closing costs and responsibilities of buyer and seller, e.g., environmental due diligence, title searches
6. Representations and warranties: Boilerplate legal statements
7. Brokerage fees: Who pays and how much
8. Timing for completion: Drop-dead date for due diligence and financing; how long before the exchange of money and final closing
9. Insurance: Proof of insurability and/or what happens with policies
10. Disposition of earnings before closing and viability of nonordinary expenditures before closing (conduct of business)
11. Access to books and records, key customers, and key employees prior to closing
12. Disclosure of any outstanding noncompete agreements or obligations with third parties
13. Statement that this is a nonbinding agreement subject to the buyer's obtaining satisfactory financing and subject to satisfactory due diligence by both parties
14. Strict adherence to confidentiality by buyer (a breach could cause the seller to sue the buyer); buyer promises not to disclose information of seller to outsiders and not to disclose that negotiations are underway
15. Statement that the seller will take the company off the market for a designated period of time of forty-five to sixty days (a breach could cause the buyer to sue the seller)

DATA NEEDED BEFORE REACHING A LETTER OF INTENT

Let us assume that you have visited the owner and CEO of a company two or three times, you have received three years of financials, you understand the owner's compensation and add-backs, and you are now ready to make an offer. The owner has not given you any idea of the acceptable price range, and before you analyze this situation any further, you want to get the seller's reaction, so you decide to use a trial balloon. Based on the information you have and using your best judgment, you tell the owner that you are prepared to draft a letter of intent with a purchase price of, say, $5 million, of which $3 million would be paid at closing. Additionally, you should state your intention of an asset purchase or stock purchase. Assuming that the seller indicates that you are close enough to draft a letter of intent, then the following items should be obtained:

1. Annual financial statements with footnotes for the last five years
2. A list of shareholders and key managers showing name, age, shares owned, current position, years of service, annual salary, fringe benefits, last raise, and breakdown of bonuses between discretionary and formula basis
3. A list of all contractual obligations
4. A list of the top twenty customers, substituting A, B, C, etc., for actual names, followed by annual sales for the last three years
5. A description of bonus or incentive systems
6. A list of aged accounts receivable
7. Add-backs or any earning adjustments that probably would not be incurred under new ownership
8. Real estate, machinery, and equipment appraisals (if any)
9. A breakdown of inventory among raw, finished, and work in process (banks do not lend against the last)
10. Amount and description of capital expenditures for the last five years and an estimate of future needs
11. If a stock purchase, a copy of loan documents

12. If a stock purchase, a list of life insurance policies showing insured, face value, any cash surrender value, and annual premium

THE DELIVERY

The next step is to deliver the letter of intent in person to the seller and explain each item point by point. As trite as it may sound, body language is very important—eye contact, sincere smile, etc. As you discuss your offer, remember that there are a number of issues:

- Price
- Terms
- Your chemistry with the seller
- Nonfinancial issues
- How fast you can close

Usually, once the seller strikes a deal, the more quickly you can secure the financing, complete the due diligence, and draft the purchase and sale agreement, the less chance there is that the seller will change his or her mind. After the letter of intent is signed, an expeditious closing will take between sixty and ninety days, assuming that there are no major glitches. Bringing the deal to a successful close will be a full-time job.

When you deliver the letter of intent, you absolutely do not want to lose momentum by having the seller say, "Thank you, I'll think it over." Ask the seller to bring advisers or other stockholders to the meeting. Allow plenty of time for the discussion, but make it clear that you expect to come to an agreement on the nonbinding letter of intent at least by the second meeting.

You should predetermine your negotiation strategy:

- Determine your top price (although you may not pay it).
- Identify key issues for both you and the seller.
- Anticipate responses by seller.

You should also determine before the meeting whether you or your adviser will be the major spokesman. Perhaps if there are some negatives about the company to divulge tactfully, it should be mentioned by your adviser (bad guy), not by you (good guy). Such negatives could include outdated machinery and equipment that is uncompetitive for the future. A few comments like the latter will show the seller that you have a good understanding of the business and that you will have to invest more money in the company after the sale is completed. Furthermore, you can tell the seller that you cannot pay more for the business because you have others with a vested interest to satisfy, such as partners, investors, and bankers.

Lesson Learned

One of my worst experiences as an intermediary happened when I represented a very successful distributor of fruit juices, coffee, tea, and hot chocolate. One of the distributor's suppliers manufactured juice-dispensing machines. The manufacturer's sales were $9 million, and its operating income was $1 million. My client and four other investors were to buy the company for $5 million—all cash at closing! If successful, my accomplishment fee as an intermediary would have been $150,000.

My client and I went to the seller's office. I was in a mood to lock ourselves in the room and throw the keys away until the deal was signed. However, while the five partners had agreed to a $5 million purchase price, the other partners did not show up at the meeting. Even though the letter of intent was nonbinding, my client would not sign it by himself. We left the office with a verbal offer, but there was no psychological commitment by the seller. The golden opportunity slipped out of our hands, because soon after, the seller received a higher bid, although with significantly less cash at closing.

THE SIGNING OF THE LETTER

While the following figures seem a little severe, Geneva Business Services, a nationwide intermediary, reports that 50 percent of all deals fail at the letter of intent stage. Another 25 percent of the deals fail at the due diligence stage, and 15 percent fail at the documentation stage. Only 10 percent of all deals make it all the way to closing!

In most cases, the LOI is not intended to have a binding effect except for certain limited provisions. The letter of intent crystallizes in writing what have, up to that point, been oral negotiations between the parties about the basic terms of the transaction.

While the letter of intent is usually nonbinding, it does create a moral commitment and allows the buyer to proceed with a feeling of confidence. However, the buyer should insist that the seller withdraw the company from the marketplace and not discuss the potential sale with anyone.

The signing of the letter of intent triggers the buyer's commencement of the due diligence process and securing of the necessary financing. However, it isn't only the seller who should be scrutinized. The seller will want to check you, the prospective buyer, out to be sure that you are creditworthy and that you are committed to completing the deal. As an individual, your credentials might be examined more closely than if you were a corporation.

Defending Yourself to the Buyer

Anticipating the seller's due diligence, verify your financial strength by presenting detailed financial statements, and emphasize your liquid assets. If asked, you should be prepared to submit a list of potential lenders or investors for this proposed acquisition. Do your homework and contact potential lenders prior to the letter of intent.

Along with your financial position, the seller will want to know about your personal characteristics, so take the time to meet with the seller socially. You want to maximize the likelihood of a successful sale and a good relationship if the seller stays involved with the company through a contingency plan.

OUTLINE THE CONTINGENCIES

The contingencies would include the arrangement with the seller if he or she stays on. If the seller leaves, the agreement would specify the length and terms of any training period and include a noncompete agreement. Other contingencies would include:

- Review of the company's financial records
- Examination of insurance policies
- Availability of vendor and customer contracts
- Assignment of lease
- Asset or stock transaction

It is customary for agents who broker companies with sales of less than $1 million to ask the buyer for a good faith deposit of $5,000 to $10,000, but it is not common for middle-market transactions. The cost for due diligence is the burden of the buyer. Depending on its complexity, due diligence can cost the buyer of a middle-market company between $10,000 and $100,000. If the seller backs out of the deal for any of a number of reasons, the buyer has no recourse unless he or she has a breakup fee written into the LOI. While the latter is desirable for the buyer, it is very hard to persuade the seller to agree. The success or failure of completing the transaction hinges on the LOI. Upon signing the agreement, both parties are morally but not legally committed to do their utmost to complete the transaction. The outcome depends on the results of the due diligence, the ability to get the deal back on track if it is temporarily derailed, and the sense of alacrity without loss of momentum.

UNDERSTAND ITS POTENTIAL RECEPTION

The buyer may be apprehensive about submitted LOIs. This lack of action is often caused by a confidence problem. From my viewpoint, buyers without M&A experience should align themselves with professional intermediaries who will encourage them to move forward. Cautious buyers should remind themselves of football quarterbacks. Even the best quarterbacks average only 50 to 55 percent completion rate, but they may throw forty passes a game. As in football, buyers have to be willing to write numerous LOIs in order to score.

The important issue is not submitting the LOI, it is signing the purchase and sale agreement after the due diligence has been completed. Of course, the buyer's greatest fear is not knowing everything about the target company—that he might be buying a pig in a poke, that due diligence did not uncover everything. At the same time, the seller is afraid that information will leak out; that his employees, customers, and suppliers will hear about the deal prematurely; or that the buyer really doesn't have enough money after all.

As the buyer, you have the right to control the drafting of the LOI and the purchase and sale agreement. While it will cost you more in legal fees, it is critical that you exercise this option in order to write your own language into the agreement.

Checklist of Items in Letter of Intent

Once your LOI is drafted, be sure it includes all of the following:

1. Description of the buying organization: place of business, owners, etc.
2. Statement of price, structure, contingencies, and exactly what is being purchased
3. Description of any notes—interest rate, term, amortization provision, secured or unsecured, negotiable or non-negotiable, and whether the buyer will have the right to offset part of the note if the seller does not meet certain conditions in the purchase and sale agreement
4. Management contracts—for whom, duration, and incentives
5. Explanation of closing costs, including intermediaries' fees and who pays what
6. A statement that representations and warranties will be a part of the purchase and sale agreement
7. Description of profit-sharing arrangements
8. A list of contingencies that have to be resolved in order for the transaction to be completed, e.g., environmental problems, title transfers, etc.

9. Planned changes to be made, such as management, and continuity items, such as not relocating the plant
10. Estimated date of closing
11. Transferability of insurance
12. Reconciliation of debts or collections with shareholders
13. The same continuity of business until closing date
14. Access to books and records
15. Description of consulting and noncompete agreements
16. The adherence to confidentiality by both parties and the understanding that the letter of intent is nonbinding and that the seller will take the company off the market for a specified period of time
17. Whether the parent company (if there is one) should also sign the letter of intent and/or if the guarantors of the selling company's obligations (if there are any) should also sign the document
18. Whether to create an escrow account to handle postclosing adjustments to the purchase price to reflect changes in inventory, final audited financials, collections of accounts receivable, etc., to offset seller's contractual claims

CONCLUSION

Writing an LOI is time-consuming. Although it is a fairly short document, it requires some serious thought. Because it is a nonbinding agreement, if so stated, you have the comfort level of knowing that you can back out. However, the chances are slight that you can materially change the price and terms of the deal after you have entered into the LOI.

One of the biggest concerns of the seller is whether the buyer has the financial resources to complete the transaction and to have sufficient reserves thereafter in case the business needs another infusion of capital. As a buyer, be prepared to share your financial information with the seller.

Putting the Deal Together

J ack Kellogg is an attorney specializing in mergers and acquisitions and has completed more than 100 transactions as well as acquired numerous companies with his business partner. Kellogg is often called upon for his sage advice, and frequently he is heard saying: "Keep the momentum going. Deals that drag don't close. Energy and zeal are critically important."

The ability to execute a transaction with alacrity gives a buyer a competitive advantage over other buyers who are not able to assemble their team of experts quickly. Once an owner decides to sell his company, he usually wants to do so as fast as prudently possible. Many of the sellers do not really enjoy the selling process, they are not familiar with the various selling procedures and they are often paranoid about a breach in confidentiality. So if a respectable buyer is one of the earliest to learn that a certain company is for sale, he may play his strongest suit first—a pre-emptive offer which excludes competitive bids until the seller either accepts or rejects that offer.

Let us assume that as a buyer, you decide your acquisition strategy will be to only buy profitable companies in your industry that are receptive to your aggressive courtship. Because of your ability to move quickly, you request the seller to temporarily negotiate only with you. In return, you will offer to pay the seller a full price and if mutually agreed, will close the transaction quickly, i.e., within the two months of original contact. Your acquisition strategy of moving quickly should not be implemented unless you have satisfied yourself on the following four items:

1. You either know or feel comfortable with the target company's industry so that you are very proficient with the due diligence in that particular industry.

2. You have sufficient equity for a deal of the estimated transaction size of the target company.
3. You have an acquisition team fully in place ready to roll up their sleeves and go to work for you immediately.
4. You are not in the middle of another transaction or otherwise overly committed to other pressing matters so that you have sufficient time to devote to this project.

The acquisition team members are usually consultants, advisers, professionals, etc., who usually work outside the buyer's entity and occasionally have a vested interest in the project. Some team members may receive reduced compensation until the transaction closes or until the buyer becomes a regular client of their firm. Successful acquisition teams have a high degree of commitment, and, as discussed, usually include the following members: intermediary, transaction lawyer, transaction financier, corporate valuation expert, machinery and equipment appraiser, real estate appraiser, and due diligence consultant. The team provides experience and insight in completing a sale. Your team members are all-important, but not all members are required all the time. Team involvement must be coordinated. A team quarterback (usually the intermediary) promotes efficiency and enhances communication. A major consideration is to assemble the team before the buyer identifies the selling company, because when the latter is "in play" the buyer who moves with alacrity very often wins.

STRUCTURING THE DEAL

Most sellers start out wanting all cash for the deal. However, a figure that appears to be fairly accurate is that only 36 percent of deals are all cash at closing. There is an old axiom that the seller sets the price and the buyer sets the terms. What is evident is that if the seller demands all cash in the transaction, he or she probably will receive a lower price for the company.

Buyers are often capable of paying all cash at closing, but are afraid they will lose all their leverage if the business does not turn out to be what was represented. The new owner often wants some hand-holding during the transition period and therefore will structure a consulting agreement over a year or two with the former owner. Terms are perhaps more important for small companies that do not have audited financial statements, particularly if the sale is a stock transaction in which the buyer assumes all the assets and liabilities on the balance sheet. Audited statements, of course, verify the accuracy of receivables, payables, inventory, etc., that are on the balance sheet, especially useful as of the closing date. Even though an asset purchase is a safer method of acquisition for the buyer, the use of terms in the structure of a stock purchase is a reasonable safeguard against any improprieties and/or oversights by the seller.

A normal structure for a deal might be the following:

Buyer's cash:	30%
Bank's cash:	30%
Note:	20%
Noncompete/consulting agreements:	10%
Earnout:	10%
Total:	100%

The cash from the bank is obviously what you borrow against inventory and accounts receivables. Typically a bank will loan you 50 percent on your inventory (excluding work in process) and 75 percent on current accounts receivables. The seller will want you to personally guarantee the note, asking for a second mortgage on your house, for example. Undoubtedly you will not want to do that, and you might offer to secure the note by subordinating it to the bank's note. These differences can often make or break a deal.

On the other hand, noncompete and consulting agreements are traditionally noninterest-bearing instruments and unsecured. The partial earnout is usually a way for the buyer to stretch to meet the seller's price. It is particularly helpful when the buyer values the company based on today's financial statements, and the seller is valuing the company on the future earnings potential. One method for a partial earnout is to structure it with 2 to 4 percent of the gross profit for a set time period, with a cap on the total dollar amount. If the seller doesn't accept an earnout, then offer him or her a claw-back whereby the buyer pays the asking price. However, if the sales or earnings are not achieved as estimated, then the purchase price is reduced and deducted from the note that is due to the seller.

From a seller's perspective, accepting terms as part of the transaction allows him or her the benefit of the installment sales tax provision, i.e., taxes are paid over a number of years. In times of a credit crunch, economic conditions often preclude deals getting done for all cash.

During the 1992–93 recession in Canada, Doug Robbins of Robbinex Business Brokerage in Hamilton, Ontario, said,

Closings are elusive partly because bank financing is nearly impossible. Of the last eight deals, none had bank financing and three had financings provided by angels with 15 percent guaranteed coupon backed by 25 to 40 percent of the owner's stock. Without bank financing, these angels are in first position on the debt, and even with equity kickers, the angels are at high risk. Deals are getting done mostly if the buyer commits to 50 percent of the purchase price with his own cash, and the seller finances the balance.

Example of a Deal Structure

A niche specialty chemical manufacturer decided to sell. It was a family-owned business, and the founder had died. While the son was successfully running the company, the heirs wished to have liquidity, since all their assets were tied up in their nonliquid stock. The basic figures were as follows:

Sales:	$20 million
Operating income:	$2 million
Long-term debt:	0
Book value: (net worth)	$3 million

The buyer used a 4.5 earnings multiple on the $2 million operating income, which placed a value of $9 million on the company. The deal was structured as follows:

Buyer's own cash at closing:	$3 million
Bank debt—cash at closing:	$4 million
Note to seller—secured by the company:	$2 million
Total:	$9 million

The above structure is very basic, but two items are noteworthy. The buyer was a private equity group with $25 million available to do deals. The group used only $3 million of its own money, and the note was secured not by the buyout group, but by the chemical company itself. The other noteworthy feature of this transaction was that the private equity group wanted the founder's son and present CEO to remain with the company in the same capacity. Therefore, the buyer persuaded the son to buy back 10 percent of the company for $300,000 (10 percent of the $3 million equity), and as an incentive the son had the option to buy up to 20 percent of the company in the next five years.

Example of Another Deal Structure

The following example was provided by Joseph Myss of Wayzata, Minnesota, in his book *Divestiture Strategies for Owners of Private Businesses*. This case involves the use of an earnout portion to reconcile the $1 million difference in value between the buyer and seller.

The two parties agreed to use EBIT as the financial benchmark, and they negotiated a minimum EBIT that must be earned each year before the earnout takes effect. Additionally, the two parties agreed upon a percentage, in this case 75 percent of the amount above the base EBIT hurdle to be paid to the seller.

ILLUSTRATION		*IN MILLIONS*	
	2006	*2007*	*2008*
	ACTUAL	*PROJECTED*	*PROJECTED*
EBIT	$1,625	$1,780	$2,000
Base EBIT (negotiated)		(1,200)	(1,300)
Excess over base		580	700
75 percent of excess to sellers		435	525
Cumulative earnout payment		435	960

Conditions

Interest expense and miscellaneous other nonoperating income are excluded from the earnout formula. Unusual items are also excluded, such as sale of nonoperating assets, sale and leaseback of plant assets, and insurance recoveries postacquisition. The seller should have reasonable control over decisions that can affect the results that will be used to measure the earnout payments.

Earnout

Structuring the transaction in order to complete the deal to your satisfaction will be one of the most challenging aspects of buying a business. In many cases, when you and the seller seem deadlocked or unable to overcome your differences, an imaginative method of structuring the deal will often overcome the obstacles. Professional brainstorming by your advisers may provide the breakthrough.

Usually the most prevalent reason that transactions are not completed is the price gap between what the buyer is willing to pay and what the seller is willing to accept. Commonly the buyer values the target company on a multiple of past earnings and the seller values the company on discounted cash flow from future earnings. A possible solution is the use of an earnout to bridge the gap.

An earnout is a portion of the purchase price that is contingent on future performance over a certain time period, such as three to five years, and may have a maximum limit. Earnouts are used not only when there is a significant price differential, but also in the following circumstances:

- When there is a major customer concentration
- When the company is about to introduce new products
- When the company is expecting a very significant contract
- When service companies are transferring relationships
- When the buyer has limited equity
- When the seller has been losing money

The benefits of an earnout are numerous:

- The seller shares in the growth of the company
- It reduces the buyer's risk of overpaying
- It reduces the buyer's cash at closing
- It reduces the purchase price payment at closing
- It quantifies uncertainty
- It protects the purchaser who was shy on due diligence

Sellers are often reluctant to accept earnouts because it is difficult to determine the true earnings and/or the buyer fears the seller will manipulate the figures to his benefit. The seller has to have complete trust in the buyer. Basing the earnout on the top line, sales, instead of the bottom line, earnings, is far less subject to manipulation by the seller.

ASSETS VS. STOCK TRANSACTION

Very early in the discussion of acquiring a particular business, it is imperative that the buyer and seller discuss whether the transaction will be an asset or stock sale.

The buyer almost always wants to buy the assets, because he or she can avoid most potential lawsuits from inherent corporate liabilities and can write up the assets, allowing greater depreciation to shelter future earnings.

On the other hand, the seller usually wants to sell stock, because for a C corporation there will be only one tax (compared to a double tax for an asset sale). Furthermore, if the seller has used accelerated depreciation for the machinery and equipment, he or she may face a possible depreciation recapture tax for selling the machinery at a higher value than that shown on the books. An asset sale is more time-consuming and more costly because there is a legal transfer of each asset, and more difficult because of the need for third-party consents on leases, loans, etc.

If the transaction is an asset sale, then the purchase price is assigned to specific assets at their fair market value (not the depreciated value on the books). The difference between the purchase price and the allocation of the purchase price is goodwill. Under the new tax laws, goodwill can be impaired and written down on the balance sheet. Further discussion on this matter is handled in Chapter 25, "Legal and Tax Issues."

Because it is so important to understand the pros and cons of asset and stock purchase, I have received permission to replicate the following analysis prepared by PricewaterhouseCoopers in their book *Buying and Selling a Business*.

Assets Purchase–Buyer's Position–Advantages
- Stepup basis of assets acquired to purchase price, allows higher depreciation/amortization deductions.
- Recapture tax on presale depreciation and investment tax credit paid by seller.
- Buyer can pick and choose assets to buy and liabilities to assume.
- Buyer is generally free of any undisclosed or contingent liabilities.
- Normally results in termination of labor union collective bargaining contracts.

- Employee benefit plans may be maintained or terminated.
- Buyer permitted to change state of incorporation.

Disadvantages

- No carryover of seller corporation's tax attributes (i.e., tax basis of assets, earnings and profits, operating and capital loss carry-forwards, accounting methods, accounting periods, install-ment reporting, or previous sales and employee benefit plan contributions).
- Nontransferable rights or assets (i.e., license, franchise, patent, etc.) cannot be transferred to buyer.
- Transaction more complex and costly in terms of transferring specific assets/liabilities (i.e., title to each asset transferred, and new title recorded; state sales tax may apply).
- Lender's consent may be required to assume liabilities.
- May lose right to use corporation's name.
- Loss of corporation's liability, unemployment, or workers' compensation insurance ratings.

Assets Purchase–Seller's Position–Advantages

- Seller maintains corporate existence.
- Maintains ownership of nontransferable assets or rights (i.e., license, franchise, patent, etc.).
- Maintains corporate name.

Disadvantages

- Taxation occurs at the corporate level upon liquidation.
- Generates various kinds of gains or losses to the seller based on the classification of each asset as capital or ordinary.
- Transaction may be more complex and costly in terms of trans-ferring specific assets/liabilities (i.e., title to each asset trans-ferred and new title records; sales tax may apply).
- Lender's consent required to assume liabilities.

Stock Purchase–Buyer's Position–Advantages

- Tax attributes carry over to buyer (i.e., tax basis of assets, earnings and profits, operating and capital loss carry-forwards, accounting methods, accounting periods, installment reporting on previous sales, and employee benefit plan contributions).
- Transaction is less complex (i.e., endorsement of stock certificates).
- Avoids restrictions imposed on sales of assets in loan agreements and potential sales tax.
- Preserves the right of the buyer to use corporation's name.
- No changes in corporation's liability, unemployment, or workers' compensation insurance ratings.
- Nontransferable rights or assets (i.e., license, franchise, patent, etc.) can be retained by the buyer.

Disadvantages

- No stepup in basis (i.e., seller's historical tax basis is carried over to buyer) unless buyer elects and incurs additional tax cost.
- All assets and obligations (i.e., disclosed, not disclosed, unknown, and contingent) are transferred to the buyer.
- Recapture tax on presale depreciation and investment tax credits falls on buyer.
- Normally does not terminate existing labor union collective bargaining contracts.
- Generally results in the continuation of employee benefit plans.
- State of incorporation remains the same.
- Dissenting shareholders' right of appraisal of the value of their shares with the right to be paid appraised value or remain a minority shareholder.

Stock Purchase–Seller's Position–Advantages

- Avoids taxation at the corporate and shareholder level.
- All obligations (i.e., disclosed, not disclosed, unknown, and contingent) and nontransferable rights can be transferred to the buyer.

- Generally provides capital gain or loss so that there is no need to calculate gain or loss by asset type.
- Generally avoids ordinary gain.

Disadvantages
- Seller cannot pick and choose assets to be retained.
- Ownership of nontransferable rights or assets is lost.
- Requires selling corporation's shareholder approval.

THE CRITICAL ELEMENT—THE TRANSACTION ATTORNEY

Often the deal hinges on the transaction attorney who may be too recalcitrant or subservient. If the attorney is too recalcitrant, the deal may not be consummated. If the attorney is too subservient, you may compromise and concede too much in the deal.

A transaction attorney is a specialist. If he doesn't complete half a dozen deals a year, then he is probably not a specialist in M&A. Beyond that, the transaction attorney may be a whiz at drafting documents, but inept at communicating. Or the transaction attorney may be very knowledgeable on creating deal structures, but lacks personal skills with clients and the other party. Further, the transaction attorney may be the star performer for a pre-eminent Wall Street law firm, but total inept at doing a small $10 million deal in a rural New England community.

Often the transaction attorney takes the lead role in putting the deal together and in the negotiations. The pressure is ever evident as the intermediary pushes vigorously to close the deal quickly. Additionally, the seller becomes increasingly nervous about further delays due to possible confidentiality leaks while the buyer needs more time for extensive due diligence. Emotions run high on both sides of the deal and unless the transaction attorney is great under pressure, the deal can explode like an oil gusher.

A major challenge you may face is when the business owner has not properly prepared for selling the company, e.g., noncompetes are not in place, technology licenses and intellectual properties are not documented, identification of critical third-party consents has not been recorded, contingent liabilities have not been resolved, etc. On the other hand, acquirers do not always bring their transaction attorney into the process during the early stages of courtship. Sometimes the buyer will submit a letter of interest or occasionally a letter of intent without the attorney's early involvement.

The success or failure of an M&A transaction often hinges on both parties' ability to communicate effectively. There are numerous constituencies such as buyer/seller; intermediaries; board of directors; attorneys; financial institutions; due diligence teams; etc. Since there are so many issues in a transaction, it is imperative that the process is organized and certain steps in the process are orchestrated by a team leader.

DEALBREAKERS

Just as expert fly fishermen lose a trout off their hook from time to time, M&A deals can crater at the later stages of negotiation. From transaction attorney Lou Katz's perspective, these dealbreakers are most likely attributed to the following factors:

- The seller does not properly prepare for the sale.
- The seller's projections are not achieved.
- There is a disconnect on the company's valuation and/or the terms of the transaction.
- Personal chemistry of the buyer with seller's management team disintegrates.
- The buyer discovers negative "surprises" regarding the seller's business, and the seller is unwilling to accept a reasonable price adjustment.
- The buyer's financing falls short.
- The deal loses momentum.

The difference between a good transaction attorney and a mediocre one is the ability to anticipate and resolve the major issues in the transaction in a manner which is fair to both parties. For example, in 10 to 20 percent of the transactions which Mr. Katz handles, there is some form of earnout to help bridge the differences in pricing and to resolve some of the "dealbreakers." In this manner, the seller is compensated for its business at a price which the seller feels is fair only if the buyer achieves the financial performance which justifies the price.

TRENDS

Sellers are demanding tighter time frames for a buyer to complete due diligence on an exclusive basis and to proceed to a closing. Offset against the seller's desire to limit the exclusivity period is the buyer's need for extensive due diligence after the letter of intent is signed as the buyer is often shown very limited information on the seller before its letter of intent is accepted. There is greater scrutiny on intellectual property and other intangible assets as we move toward a more technology-driven economy.

Mr. Katz suggests that the tension between the seller's desire to limit exclusivity and the buyer's desire to obtain adequate time for its due diligence can be satisfied by a well drafted letter of intent that sets milestones which the buyer must achieve to continue the exclusivity. As different thresholds are met (i.e., satisfaction of environmental compliance), you can sign off on this stage of your due diligence and receive more and more confidential information from the seller and the continuation of the exclusivity period. Using this "staggered" exclusivity period for due diligence, the seller can get comfortable that the deal is moving to closing and you can have sufficient time to adequately perform your due diligence on the target company.

CONCLUSION

It is important for the company about to embark on an M&A transaction to assemble a qualified team of advisers. One key member of the team has to be a transaction attorney who is experienced in your industry and who knows how to get deals done in a timely and efficient manner. The match of the attorney's firm to your company and your transaction should also be appropriate. You want to make sure that the deal size will get the attention of experienced attorneys in the firm you choose. The firm you select needs to be able to help you develop and implement the road map in getting from the inception of the M&A transaction to the successful completion of the deal.

The attorney has many roles to play in the transaction, i.e., business adviser, legal counselor, and a principal negotiator. When the deal is stalled, the attorney frequently brings the two parties together. When the deal hits an impasse, the attorney needs to advise his client what items to concede, what items to hold firm, and what tradeoffs can be negotiated. Many transactions come close to the finish line, but don't close. Oftentimes, the transaction does not close due to valid business and legal considerations. However, the right transaction attorney and other advisers may help find creative solutions to put the deal together in the manner appropriate for the risks assumed by the parties.

CHAPTER 20

Due Diligence

To my knowledge, no one has done a documented study of why many mergers and acquisitions do not live up to expectations. Without discussing all the various possibilities, it is reasonable to say that many acquisitions fail principally because due diligence was inept.

A comprehensive due diligence study is time-consuming, expensive, and very broad. The majority of the work takes place after the letter of intent is signed and goes far beyond such items as environmental disclosures and whether the owner has the legal authority to sell the business. For the purposes of this chapter, I have used the term due diligence to refer to investigating the company after the letter of intent has been signed, as opposed to the assessment of the business prior to this period. The purpose of the due diligence is to help you determine whether you want to go forward with the transaction or whether you want to renegotiate the price and terms of the deal based on your findings. If you are going forward with the deal, you want to be sure that you will be receiving the assets you expect, and that there will not be any unexpected liabilities or unexpected expenses postacquisition. One resource to reference during the process is the publication by PricewaterhouseCoopers, *Checking Into an Acquisition Candidate.*

The following suggestions are merely ten items that I have highlighted to give you a flavor of the enormous variety of due diligence matters.

1. In buying the assets of the business, as opposed to the owner's stock, supplier and customer contracts will have to be reassigned to the buyer in order to maintain a valuable right.
2. Review the customer list and corresponding annual sales volume. Numerous middle-market companies have one

or two major customers, which places the company in a very vulnerable position if such an account is lost. It is not uncommon to have 80 percent of the sales produced by 20 percent of the customers. Obviously a more balanced distribution of sales is desirable.

3. Some businesses have subtle and unorthodox ways of conducting business that may be foreign to the buyer's comfort level. It may be necessary to give favors to key people in order to procure the sales. Try to understand the intricacies of each particular business.

4. Knowledge of personnel issues is a key factor to prevent surprises after the company has changed ownership. Obtain an organizational employee chart. If the company is a family business, are there nonworking members on the payroll, and/or are there members working without pay? Find out what each employee earns in the way of salary and fringe benefits, and how and when raises, benefits, and stock options have been exercised. What employment contracts and other deferred compensation agreements exist?

5. Obtain a complete list of all machinery and equipment to appraise its approximate value and to ascertain whether it is outdated. Sometimes buyers assume that they are acquiring all the machinery on the factory floor, only to find out later that certain pieces have been leased.

6. It is prudent to find out early on in the company buyout whether there is any litigation. Obviously, the extent of the litigation may affect whether you want to proceed with the acquisition; if you do, you would certainly be more inclined to buy the assets of the business than the stock.

7. Carefully assess the financials. Audited statements are vastly more credible than unaudited statements. With audited statements, accounting firms verify such items as accounts receivable, inventory, promissory notes, etc. As a buyer, you should be receiving timely statements as you evaluate the company, if not on a monthly basis, at least

on a quarterly basis. Be sure you analyze the aging of the accounts receivable to determine the nature of the customers' paying habits. Your banker will be particularly interested in this aging list, as it represents collateral for your borrowing. Analyze the inventory breakdown among raw materials, work in process (WIP), and finished goods. Most banks do not lend money on WIP inventory. The inventory turnover rate varies with different industries, but it is an important number to measure. The last-in, first-out (LIFO) method of inventory calculation understates earnings because it reports inventory costs at the older prices (which are usually lower, given the inflationary trend in our economy). Therefore, companies using LIFO instead of first-in, first-out (FIFO) report more conservatively.

8. It is important to understand the company's return policy and guarantees. Some companies have an open-ended arrangement on returns, which can be costly. One distributor that imports in-line skates from Asia and sells to discount chains let its return policy get out of control. The distributor's total sales were $20 million. Gross margins were a very tight 20 percent and returns amounted to 2 percent—or $400,000! The discount chains were taking advantage of the distributor and returning merchandise for reasons that were unwarranted. As a buyer of a new company, you want to be sure that sales are not generated in part by very liberal return policies and/or by overly generous payment terms (net ninety days) or consignment sales.

9. Pay attention to the expense item "Professional Services," to be cognizant of what and why the services were provided. For example, if the accounting fees showed an unusual increase for the last year, perhaps it was a result of an IRS audit. If so, you should know the details. If the legal fees were considerably higher, perhaps this was for defense of a lawsuit. Other professional services like environmental consultants might reveal the tip of an iceberg.

10. If the company has a pension plan for the employees, be sure that it is not underfunded.

Due diligence is a process that starts as soon as you are introduced to the target company and is ongoing even after the final purchase and sale agreement has been signed. Because some transactions are rushed in order to minimize the disruption for the selling company, a buyer should then try to incorporate more extensive representations and warranties into the selling document.

Only 10 to 15 percent of small- to medium-size companies have audited financial statements. Audited statements, while costing a company 50 to 100 percent more, are significantly more comprehensive than an accountant's review or compilation. As a buyer, you should rely less on the accuracy of reviews and compilations, as such items as accounts receivable and inventory have not been verified by the accounting firm. The name of the game in due diligence is not to assume anything. For example, if you are looking at plastic injection-molding machines, do not assume that the company owns the molds, tools, and dies. They may be consigned from the customer of the parts. If the selling company does not have noncompete agreements with key employees, do not assume that the top engineer or sales manager will not leave the company and go to a competitor as soon as the acquisition is completed. The entire process of due diligence boils down to whether you should buy or not buy the target company based on certain price and terms. If the target company does not pass the due diligence process, you should not buy the company.

There is a significant difference in the degree of due diligence depending on whether the purchase is an assets or a stock transaction. Obviously, if you buy the stock of the company, you are assuming all the assets and liabilities, with all the inherent ramifications, subject to the modifications of the representations and warranties. On the other hand, if there is an environmental problem on the real estate, just because you lease the property does not allow you to escape the penalties of the regulatory authorities.

Due diligence is more difficult when you are acquiring a division or a subsidiary of a larger company, particularly when the financials have been consolidated. The four areas of concern are as follows:

1. That all costs are properly reflected, whether they involve products or services being bought or sold between the two entities.
2. That business between the two entities is on an arm's-length basis, and items are not bought and sold because of the inter-company relationship.
3. That the division or subsidiary has the quality and depth of management to successfully operate independent of the parent company.
4. That the extent the parent company's access to services at favorable rates, e.g., accounting, tax, legal, insurance, benefits, information services, etc., substantially reduces the cost to the division or subsidiary.

PROCEDURE

Let's swing into action! Both parties have signed the letter of intent, in which the ground rules for conducting the due diligence have been outlined. At this point, another, more comprehensive confidentiality agreement should be executed, which among other items states that you will return all information if the deal crumbles.

Now, you will need to put together a team of due diligence experts, one of which should be an experienced accounting firm. Usually the seller will want to keep this investigation stage to between thirty and sixty days. Your team of experts would include:

Appraisers: For real estate and machinery/equipment
Engineers: To evaluate the plant and its equipment
Accountants: For financial advice
Lawyers: To handle all legal issues

Environmentalists: For inspection of ground/water/asbestos, etc.
Intelligence professionals: To manage the audit

What you should expect to receive is the following:

1. Documents—meeting minutes, financial statements, engineering assessments, tax certificates, patents, etc.
2. Statements—liens (if any), encumbrances, Uniform Commercial Code (UCC)
3. Reviews—litigation risk review
4. Audits—environmental assessments
5. Market studies
6. Contracts—with suppliers, customers, employees/ employer, consultants; leases/mortgages; loan agreements; licenses; agreements with shareholders; pension plans/profit sharing plans/ fringe benefits; insurance policies; stock options; product warranties

One way to organize the due diligence process is to set up a matrix of assets and liabilities with three categories to determine the real underlying values.

AMOUNTS RECORDED IN DOLLARS

ITEMS +	UNDERVALUE –	OVERVALUE –	UNRECORDED =	DIFFERENCE
Plant/equipment	Depreciated			
Joint venture	Not recorded			
Lease	At favorable rate			
Inventory		FIFO		
Accounts receivable		Uncollectible		
Pension		Less than obligation		
Pending litigation			No reserve	
Pending severance			No reserve	
Product reserves			No reserve	
Etc.				
Total				_____

DISCLOSURE

Some states require that you as the buyer must obtain a disclosure statement from the seller. For example, California has licensing requirements for the business brokerage industry, in which one aspect is the use of proper disclosure. The following questions are taken in part from the California Association of Business Broker's Seller's Disclosure Statement. This series of questions with answers is to inform prospective buyers about the particular business. It is supplied by the seller to provide relevant information and to answer frequently asked questions, but it does not take the place of the buyer's inspection of the business and its financial and other records. Those must be carefully examined and approved by the buyer.

If the seller responds in the affirmative, then an explanation is required on the addendum. The following fifteen questions and corresponding answers could eliminate a lot of surprises. The following disclosure statement herewith only covers the business conditions and does not include the other sections of the disclosure statement, i.e., regulation, legal considerations, etc.

1. Are you aware of any circumstances in the industry or market area that may adversely affect future profitability of the business?
2. Are there any revenues or expenses of the business that are not clearly reflected in its financial statements?
3. Is the business in default of any of its financial or contractual obligations?
4. Has the business or any of its owners been the subject of any bankruptcy filings, assignments for benefit of creditors or insolvency proceeding of any kind during the last five years, or consulted with any attornies or advisers regarding such proceedings?
5. Are there any individual customers who account for more than 10 percent of annual gross sales? If yes, list each by name and indicate the approximate percentage of annual gross sales and any relationship to the business or its owners.

6. Are there any commitments to employees or independent contractors regarding future compensation increases?

7. Are there suppliers who have a personal or special relationship with the business or its owners? If yes, list each such supplier, the nature of the relationship, and the approximate amount of annual purchase.

8. Are any of the employees or independent contractors related to any of the owners of the business, or one another? If yes, list them by name and describe their relationship.

9. Have you had or do you anticipate any disputes with the landlord or problems with the premises the business occupies?

10. Are there any terms or conditions of the premises lease with which the business or the landlord is not in full compliance?

11. Have there been any deaths, violent crimes, or other criminal activity on the premises within the last three years?

12. Are you aware of any substances, materials, or products on or near the premises which may be an environmental hazard such as, but not limited to, asbestos, formaldehyde, radon gas, paint solvents, fuel, medical waste, surface or underground storage tanks, or contaminated soil or water?

13. Is there any equipment used in the business that it does not own?

14. Is there any equipment used in the business that is not in good or operable condition, or for which maintenance has been deferred?

15. Does the business have a franchise, distributorship or licensing agreement? If yes, please provide a copy of each.

In Review

In reviewing the highlights of due diligence, it is important to keep three points in mind.

1. Verify the critical elements of the acquisition. Concentrate on the key issues of the target company and its industry. If you are buying a high-tech company, concentrate on transferring intellectual property without encumbrances. If you are buying a consumer product company, concentrate on possible product returns or recalls. And if you are buying a heavy manufacturer, concentrate on environmental issues.
2. Weigh the risk/reward factors of doing the deal. Small repercussions may be acceptable, but disasters must be avoided.
3. The net result of due diligence is not necessarily a go or no-go on the acquisition. You may still want to buy the company, but because of certain circumstances you may deem it necessary to renegotiate the deal by changing the price or structure.

TYPES OF DUE DILIGENCE

As you proceed through this process you need to be aware that there are four specific types of due diligence. Each one carries its own specific particulars that need to be addressed. The four types of due diligence are financial, legal, business, and management.

Financial Due Diligence

The acquisition audit should be conducted by an accounting firm that has a lot of experience and expertise in this extremely important type of investigation, particularly if the financials are unaudited. The objectives are twofold. One is to verify the figures in case there should be an adjustment to the purchase price. The second and more important is to determine whether the selling company is guilty of deceptive bookkeeping in order to spruce up the financials.

There are a number of items that will tip off the due diligence team that the books are being cooked, such as recording sales before the order has actually been shipped, recording consignment sales as actual sales, overvaluing the inventory, or not posting all the accounts payable. Your investigation should compare the company's income tax records with its financials, ascertain that withholding taxes have been paid, and check original documents to see if they have been altered, as well as conduct other audit procedures such as verifying payables and receivables.

A good due diligence team will red-flag rising selling expenses, inventory dead wood, extended terms on sales, slowdown on accounts receivable collections, or rising inventories, especially in finished goods. The following items are matters that some buyers might overlook.

The compensation: You should assess the target company's compensation of personnel at comparable levels of responsibility. For example, a high-tech public company from Boston made an offer on a smaller company with a proprietary product. Part of the reason the target company was so profitable was the owner paid his employees minimum wages with virtually no benefits in a facility with minimum overhead. If you absorbed the target into your own system, you would be compelled to equalize the compensation of the seller's employees, thus vastly reducing the stated profitability of the target. Conversely, if the target's management and employees had a much higher compensation than the acquirer, it will be difficult to merge the two companies without having personnel problems.

Capital expenditures: You should determine to what extent the machinery and equipment of the target company needs to be replaced in order to be up to date with the competition, thus adding a further cost to the acquisition price. Or, rapidly growing companies may require annual capital expenditures that exceed the normal depreciation expense, thus modifying projections and ultimately affecting the transaction price.

Internal controls: A buyer, especially one representing a public company, is often far more sophisticated in financial controls, systems, and reporting than the target companies. Some companies grow so fast they do not have time to put proper controls in place. For example, an $11 million retail chain came very close to selling a minority interest to raise essential working capital. The potential investors ultimately lost confidence because the financials were not audited and the five stores did not control their inventory through a point of purchase (POP) perpetual inventory control system at the checkout counters.

Inventory obsolescence: You should pay particular attention to the target company's product life cycle, particular in the high-tech industry. The buyer should question the seller's inventory reserve policy to be sure it is adequate to cover the inevitable writedowns.

Cash flow statements: For buyers, evaluating cash flow statements is more important than evaluating the target's balance sheet and income statement. You should verify that the seller will continue generating positive cash flow after the acquisition when the extraordinary and nonrecurring items have been eliminated and the new debt service has increased.

Discretionary costs: You should be aware that some sellers prepare the company for sale by maximizing profits through a reduction of managed costs such as advertising, promotion expenditures, research and development expenses, and maintenance. These cuts will eventually hurt the company's long-term prospects.

Financial covenants: If you plan to exercise a stock transaction, one of your major concerns should be the covenants that will be assumed with the bank notes, leases, and rentals. The lenders, leasers, and landlords will have enforceable covenants such as balance sheet ratios, debt coverage percentages, etc. If an asset transaction is to occur, you should not be rushed into agreements without proper time to negotiate the covenants.

Legal Due Diligence

From a legal standpoint, a thorough investigation would include the following items:

- Authenticity of trademarks and patents
- Adequacy of insurance coverage
- Assumption of license rights

- Environmental liabilities
- Notification of underfunded pension plans
- Status of contracts

In the case of contracts, if there is a need to bring them all up to snuff, a portion of the purchase price might be adjusted downward. For example, there might be a plethora of contracts ranging from key employees, unions, vendors, customers, leases, agents, etc., and so the legal expense to update the contractual arrangements could be sizable.

Business Due Diligence

The business due diligence includes the company's products, markets, competitors, employee relations, and industry regulations. In many cases, the buyer is searching for the real reason the company is being sold. The first order of business is to evaluate the company's key operating ratios over the past five years and compare them with the average for its particular industry as documented by Robert Morris and Associates. Key ratios would include:

- Gross profit/sales
- Cash flow/sales
- Selling, general, and administrative/sales
- Selling expense/sales
- Cost of goods sold/sales = inventory turnover

The three major items on which to focus are as follows:

The industry: As part of an acquirer's assessment of the target company, he or she should review the industries in which the potential seller's customers and suppliers operate. This method of due diligence is frequently called a SWOT analysis. The buyer reviews the strengths, weaknesses, opportunities, and threats of the potential acquisition candidate's competitors.

If an entire industry is growing, then all boats rise with an incoming tide. Nelson Gifford, former CEO of Dennison Manufacturing Company, reflecting on his three dozen transactions, said that you can often overcome paying too high a price for a business if it is in a fast-growing industry. On the other hand, you can underpay for a company in a declining industry and the outcome will be a poor acquisition in the final analysis. Also, it is important to understand the ramifications in a down market. If the proposed transaction is highly leveraged, then a target company selling heavily into the defense industry or a target company in a cyclical industry may not survive a down market.

Sales/marketing: To properly measure sales growth, it is important to divide the total number of employees into total sales to determine the sales per employee. The resulting figure is indicative of a company's efficiency. Most manufacturing companies should have sales between $150,000 and $200,000 per employee. If sales costs are rising faster than actual sales, then perhaps the market is maturing and there will be a market slowdown. While this discovery may be of concern, it may not be a dealbreaker. However, it does require further investigation to determine why noncustomers buy from the company's competition, what marketing is necessary to target noncustomers, and what other channels of distribution should be pursued.

The previous statements are just a snapshot of market examination which is much more important than the average individual acquirer might realize. A few years ago, Hillcrest Associates of Holliston, Massachusetts, conducted a comprehensive survey with buyout groups, corporate development officers, and venture capital companies in which the results showed an overwhelming preponderance toward marketing due diligence. Some of the marketing issues in this survey were as follows:

- The relationship between the company and individual customers
- The risk of technology change, the threat of substitution, and the product life cycle—its reputation, quality, and service
- Whether on an industry-wide basis the profits are increasing or decreasing

- What are the risks on the horizon and the opportunities
- To assess the stability on the top line for about twelve to twenty-four months so that there is time to concentrate on internal cost structure

Generally speaking, it is better to engage an outside firm to conduct the business due diligence. There are certain questions an outsider can ask that an insider cannot. For example, it is easier for an outside consultant to gather competitive intelligence, to ask probing information of a customer about a company's performance, and to gather objective information about a market without revealing the purchaser of the information.

Products: In evaluating a company, there are some items, like lack of profitability or perceived poor management, that can be rectified. However, if the industry is declining, the sales are declining, and the product is suspect, then it is safe to say that you should not have to do much more in the way of overall business due diligence.

Management Due Diligence

There are agencies that will conduct an investigation of the CEO of the selling company to determine such things as whether he has a criminal record, was dishonorably discharged from the military, has declared personal bankruptcy, or has encountered IRS problems. If you are investing millions of dollars and committing your energy to an enterprise, you would be remiss if you failed to determine whether the person currently representing that enterprise has a dubious background. Some firms provide comprehensive, insightful analysis of the strengths and weaknesses of management. They assess the attributes, capabilities, and direction of a company's management. Historically, very little due diligence in M&A has been conducted on senior management. One national firm is New London Management Associates run by Hardy Hasenfuss, a professional human capital expert.

As Mr. Hasenfuss explains: "The buyer's dilemma is not really knowing about the top management team of the selling company." Of course, the buyer will have received:

1. Information on the management team's employment record
2. Input on the management team's technical and product expertise
3. The management team's industry knowledge

Mr. Hasenfuss' skills in the management due diligence is evaluating the following subjective issues:

- Leadership ability
  - To articulate their vision
  - To inspire others
  - To attract top talent
  - To motivate employees
- Operating ability
  - How they handle conflict/controversy/problems
  - How they make decisions—fast, deliberate, or slow
  - How they communicate—clearly, proactively, friendly
  - How open they are to listening
- Strategic ability
  - In handling and adapting to change
  - In taking risks—not too much, not too little
  - In seeing the big picture but not missing the details
  - In anticipating market and technology trends

Mr. Hasenfuss continues, "While many times we rely on our gut feelings or our experiences with having done the management evaluation so many times, in most cases we are relying on luck to make the right decision. The stakes are too great and prudence would dictate that this is where professional assessments and personality profiles are critical. After all, many buyers would say that the quality of management is the most important aspect of the company."

CONCLUSION

Some buyers instinctively make the assumption that if the balance sheet is healthy, everything else must be too. Not so. Due diligence is a critical component in a successful acquisition. You can never know too much about buying a business, but you can certainly know too little. If knowledge is power, the lack of it can only mean vulnerability.

CHAPTER 21

Representations and Warranties

Representations and warranties, commonly referred to as reps and warranties, are indemnifications and covenants written into the purchase and sale agreement that provide factual information that is important to protect the buyer in the event of future problems. The reps and warranties reflect the situation as of the date of signing the purchase and sale agreement. The representations are designed to uncover certain operations, such as business dealings that are not at arm's length, deferred compensation arrangements, unknown liens on assets, or penalties resulting from late tax filings. If a seller fudges on any reps or warranties, it is a breach of contract. According to the book *The Art of M&A* by Stanley Foster Reed:

> *These conditions are intended to disclose all legal, and many financial, aspects of the business to the buyer. The seller also gives assurances that the transaction itself will not have adverse effects upon the property to be conveyed. The buyer should be aware that lenders providing acquisition financing will require the buyer to make extensive representations and warranties about the target as a condition to funding.*

Reps and warranties are very important in an acquisition, and according to Reed, cofounder of the "Merger Week" at Northwestern, "a buyer or seller will be able to back out of the agreement if it discovers that the representations or warranties of the other party are untrue to any material extent." Equally important is that to the extent of the documentation, the reps and warranties safeguard you postacquisition from facts that were misrepresented by the seller.

When paying up for a company, one way you can try to protect the investment is to have extensive reps and warranties. This complex document takes time to negotiate and frequently delays the closing. The rationale for you to draft a comprehensive reps and warranties document is that if you are forced into paying a high price due to a competitive bidding process, then you must protect your downside as best as possible. Hence, you need a carefully drafted reps and warranties section.

THE PURCHASE AND SALE AGREEMENT

The purchase and sale agreement defines the parameters of both yours and the seller's reps and warranties. The heaviest negotiating near the closing date usually involves the reps and warranties and the indemnifications. Also, the seller's reps and warranties normally account for the largest part of the purchase and sale agreement. The investigation follows the execution of the purchase and sale agreement and obviously precedes the closing. If an adverse material fact surfaces after the closing, then the seller will have to compensate you based on a breach of representation. The following seller's reps and warranties are the most important:

1. Financial statements. A closing audit is imperative to verify the authenticity of all the items, particularly inventory, receivables, and payables. Then a postclosing adjustment is factored into the final floating payoff at closing.
2. Assets. As the buyer, you want to be sure you are gaining full title to the assets, particularly to such items as intellectual property, patents, etc. Also, you want assurances that the machinery and equipment are in good working order.
3. Taxes. Not only is it critical to verify the seller's tax liability if it is a stock purchase, but if it is an asset purchase, you want to be sure that there are no liens on assets because of failure to pay taxes.

4. Employee relations. Employment contracts and employee benefits are very important even in an asset sale, because if a new owner knowingly or unknowingly takes away an employee's privilege, then he or she will walk into a hornet's nest.

5. Environmental problems. Many transactions today are being canceled because of environmental liabilities. Just because you lease the premises instead of buying the property does not mean that you will not be held responsible in part for the contamination caused before your arrival.

6. Pending and potential litigation. This becomes a bigger issue with a consumer product company because of our litigious society. The seller will want to place a time period and/or cap on the total responsibility. Usually the buyer ends up sharing some of the risk for previously made products.

7. Authorization. The seller must have any necessary authorization to sell the company from stockholders, directors, and/or third parties such as the bank.

The seller will in effect be expected to ensure to the buyer that:

All liabilities are represented.
All contracts are disclosed.
All wages and taxes are current.
All insurance is current.
All bonus plans are disclosed.

One of the recent trends is the increased use of the Material Adverse Change (MAC) section in the reps and warranties section. In one survey by the Kaye Scholar firm of 300 M&A transactions, over 80 percent of the deals surveyed contained MAC provisions—which state that if there are material adverse changes in the company's performance and/or its assets from the time the deal was struck and the closing that the buyer has the right to renegotiate the deal. If there is a MAC event, it may not stop the closing, but it would affect the indemnifications position of the contract. MAC arises from unknown events, and it must substantially threaten the overall earnings potential of the selling company in a durationally significant manner.

THE BASKET PROVISION

About ten years ago, I sold a sporting goods store that I personally owned. Not knowing whether the pending sale was to be consummated, I ran the business in a normal manner. To promote our new line of Fuji bicycles, I placed a discount coupon advertisement in a certain publication. Over the next few weeks I either forgot about the impending advertisement, or it seemed irrelevant as my attention focused on the sale of the business. The day after the sporting goods store was sold, customers started to redeem their discount coupons with the purchase of bicycles. As this undisclosed liability amounted to only a few thousand dollars, this example could be considered a frivolous claim and hardly a material amount. However, other such incidents and amounts could add up, becoming a significant aggregate loss for the buyer, even if there is no single breach that has a material adverse effect on the business. According to Reed, "the precise effect of the basket amount on all of this is uncertain. It might be argued that the basket amount is a numerical definition of the word material."

The basket provision is also used to protect the seller by indemnifying him or her for damages only up to a certain amount. Furthermore, there is usually a cutoff date for the buyer to make claims against the seller, e.g., three years is the outside limit. One way to facilitate the buyer's claims is to allow him or her to offset these amounts against the note due to the seller. Another method is to set up an escrow account equivalent to 5 to 10 percent of the purchase price. The phrase "no material adverse change" or "not material to the transaction" is the key. In fact, the seller may insist on inserting the word material when referring to liabilities, litigation, etc. While the word material can be construed as ambiguous, the parties can set a dollar threshold, the basket amount, that defines materiality in particular circumstances.

While most of the burden for reps and warranties lies with the seller, you may be required to warrant that the acquisition does not violate your loan agreements or, if stock is to be used, it is properly authorized.

Obviously, if the transaction is a stock sale in which you assume all the assets and all the liabilities, the reps and warranties are more lengthy and complex. Often the buyer's willingness to undertake a stock transaction depends on the tightness and thoroughness of the reps and warranties. For the seller, the important issue is which reps and warranties survive the closing and which ones cease. Those that customarily cease at closing include warranties on equipment and guarantees on licenses. Those that often survive the closing include matters of litigation.

Other Postclosing Instruments

For middle-market deals, about 80 percent have purchase price adjustments after the closing with over half related to net working capital adjustments. Other instruments postclosing not discussed above are the following:

Contingent payments are future financial obligations like earnouts or royalties that are dependent on contractual events taking place. Escrow is money that is delivered to a third party and held on deposit until the party to receive it fulfills certain conditions. Most escrow accounts range from 10 to 15 percent of the purchase price.

Holdback is a provision stating that if a buyer winds up having to pay a debt that the seller did not disclose, it will be paid from an amount that was held back at closing and placed in an escrow account.

Indemnification is the exemption for the buyer from incurred penalties or liabilities after the closing as a result of incomplete reps and warranties of the seller. The average "cap" for indemnification claims for middle-market deals is close to 30 percent of the purchase price. About 50 percent of the deals have a survival period of one to two years for indemnification claims after the deal closes.

Noncompete is a contract in which the former owner, CEO, or key management employee receives compensation in consideration for not directly competing with the company in which he or she was previously employed. Some states like California do not enforce these agreements. For enforceable noncompete agreements, about 40 percent of them last about three years; others tend to last fewer years.

It is nearly impossible for the buyer to do *enough* due diligence before the closing, hence the importance of reps and warranties reinforced with an escrow account until the claim period expires. In the absence of an escrow fund, require that the seller and/or the shareholders give a security interest in some form of collateral to secure the liability on their indemnification undertakings.

Philip Chapman, an attorney specializing in the buying and selling of businesses, takes special effort to safeguard his buyer's claims postclosing. Mr. Chapman's advice is as follows:

The best protection the buyer can obtain is the escrowing of a portion of the purchase price at the closing. However, the provisions of the escrow arrangements are complex and need very careful attention.

First, the amount of the escrow and the time period for keeping the money in escrow have to be addressed. Each deal will have its own solutions. What will be appropriate will depend on many variables, among which are the sophistication and degree of careful attention to details by the seller in the conduct of its business, the nature of the business, the familiarity of the buyer with the business and the extent of the buyer's due diligence prior to signing of the agreement.

The seller's resistance to the amount which the buyer wants escrowed may be overcome by providing for the release to the seller of portions of the escrow fund from time to time if no claims are asserted against the seller.

The establishing of the escrow requires detailed provisions for the investing of the escrow funds and the duties and liabilities of the escrow agent.

Lastly, the escrow agreement and/or the indemnification provisions of the Asset Purchase Agreement, have to deal carefully with the procedures for the giving of notices of claims, response thereto and defense and settlement of claims.

Aside from the use of the escrow method to enforce the terms of the reps and warranties, the buyer should get *all* the shareholders to sign reps and warranties agreements. Mr. Chapman further advises:

If there is more than one shareholder, all of the shareholders should be required to join in the warranties and representations and indemnification undertakings, or, at least in the indemnification undertakings.

While as among themselves, the liability of the shareholders should be apportioned based upon percentage of stock ownership, their liability to the buyer should be joint and several. Shareholders who are not active in the business should not be excused from signing personally—their lack of knowledge as to the seller's affairs can be covered by their getting indemnification from the active shareholders.

CONCLUSION

The following advice from Nelson Gifford is noteworthy. As former CEO of the Dennison Manufacturing Company, he said that from the buyer's point of view:

The critical aspect of negotiations is what is stated in the representations and warranties such that the document reflects the following:
Everything you know, you told us.
Everything you told us is true.
Everything you didn't know, you should have known.

CHAPTER 22

The Closing

The closing is the formal transfer of the business. There are four key elements that must take place prior to closing:

1. Both parties must agree to the price and terms, and the seller has to show evidence that he or she has legal authority to sell the business.
2. Due diligence needs to be completed by you—the buyer—and the seller's representations and claims have to be substantiated.
3. The financing has to be secured and the proper liens put in place so that the lender can release the funds for the acquisition financing.
4. Remedies must be available to you in case the seller breaches the representations and warranties.

Clearly the closing is no time to cut corners financially. You need expert legal advice, as a foolish mistake at this juncture could cost you ten times the amount in the future. As the buyer, it is your prerogative to have your lawyer draft the purchase and sale agreement. Doing so will put you in the best position to control the process, from drafting the contract to writing the checklist used at the closing. It is customary for the buyer's attorney to draft the original agreement, then the seller's lawyer handles the revision, and finally the buyer's attorney completes the final agreement.

Be aware of red flags prior to closing so you can take proactive steps. One of the red flags in the later stage of a deal is a difficult, inexperienced, or overly aggressive transaction attorney for the seller. Attorneys can be the most difficult element in a transaction, and as the buyer you may not be able to complete the transaction. If, at this point, you have not established a rapport with the owner, you are in trouble. Since to override the difficult attorney, you may have to caucus with the owner and explain that your relationship has to prevail if the deal is to be completed.

Other types of red flags at the closing should be cause to overcome them rather than to abort the transaction. It is, however, in your best interest to recognize the red flags so that you can deal with them accordingly.

Emotions can run high at the closing. Hopefully, mutual trust has developed between you and the seller during the many months of courting and negotiating. You will have spent thousands of dollars on inspections, due diligence, and obtaining the proper financing. Occasionally, sellers will ask for a security deposit. Do not do it—maybe in the sale of small mom and pop operations, but not for middle-market companies. You have already spent serious money on due diligence. But remember, it is important for both sides to maintain a positive attitude, approach problems reasonably, and not hold out for the last dollar. There are two major elements of the closing that happen simultaneously:

Corporate closing. This completes the transfer of the stocks or assets pursuant to the acquisition agreement. Representations and warranties should be true in all material respect. All covenants and required agreements have been performed. All stockholders' approvals have been obtained. Litigation has been settled, noncompete agreements have been signed, and, where appropriate, resignations of officers and directors have been obtained. And all third-party consents such as those of insurers, landlords, and intermediaries, have been obtained.

Financial closing. Unless all the conditions of the deal that affect the lending institution are met, all the liens are in place, and there is an enforceable sales contract with all terms and conditions spelled out, the lending institution will not release the funds. Alternatively, the funds will be held in escrow by the title company or an escrow attorney until all the contractual conditions are met. Once these conditions are met, escrow can be closed (transfer possession), and titles and assets are passed from seller to buyer.

Structure of the Purchase and Sale Agreement

The purchase and sale agreements usually have four sections.

1. Description of the transaction, such as a stock or an asset sale.
2. Terms of agreement, such as price and method of payment (cash, notes, stock, etc.). This section also includes the agreed-upon role of the remaining management team, such as corporate position and remuneration.
3. Representations and warranties, usually the most heavily negotiated items after the letter of intent is signed, they protect both parties against any misrepresentations. A warranty is a guarantee or assurance that the property or item is or shall be as represented.
4. Conditions and covenants include noncompete agreements, identifications, and promises.

PUTTING THE CLOSING IN MOTION

You should have a preclosing one week in advance, making sure that all the documents have been distributed, all conditions have been satisfied or waived, and any open matters have been negotiated to conclusion. If not all the conditions have been met or if a vital signature or an important document is missing, then an escrow closing takes place. Instead of the euphoric high of a successful closure, the closing becomes conditional.

The closing usually takes place at one of the attorney's offices or at the buyer's bank. Along with the principals, there are attorneys for the buyer and seller, the attorney for the seller's bank, intermediaries, and perhaps a real estate broker. There could be six to twelve people in attendance, and the ordeal can take from one to five hours. There are numerous documents to sign, such as loan agreements, leases, personal guarantees, etc.

A stock transaction is much easier than an asset deal because buying the company is like getting onto a moving train. You buy the company "lock, stock, and barrel," including all assets and all liabilities. With an asset purchase, you have the following items to contend with:

- Purchase price adjustments
- Utility and tax prorations
- Vacation accruals
- Deposits
- Lease and insurance transfers
- Bulk sales law compliance (only in some states)
- Transfer of telephone numbers
- Patent assignments
- Bills of sale and/or deeds
- Licenses to be transferred

The best way to ensure a smooth closing is to set up a checklist to avoid any last-minute mishaps. The model checklist below was developed particularly for asset purchases by C.D. Peterson, author of *How to Sell Your Business*. You should make sure you have each of the following in order:

- Time and place of closing
- Who needs to attend
- Documents required
- Amount of funds to be disbursed in the specified form
- Corporate tax and employer identification numbers
- Licenses transferred or obtained, e.g., liquor license
- Prorating calculations for taxes, wages, utility bills, etc.
- Adjustments for landlord, supplier, or utility deposits
- Transfer of banking arrangements
- Transfer of keys, alarm, and computer codes
- Transfer of telephone number
- Customer lists
- Clearance of outstanding liens or encumbrances
- Compliance with bulk sales law
- Assumption or discharge of leases or mortgages
- Definition of seller's obligations in business transition
- Provision for continuity of insurance
- Adjustments for inventory and receivables at closing

- Provisions for uncollectible receivables
- Disposition of outstanding claims
- The real estate lease or purchase agreement
- Consulting and noncompete agreements
- Allocation of the purchase price to assets, goodwill, etc.
- Provision for intermediaries' fees
- Representations and warranties
- Buyer's security for seller's notes

A preacquisition contingency is an unresolved situation that exists at the closing and is resolved later. Obviously such contingencies should be kept to a minimum, but we live in an imperfect world and sometimes closings are not perfect, and so it is better to resolve minor issues in the fashion described herewith than to abort the entire closing.

1. It is important that both parties to the transaction be represented by the principals of their respective companies so that changes, material or otherwise, are not challenged for lack of authority.
2. Closings should not take place on a Friday or the day before a holiday in case the closing continues into the following non-business day without the ability to transfer or invest funds.
3. It is important to have adequate support staff to make last-minute revisions in documents. I heard of a transaction that did not close because of improper instructions for wiring funds from one bank to another. The next day the seller changed his mind about selling. The best types of risk-free checks are bank certified and cashier's check.

For you, the buyer, the closing represents the apex of the acquisition search and perhaps the single largest monetary transaction in your business career. Upon completion of the closing, you will embark on an adventure full of opportunities, rewards, and risks. It probably will begin with corks popping and bubbles flowing, followed by statements of confidence but feelings of apprehension. For the moment, optimism prevails.

CHAPTER 23

Postclosing—How to Make the Acquisition Work

Tennis great Rod Laver is known for his statement: "You are most vulnerable when you are ahead." This is very true in business acquisitions.

The acquirer of a business is susceptible to making mistakes during the delicate period of ownership transition. You are apt to experience an emotional and physical letdown following the lengthy and intense process of negotiating and finalizing the acquisition. The purchase of private companies is usually conducted without the knowledge of the employees; therefore, your initial concern should be gaining the confidence of all the employees. Your introduction by the former owner should take place the day after the closing to create as much harmony and confidence as possible.

The employees will naturally be apprehensive because a major change in the company represents uncertainty and the unknown. The old owner should assemble all the employees so that he or she can introduce them to you. You should then deliver a straightforward, sincere speech to gain the employees' confidence and calm their fears. If asked, you should not guarantee that there will be no job losses, as honesty is paramount. The best response is to explain that it will be necessary to fully understand the company before making any decisions. However, the first order of business is to prevent employee defections or a slowdown in productivity due to lack of employee enthusiasm.

Obviously there is so much to do postclosing that your real challenge is to be sufficiently organized and patient so that you do not make many mistakes. Successful acquisitions often start with a comprehensive postacquisition plan that evaluates the company's strengths and weaknesses as well as an initial overview of:

- Customers
- Employees
- Markets
- Research
- Financial controls

- Suppliers
- Products
- Manufacturing
- Organization structure
- Reporting methods

According to George Berbeco, CEO of the Devon Group in Waltham, Massachusetts, which has acquired four middle-market companies, he initially spends several hours with the key employees. For example, Berbeco may try to help the production manager improve the back-order situation and thereafter spend less time monitoring his or her progress. Berbeco goes on to say that as soon as possible, he personally visits the company's top ten customers to solidify their ongoing relationship. Finally, Berbeco says that if he does make employee cuts, he does it as a one-time event instead of letting employees go individually.

In making major decisions, it is important to initially go slowly enough to understand the company's strengths and where it is most profitable. If the company is not too large to interview every employee, individually or in groups, do so. Their input on how to improve the business is usually most insightful. The key to success is to listen carefully and *communicate, communicate, communicate.* And if you do have to discharge employees, either subsidize part of their outplacement or pay them a severance package. Not only is it morally correct, but the remaining employees will respect you accordingly.

Aside from the operational segments of the business, it is also important to put the succession plan together without delay. For example, if you buy a business with a 50 percent partner, then a buy/sell agreement should be signed so that if one of the partners either wants to leave or dies, there is a predetermined buyout arrangement consisting of a buy/sell financial formula that will leave the remaining principal in free reign to run the business.

Second, you should have life insurance payable to the company in order to buy out the stock of the deceased partner or to subsidize the company's operations going forward.

Third, if real estate is part of the business acquisition, then it would be wise to separate the two parts because it facilitates analyzing the company's operations and makes it easier to sell the company in the future. Another option is to implement sales-leaseback on the property so that the resulting cash is used for working capital or to pay down the debt. To go one step further, the machinery and equipment can also be separated and leased to the company.

One of the ways to demonstrate continuity after the acquisition is to retain the name of the business. However, the ego of many new owners compels them to use their own name. If you do plan to change the name, it is better to phase in the name change over several years by incorporating both names during the transition. The goodwill from a well-recognized name is often worth keeping.

REFLECTIONS ON THE POSTCLOSING STAGE

Some years ago, Tom Tremblay acquired Guardair Corporation of South Hadley, Massachusetts, an industrial power tool manufacturer. A year later Tom reflected about his postclosing experience, and in order of importance listed the following advice:

1. Without hesitation and immediately, buy your spouse a gift and take him or her out to the finest restaurant in the area. Not only is the acquisition stressful for you the buyer, but the repercussions of this intense process will affect your spouse and tax the marital relationship. It is quite possible that your spouse has provided encouragement when necessary and counseled you during the darkest moments of the acquisition process. Recognition and appreciation of your marital partner is the first priority.

2. The deal is done, and there are people to thank, business associates to inform, and community members to acknowledge. When you buy a middle-market company, there are bankers, lawyers, intermediaries, consultants, accountants, and advisers who helped you. A letter to the president of the

bank praising the particular loan officer or an announcement to your corporate neighbor in the industrial park will help you build important business relationships and solidify your support group for the next time you reach out for their cooperation. You may want to buy another company in a few years, so don't forget all those who have helped you grow, even if they were not involved in this particular transaction.

3. There is so much to do upon buying a business that you scarcely know where to begin. Start with the life blood of most organizations: the employees—in the office, on the factory floor, at their sales representative's office. Let them see that you are interested in their work and their input.

4. After interfacing with the sales side of the business, it is logical to visit the major vendors. Each year vendors become more critical to the success of middle-market companies because there is more reliance on just-in-time deliveries and a trend toward relying on fewer vendors. Using fewer vendors can improve quality and price, but it also results in higher risks regarding on-time deliveries. Visiting major vendors and assessing their financial status is one of the top priorities.

5. Within a month, you should be ready to visit your major customers. The objective is not only to keep their business under the new ownership but to increase the volume. This effort of calling on major customers is akin to marketing intelligence in which one elicits criticism of the product, the service, and/or the organization of the newly acquired company. Feedback may include recommendations for product improvement, discount schedules, data sheets, etc.

In another example of how to make the acquisition work postclosing, I interviewed Brad Yount, president of Odyssey Bay Ventures of Andover, Massachusetts, who acquired three companies along with some investors. Mr. Yount acquires companies with flat sales and weak operating margins. His postclosing approach is as follows:

1. Forego the external growth until the internal problems are corrected thereby focusing on improving operating margins as quickly as possible.
2. Implement an operating plan right after closing based on the preclosing financial due diligence by his accounting firm and his own preclosing operational due diligence.
3. Build trust quickly with the employees by sharing with them his vision of the company's future, touching on points like:

   - Mediocre financial returns and operating performance are unacceptable
   - Change will be a standard procedure
   - Create higher expectations by raising the bar significantly
   - Every job must be justified
   - A new infrastructure will be developed quickly
   - Everyone will be given a fair appraisal
   - Key management will select the new organization

4. Be the catalyst but let the management execute. Because the "people part" of the equation is so important, a degree in human behavior is probably more important in turning a company around than an engineering degree. One of his techniques is to ask the same questions to most of the employees to better understand the problems of the business. He is also upfront and keeps few secrets from the employees, and significantly raises the bar for all those to work to higher standards.
5. Lay out the new ground rules for how he plans to progress. The resulting impact on the corporate culture is enormous and the increased productivity is clearly evident. To help find the problems, Yount will skillfully find the bottlenecks, whether it is in the manufacturing or ordering departments, by talking to the folks working on the loading dock or in the office. Such inquiries often surface the future leaders of

the organization who currently may be on the plant floor. Repositioning the employees, releasing unproductive workers, and focusing on the agreed upon deficiencies should be implemented by Yount within a few weeks after the acquisition. Then the new management team is expected to "run with the ball."

Another expert in the M&A business, Tibor Toth, managing director of Babson Capital Management in Springfield, Massachusetts, has the following procedures postclosing:

1. Put the all-important business plan in place that was drawn up preclosing, and then monitor it religiously.
2. Execute employment contracts with managers that are crucial to the success of the business. These contracts are written for terms of one to five years, and include terms of regular and incentive compensation, terms of termination and severance, and noncompete clauses which continue for a period beyond termination of employment.
3. Establish an operating cost structure and sourcing strategy for vendors if not already refined.
4. Diversify the business by establishing other channels of distribution.
5. Analyze the human resources with expectations to prune and/or add key employees.
6. Review the capital structure in order to support the working capital and marketing expenditures which are necessary to grow business aggressively.

Based on the above information, you can proceed to make the necessary changes in the company and hopefully will be on the way to making the acquisition work.

CHAPTER 24

Why Deals Fail

W hen deals fail to close, everybody involved with the transaction is disappointed. Sometimes the differences between buyer and seller are insurmountable; other times the differences are miniscule. There are dozens if not hundreds of reasons why deals do not close. Of course, the critical stage of any transaction is the letter of intent stage when the expression of interest is transformed from verbal communication to a written document as a prelude to the purchase and sale agreement. While the basic price and terms will have been agreed upon, the devil is in the details. The reps and warranties, the indemnities, the extent of the escrow account, employment contracts, noncompete agreements at several levels—all loom as serious dealbreakers. Then there is the potentially explosive personality conflicts between the attorneys and advisers before, during, and after the due diligence process when differences of material facts cannot be resolved. One cannot overlook the final decision by either party's board of directors who can quickly and unexpectedly squash the deal.

When deals fail, it is the responsibility of both the buyers and the sellers. The following are some basic reasons for why deals fail to close.

For Buyers:
- They lose patience and give up the acquisition search prematurely, maybe under a year's time period.
- Some are not highly focused on their target companies and have not thought through the real reasons for doing a deal.
- They are not willing to pay up for a near perfect fit realizing that such circumstances justify a premium price.

- Others are not well financed or capable of accessing the necessary equity and debt to do the deal.
- Inexperienced buyers are unwilling to lean heavily on their experienced advisers for proper advice.

For Sellers:
- They have unrealistic expectations for the sales price.
- Second thoughts about selling, commonly known as seller's remorse and most frequently found in family businesses, cause them to abort.
- Some insist on all cash at closing and/or are inflexible with other terms of the deal, including stringent reps and warranties.
- They fail to give the intermediaries their undivided attention and cooperation.
- They allow their company's performance in sales and earnings to deteriorate during the selling process.

My definition of a deal, before closing, is that the two parties appear to have a verbal agreement sufficient for the buyer to draft a letter of intent. For a variety of reasons, which will be discussed shortly, about 50 percent of the deals that reach the letter of intent stage fail to result in actual transactions. It is important to differentiate this from a buyer who merely submits a letter of intent and/or letter of interest without discussing the proposal on the supposition that the seller might either accept it or at least counter with an alternative proposal. The following items are dealbreakers that kill potential transactions even after a verbal understanding has been reached.

Dealbreakers
- The seller realizes that after paying taxes and reinvesting the money, his or her income will be vastly reduced from what he or she is currently taking out of the business.
  - *Response*: While there is a certain element of truth to this reasoning, most owners sell out for reasons other than financial, i.e., burnout, no successor, lack of funds to grow

the business, competitive pressures. There is usually some *event* like death, divorce, or despair which solidifies the owner's resolve to go through with the sale.

- The seller or buyer is negotiating with another party, and the other arrangement is more attractive than this letter of intent.
  - *Response:* The highest price is not necessarily the winning offer. Other factors such as personal chemistry between buyer and seller can be more important. Buyers who move quickly and professionally increase their chances of success.
- Due diligence on either side brings to the surface undesirable factors that cause a withdrawal from the letter of intent.
  - *Response:* A more upfront detailed analysis of the other party will help obviate aborted letters of intent.
- The buyer is unable to secure the acquisition financing and/or the seller wants more upfront payment than the buyer is willing to provide.
  - *Response:* Buyers often underestimate the amount of cash required to do a deal. Aside from the cash at closing, there are sizable expenses for the intermediary, lawyers, accountants, appraisers, etc., and more money may need to be invested in the company for working capital. Financing is often left as a final detail in structuring an acquisition. Many failed acquisitions are attributable to inappropriate capitalization.
- The buyer and seller cannot agree on particular aspects of the transaction, especially when their respective advisers become involved.
  - *Response:* While letters of intent are usually brief, ranging from one to ten pages, basic issues should be predetermined, such as whether it is a stock or an asset transaction, key management compensation, security for the notes, severance package for employees if the business is to be moved, rent on the real estate, etc.
- The stockholders of the selling company do not agree with the proposal or do not want to sell the company under any conditions. Often a buyer will be negotiating with the CEO of the

selling company who has a minority ownership position. The power lies with the outside inactive majority owner. This situation frequently happens in family businesses.

- *Response:* More experienced buyers realize that they should be communicating with the real decision makers as early as the second or third visit.
- Seller's remorse results in the owner's backing out of the transaction because so much of his or her life is tied up in the company that he or she cannot bear to part with it. Sellers may realize that they would not know what to do with themselves if the business were sold.
  - *Response*: It is very important to understand the real reason the owner is willing to sell the business, not necessarily the stated reason. Sometimes a business that is for sale because it is losing money will show a dramatic turnaround. The owner may regain confidence and take the company off the market. A buyer should appeal to this seller by allowing the seller to phase out gradually—making him or her the chairman, a director, or a consultant to the company.
- The buyer's sensitivity to earnings! If the company shows a bad earnings quarter after the letter of intent, the buyer often becomes apprehensive about the entire transaction.
  - *Response*: Aside from reasons beyond the CEO's control, some businesses suffer when the CEO spends full time on the sale of the company. The lower earnings may be a result of this distraction.
- Deterioration of trust between the principal buyer and the principal seller.
  - *Response:* The principals should make an effort to get to know each other in a social setting outside the business environment in order to build personal chemistry and rapport.
- Impatience—some deals take a lot of time to put together because of dissenting stockholders, environmental problems, buyer's financing, etc.

- *Response:* There is a difference between lack of momentum when little is being done to move the project forward and hurdles that are complicated. In the latter case, patience is necessary.
- Reserves and escrow accounts: Some buyers get carried away with caution and legalese to the point that they do not want to assume any risk on such matters as accounts receivable, environmental matters, etc., and therefore try to set up full reserves and escrow accounts.
  - *Response:* There is a point in acquisitions at which the buyer has to decide the dividing line between a businessman's risk and a prudent man's decision.
- Inexperienced transaction lawyer: The jargon in the M&A business is that lawyers are either dealmakers or dealbreakers.
  - *Response:* Negotiating transactions usually requires compromise on both sides. Attorneys who try to win every point end up losing for their client.

Even if the deal makes it past the verbal agreement, the LOI, due diligence, and the purchase and sale agreement, there is a still a chance of failure. The following highlight potential causes for the bottom to fall out of your deal:

Postclosing: Reasons for Failure

- Overpaying for a company, particularly when most of the money is up front, may leave you with no reserve to improve working capital or to overcome shortfalls.
  - *Response:* Profitable, fast-growing companies can often compensate for the buyer's overpaying because they will grow their way out, but moderately profitable companies with slow growth will not redeem the buyer's mistake of overpaying.
- Overleveraged transactions in which operating income barely covers the debt service, leaving little for capital improvements. Business is so competitive that successful companies must constantly reinvest in their future.

- *Response:* Usually a transaction should have at least 30 to 40 percent equity in the deal, the balance being bank debt, seller's paper, and/or noncompete or consulting agreements.
- The buyer does not really understand the business. Perhaps the buyer has previously been successful in a low-tech business and then buys a high-tech business, or was successful in a white-collar business and buys a blue-collar business.
  - *Response:* Some buyers do not see enough deal flow and buy one of the first businesses that is available, or they are overconfident and misjudge their capabilities.
- Placing too much faith in existing management and failing to bring in new blood.
  - *Response:* Many middle-market companies succeed because the owner/CEO is extremely capable; however, the middle management is often subservient. When the owner/CEO leaves, the remaining management does not perform as well on its own.
- Some buyers assume that sales will remain stable after the acquisition, not realizing that competitors view a change of ownership as an opportunity to strike at the existing customer base.
  - *Response:* Service businesses are most vulnerable, and so anything that accentuates the new ownership, like changing the company's name, is a mistake.
- There was an overestimation of the company's growth potential, when in fact its market is mature. Gaining market share in a stable industry is more difficult than growing in an improving market.
  - *Response:* Many buyers should base their near-term profit projections as much on cutting costs and reducing overhead as on increasing sales.
- The buyer acquired a business in a fundamentally unprofitable industry.
  - *Response:* In the last ten years there has been some sensational acquisition consolidation plays in moribund industries such as steel, railroads, and coal, but generally speaking the expression that "all boats fall in an outgoing tide" is relevant in the M&A business, especially as it pertains to individual buyers.

- The buyer did not adopt the deal structure to the specific business.
  - *Response:* When buying a manufacturing business with considerable assets in plant and equipment, one can afford to leverage the balance sheet and pay a hefty portion of cash at closing. With a service company where employees and customers are the principal asset, the buyer should only pay 50 percent cash at closing.

HOW TO DEAL WITH FAILURE

Having acquired a company, how does one mitigate the chances of failure? The following suggestions are provided by PricewaterhouseCoopers in its book, *The Buying and Selling a Company Handbook*:

> *Formulate a plan: Whatever the size of the business you are buying, developing a strategy for after the deal closes is extremely important to a smooth transition. Before closing, you should understand the business, including its strengths and weaknesses, and how you will run the business when it's yours. A detailed written plan will serve as your touchstone for monitoring performance of your new company, including the transition. Successful buyers always have a plan and monitor every action against it. Problems that arise during the transition period were probably foreseeable—and avoidable, had buyers adequately planned ahead.*
>
> *Understanding: Until you fully understand the new business, its employees, its customers or markets, its products and its competition, it makes little sense to implement major changes.*
>
> *Timing: Once you understand the business, then proceed with your post acquisition plan as quickly and efficiently as possible so that you can prevent further financial problems, unfavorable employee morale and/or shortcomings in productivity. Announce major changes (especially in personnel) as quickly as possible.*

Employee relations: New owners often overlook the impor-tance of retaining existing personnel. These people know the business; overlooking their experience can be detrimental. Employees are intangible assets and successful acquisitions begin with the proper management of existing employees.

Customer relations: Sellers know their customers well and are often in a position to transfer their customers' accumu-lated goodwill to new buyers. Negotiate an employment con-tract with the seller. Customer retention is vital for a successful acquisition.

Supplier relations: Often buyers automatically keep the same suppliers used by prior owners and ignore all the other prospective suppliers knocking on the door. As a result, they may be unaware that they are not receiving the best prices or terms currently available. Present suppliers may have stopped offering competitive prices or terms years ago when they real-ized previous owners would never consider switching to new suppliers. It does not hurt to shop around.

Goodwill: Buyers often undervalue the acquired business' existing name. Many times names are changed simply because the new owners want to see their own names on neon lights. If you have purchased a successful business with a reputation for outstanding products or services, the last thing you should do is change the name and in so doing, signify a change in ownership and a perceived change in the quality of the busi-ness' products or services.

The real message is the days of easy deals in the 1990s are over—at least for now. Deals are definitely more difficult to close nowadays, and when closed, they are more difficult to sustain as a successful business.

CHAPTER 25

Legal and Tax Issues

Inevitably the buyer and seller are confronted with the question of how the transaction should be structured as it is a tax issue. You as the buyer should want an asset purchase in order to step up the value of the inventory, plant, and equipment in order to increase future depreciation deductions, while the seller most likely wants a stock sale to mitigate the capital gains tax and avoid the recapture tax, which occurs when the capital gain of the business exceeds the depreciation already taken. The end result is frequently a significant amount of income that the seller must recognize.

If the decision is to purchase the business in an asset deal, then the various components of the business should be broken down, e.g., land, buildings, equipment, inventory, patents, and goodwill. You obviously want the least amount of goodwill on the books because it is considered a soft asset. Also, you will want a lower value placed on land than on buildings because it is not a depreciable item.

On the other hand, sellers of a C corporation are faced not only with a double tax if they sell the assets instead of the stock but with the possible recapture of some depreciation previously taken on the equipment of the corporation. With heavy capital equipment-based companies like plastic injection molders, the depreciation recapture may be substantial, will be taxable at the maximum rate of the corporation, and will ultimately erode the purchase price available to the seller.

COVENANTS: CONSULTING AND NONCOMPETE AGREEMENTS
Aside from the basic motive of employing key personnel part time and preventing them from competing, you have a tax

reason for including these covenants in the purchase and sale agreement. Payments made by a buyer to a seller for these covenants are deductible by the buyer as a regular expense in the year in which payments are made. Conversely, payments received by the seller for these covenants are taxable as ordinary income instead of being taxed at the lower capital gains tax rate. Furthermore, a $1 million noncompete agreement in which $333,333 is paid at the end of each year for three years has a total present value of $828,951 using a 10 percent discount rate. One advantage for the seller is that the tax payments are spaced over a three-year period.

While the buyer in many cases wants the covenants for consulting and noncompete agreements for these genuine reasons, you may also intend to use the covenants to pay the seller over time and to allocate the purchase price to intangible assets, thus reducing the goodwill on the balance sheet of your new company. These covenants are, however, more advantageous to you than to the seller because they will generate ordinary deductions to you but ordinary income to the seller, and the tax on income is higher than the tax on capital gains.

To the extent that the overall purchase price can be reduced by allocating payments to covenants with the seller, there will be that much less residue of purchase price to be allocated to goodwill.

REAL ESTATE

Real estate is a very important issue in a transaction. The following are various possible situations:

- The selling company owns the real estate and wants the buyer to move the business, buy the building, or lease the building.
- A real estate trust associated with the selling company owns the building and currently leases below market rents, or leases above market rents.
- The selling company rents from a third-party landlord and can either sublet or not sublet.

Since the real estate is a major consideration, you should address the potential problems early on, and if necessary have discussions with the third-party landlord, if there is one. Perhaps the seller will be held liable by the landlord if he or she subleases. Perhaps you will have to show the bank and other lenders a definitive lease agreement before the acquisition financing is in place. From a buyer's perspective, if you foresee the need for additional space, zoning and compliance matters should be determined prior to the purchase.

For retail companies, the terms and conditions of the individual store's lease are probably one of your most important considerations in whether to acquire the business. Many retailers have gone out of business because their lease expired without reasonable renewal terms. It is not unusual for a retailer to sign a three-year lease with renewable lease options in three-year traunches for twenty years on an agreeable rental increase based on the cost of living index.

SECURITY ON THE SELLER'S NOTES

Most transactions are structured so that there are three or four components.

- Cash at closing
- Seller's notes
- Covenants: consulting and noncompete agreements
- A partial earnout

The issue of how the buyer will secure the notes always seems to be a negotiated item. Usually the buyer has pledged the key assets to the bank for the acquisition financing and normal credit lines. If the bank requires only accounts receivable and inventory as collateral, then the seller can take a first position on the machinery and equipment and a second position on the bank's collateral. On smaller transactions, it is common for the buyer to personally sign for the notes and perhaps offer a lien on a summer home or whatever applicable asset. If there are two individuals buying a business, the seller's lawyer will probably want the buyers to personally sign a "joint and several" agreement, which means if one partner fails to live up to the commitment, the other partner is responsible for the shortfall. As a buyer, you should avoid joint and several agreements.

TAX-DEFERRED TRANSACTIONS

An installment sale, by definition, is when at least one payment is to be received after the close of the taxable year in which the sale occurs. In other words, the recognition of the capital gain is postponed. If such a sale is structured properly, both you and the seller benefit. In the case of the seller, the taxes are deferred, and in your case, the payments are also deferred.

From a seller's perspective, the deferred payment may be exchanged for a promissory note by a third party or a standby letter of credit; however, installment obligations secured by cash or certificates of deposit of U.S. Treasury instruments do not qualify.

CHAPTER 26

Letters, Memos, Forms, and Contracts

E arlier in the book, I discussed the three elements required for a successful acquisition search, namely process, professionalism, and persistence. The use of certain forms in the acquisition search not only is important in organizing the process, but ensures a higher degree of professionalism.

BROCHURE

The first order of business is to print a rather simple, straightforward brochure or investment proposal about yourself and your acquisition entity. In Chapter 8, "Assessing Your Acquisition Strategy" under the subheading "Business Entity," an outline of this document was presented. Whether your investment proposal runs for many pages or you decide to prepare a one-page, three-fold brochure, you have conveyed a message that is not only informative but professional. Some individuals who are seeking credibility in the eyes of the potential seller may make a greater effort to gain this respect through association; for example, listed on the brochure might be the following:

Accountant:	PricewaterhouseCoopers
Attorney:	Ropes & Gray
Bank:	Bank of America
Directors:	Recognizable industry names

Many of the suggestions on how to present yourself in the brochure may be considered "smoke and mirrors" or purposely deceptive. I am not urging you to do anything dishonest or to say anything that is not true, but I am suggesting that you do everything legitimately possible to overcome your perceived disadvantage as an individual buying a middle-market company. Following are a list of suggestions on how to achieve this:

- Choose the name of your company so that it does not sound like a consulting firm, an investment company, or a sales business; otherwise, when you telephone or write the target company, the recipient's first impression will be to avoid the communication. I have a friend who has a background in the valve business and wanted to buy a valve company for himself. He printed a terrific brochure for his acquisition search, but he made one mistake. The name of his company was XYZ Management Company. It should have been XYZ Valve Company or just XYZ Company. A word such as management, partners, group, etc., is a tipoff to the recipient that you are not an operating company. Although you may not be an operating company, you do plan to become one upon an acquisition. Potential sellers by nature are apt to take more seriously an overture by an operating company than by an investment or holding company.

- Just as I suggested earlier that you gain credibility through association, think twice about using your hometown street address on the brochure. Street names like "Sandy Pond Lane" or "Cherry Hill Road" are a dead giveaway that you are operating out of your house. Using a post office box number is an alternative, and subleasing an office in the downtown area of a major city is worth considering.

- When people are job hunting, they often have several sets of resumes that differ in the "objectives" section at the top of the page. Let us suppose that you are seeking both manufacturing and distribution companies or both office products and food manufacturers. It is more effective in your literature if you customize your presentation accordingly, just as people do with resumes. While some buyers feel that it is advantageous to present themselves to business friends and intermediaries as generalists or opportunists, it is usually less effective. Certainly the owner of a target company is more likely to discuss the sale of the business if your acquisition objectives have some relevance to the business.

SEARCH LETTER

In Chapter 13, "Finding the Deal," there is mention of mass mailings and individual letters to the presidents of target companies to uncover interest on the part of possible sellers. While the response rate will be predictably low, the effectiveness will depend on a number of factors. Here are some suggestions:

- If you are obtaining the name from a directory and it is not a current edition, you should call the company to be sure the listing for the CEO is correct.
- Print "Personal & Confidential" on all envelopes. Use of an actual stamp instead of the postage meter will help personalize the letter.
- The more personal the letter, the better. Almost anything you can do in this regard will help, especially in the opening paragraph. Also, before writing the letter, go onto their Web site in order to better understand the target company.
- The search letter is only the opening gambit. Using a copy of this letter as your guide, you should then be persistent by following up within ten days with a telephone call. If you are unable to reach the CEO by telephone, write another but different letter, then telephone again, followed by a very discrete fax, and finally, if you are still undaunted, send a Federal Express communication to emphasize your determination. Obviously, you should use the latter technique only with companies in which you have a very keen interest.

MEMORANDA ON COMPANY VISITS

As a way to stay organized, set up a three-ring binder to log in all company visits with ensuing information. I have found the following format for a one-page memo the most useful.

TO:	File Name
FROM:	Yourself
DATE:	
RE:	ABC Company
	Address, telephone number, and email address
1. Background:	When company was organized
	Name and age of CEO
	Ownership breakdown
2. Business:	Describe the basic operation
3. Distribution:	Sell through what channels?
	Sell by own sales force, sales reps, distributors, small dealers, super stores?
4. Plant/employee:	Own or lease?
	Size of plant, number of employees
	Union or nonunion?
5. Financial:	Sales
	Gross profit
	EBIT
	Book value
	Growth rate
6. Competition:	Who?
7. Conclusion:	Opinions of the company

CONFIDENTIALITY AGREEMENTS

It is customary for the owner or CEO of the prospective selling company to require you to sign a confidentiality statement. Unless the seller is actively selling the business, he or she will not have such a form in the file. Therefore, I recommend that you carry your own confidentiality agreement in your briefcase in order to expedite matters. This format is fairly standard:

Confidentiality Agreement

In connection with our interest in purchasing the assets and/or stock of _____ (the Company), we have requested that we be permitted to examine the financial and other business records of the Company. We understand and agree that the information contained in these records is of a confidential nature and that it will be used by us solely for the purpose of making an offer for the assets and/or stock of the Company. We will not disclose, nor will our agents, servants, employees, or attorneys disclose any of the information contained in these financial and other business records, including the identity of the company, to any other person except to such investors, bankers, attorneys, or other persons necessary to consummate the sale to the undersigned.

Signed: _____ Date: _____
(Print)

_____
(Signature)

FEE AGREEMENT WITH INTERMEDIARIES

Intermediaries, of course, have their own fee agreements, but if they do not have a signed agreement with you and they do not have one with the seller, you will not hear about the deal from them.

I urge you to be proactive and tell intermediaries that you will be pleased to pay intermediary's fees; in fact, go one step further and send the intermediary your own version of an agreement. If you have your own fee agreement, you can simply mail the signed form to every intermediary with whom you want to do business. It will show the intermediaries that you are aggressive, anxious, professional, and ready to review deals. Here is a form you might consider using.

Your Company Inc.
Address

TO: XYZ Intermediary

1. WE ARE AGREEABLE to paying you and/or your associates a fee based on the purchase price or other consideration for any company, agency, distributorship, or other business entity or organization, whether expressed in cash or stock or any other remuneration; whether payable at closing of transaction or on extended payout; and regardless of which party pays the remuneration, when you are instrumental in helping us purchase, sell, or acquire any substantial interest in such company which we agree to accept. Of the purchase price, the fee to you and/or your associates would be:

5% of the first	$1,000,000
4% of the second	$1,000,000
3% of the third	$1,000,000
2% of the fourth	$1,000,000
1% of the value thereafter	

The payment of this fee shall be due and payable in cash at the time of closing.

2. Your Company Inc. will confirm in writing any introduction or referral.

3. If any of the principals of the parties introduced to Your Company Inc. become involved in a transaction as contemplated herein and such transaction is consummated, an intermediary's commission will be due XYZ Intermediary irrespective of who conducts the negotiations.

4. This agreement shall be binding upon and inure to the benefit of the parties hereto, their administrators, executors, heirs, successors, or assigns, any corporation and other entities now existing

or to be formed having substantially the same principals as either of the parties hereto.

If you accept this understanding, kindly countersign and return the enclosed copy of this agreement.

Your Company, Inc.
By: _____

Accepted:
XYZ Intermediary
Street Address
City, State, Zip
Telephone
By: _____ , _____
Title
Date: _____

GENERAL PROPOSAL LETTER

While most buyers prefer to "talk out" their general proposal with either the CEO of the target company or their intermediary, an alternative is to send a letter that broadly describes the proposal. Here is an example of such a letter.

Dear Mr. Smith:

The following is a proposal to acquire the assets of Big Time Inc. (the "Company"). This letter is an outline of a proposed transaction and is not meant to be binding on any party at this time, and is subject to the signing of a mutually acceptable, definitive purchase and sale agreement. In addition, this offer is subject to the requisite due diligence effort normally attendant on a transaction of this magnitude. With the aforementioned kept in mind, our offer is as follows:

Transaction: A new corporation ("Newco") will be formed by Your Company Inc. to acquire the assets of the Company.

Terms and Estimated
Purchase Price $4.0 million to $5.0 million cash at closing.
We would be willing to purchase the Company without the real estate and enter into a lease at current market rates and terms. In this case, our offer would range between $3.5 million and $4.5 million.

Conditions of Transaction
A. We anticipate that a transaction could be consummated and closed within 120 days.
B. This proposal is subject to financing commitments satisfactory to us. We are happy to provide you with references regarding our ability to finance the transaction.
C. Representations and warranties of seller with respect to accounts receivable, inventory, fixed assets, disclosure of liabilities, litigation, labor matters, corporate existence, etc., will be required.
D. We would anticipate completing our due diligence process within thirty to forty-five days, whereupon we would want to move immediately to the execution of a purchase and sale agreement.
E. If in the due diligence process and prior to the closing, we, in our sole judgment, wish to excuse ourselves from this transaction, we may do so without any liability, fee, penalty, or cost.
F. All fees and expenses of this transaction, including but not limited to legal, investment banking, accounting, broker, and due diligence, will be paid for by each of the respective parties.

Should you have any questions regarding this proposal, please do not hesitate to contact me at (000) 111-2222.
Very truly yours,

TERM SHEET

If you and the potential seller have verbally agreed on the price and terms of the transaction, then it would be helpful to put the basic financial arrangements on one piece of paper before you go directly to the letter of intent. Such an example would be as follows:

Term Sheet

Carlisle Corporation
Outline of Preliminary Proposal for an Asset Purchase

Gross purchase price	$5,000,000
Less debt assumed*	(500,000)
Net purchase price	$4,500,000
Form of consideration:	

John Smith (50 percent owner):	
Cash	$1,850,000
Four-year consulting and noncompete agreement ($100,000 annually)	400,000
John Smith's consideration	$2,250,000

Joe Doe (30 percent owner):	
Cash	$675,000
Carlisle stock	$675,000
Joe Doe's consideration	$1,350,000

Employment contract for Joe Doe: Three-year contract for $100,000 annually with additional annual bonuses of $50,000 provided company's annual operating profit of $700,000 is maintained.

Mary Jones (20 percent owner):

Cash	$450,000
Carlisle stock	$450,000
Mary Jones's consideration	$900,000
Employment contract for Mary Jones:	
Two-year contract for $70,000	
annually	
Total Consideration Paid	$4,500,000

*Interest-bearing debt (usually bank debt)

LETTER OF INTENT

The importance of the letter of intent is emphasized in Chapter 18. My experience is that it is best to draft an agreement of one or two pages that is not legalese. The simplicity of such a letter of intent makes it less threatening in the eyes of the potential seller than a document with legal jargon and lengthy qualifications.

The letter of intent has two contractual elements, i.e., that the seller will take the company off the market for a specified period of time and that both parties (particularly the buyer) will keep all confidential information confidential.

All letters of intent should specifically state that this is a non-binding agreement and of course should state the price, terms, and whether the purchase is an asset or stock transaction. It is customary for the buyer to draft the letter of intent as well as the purchase and sale agreement. This is a sample of the letter of intent.

Letter of Intent

Esterbrook Corporation Incorporated proposes to purchase all the assets of Mercury Security Corporation (MSC) of Boston, Massachusetts, including goodwill, customer list, and all other intangible and balance sheet assets, to be substantially the same as those set forth on the balance sheet of MSC as of _____, 2008 (Exhibit A). The name Mercury Secu-

rity Corporation or any derivation of the word Mercury is not transferable.

1.   Purchase Price: The purchase price for the assets will be $_____ payable in cash at closing.

2.   Noncompetition Agreement: The principals of MSC agree not to compete, directly or indirectly, with the business of Esterbrook as it pertains to MSC in any of its markets for a period of five years after closing. For such consideration, Esterbrook will pay $_____ per year for five years to John Smith.

3.   Lease of Building Space: It is agreed that MSC will use its best efforts to transfer the lease to Esterbrook at current or market rental as permitted by lease.

4.   General and Specific Liabilities: Esterbrook will assume the liabilities as shown on the balance sheet dated _____, but will not assume any other liabilities past, present, or future.

5.   Audit: Esterbrook will cause an audit to be conducted by Esterbrook's auditors at Esterbrook's expense as of a date to be selected.

6.   Expenses:
   a)   The stockholders, Esterbrook, and MSC will each pay their own expenses, including legal expenses, up to the time of the closing.
   b)   Esterbrook and MSC agree that no intermediary is involved in this transaction other than _____, of _____ ___, whose compensation is the responsibility of MSC.

7.   Letter of Intent: This letter of intent is nonbinding and may not be construed as an agreement on the part of any party. In the event that the

parties are unable to agree on a mutually satisfactory definitive agreement providing for the transactions contemplated by this letter of intent, none of the parties shall be liable to any other party or to any other person. The conclusion of any definitive agreement will be subject to the following:

a) Approval of all matters relating thereto by counsel for Esterbrook and MSC;

b) Review of all business, legal, and auditing matters related to MSC, the results of which are acceptable to Esterbrook;

c) Approval of all matters related thereto by the Board of Directors of Esterbrook and MSC and the voting shareholders of each company, if required;

d) Completion of such financing as Esterbrook may require to effect a closing;

e) Preparation and completion of all closing documents;

f) The closing date to take place in or within 90 days of the execution of this agreement.

8. Continuing Obligations: Until termination of the letter of intent, MSC shall not, and all of MSC's officers, directors, employees, agents, or representatives (including, without limitation, brokers, advisers, investment bankers, attorneys, and accountants) shall not, directly or indirectly, without prior written consent of Esterbrook, entertain negotiations with or make disclosures to any corporation, partnership, person, or other entity or group in connection with any possible proposal regarding a merger, consolidation, or sale of capital stock of MSC, or of all or a substantial portion of the assets of MSC, or any similar transaction.

9.   Confidentiality: Both Esterbrook and MSC agree to maintain complete confidentiality of all confidential material each company exchanges with each other as outlined in separate confidentiality agreements.

All documents in respect to this transaction will be prepared by an attorney or law firm selected by Esterbrook, subject to such documents being reviewed by and being acceptable to legal counsel for MSC.

Mercury Security	Esterbrook Corporation
Corporation	Incorporated
By_____	By_____
Title_____	Title_____
Date_____	Date_____

PURCHASE AND SALE AGREEMENT

In the book *The Art of M&A*, the author writes: "It is very important for the buyer to protect its customary right to control the drafting of the documents. It is the shortsighted buyer who tries to save legal fees by letting the 'other guys' do the drafting." Furthermore, the purchase and sale agreement, also known as the P&S agreement or acquisition agreement, has the following characteristics:

1. It is a legally binding agreement.
2. The buyer will seek to protect itself in such areas as pending litigation, undisclosed liabilities, and environmental problems.
3. The seller rarely sells for "all cash," leaving the buyer leverage to hold out on further payments if the transaction is not what the seller represented it to be.
4. The seller may opt for a lower price at closing for all cash rather than risk postclosing adversity.

5. The conditions section lists issues that must be satisfied before the parties become obligated to close the transaction.

6. The indemnity section relates to discoveries after the closing.

7. The representations and warranties section assures each party of the other's legal and financial ability to consummate the transaction.

8. The covenants section of the agreement defines the obligations of the parties with respect to their conduct during the period between the signing and the closing, e.g., the seller conducts the business in the ordinary manner.

The following is a sample purchase and sale agreement (an asset purchase).

*Date*_____

Asset Purchase Agreement

This is an agreement among RST, Inc., formerly known as Carlisle Inc., a Massachusetts corporation with a place of business at _____ ("Seller"); John Doe of _____ _____ ("Stockholder"); and Carlisle Inc., a Massachusetts corporation with a place of business at _____ _____ ("Buyer"). For consideration paid each other, the parties covenant and agree as follows:

1. Assets to be sold.
   Seller will sell, transfer, and deliver to Buyer free and clear of any liens or other encumbrances, Seller's business and the assets and properties of Seller, tangible and intangible as listed herein. Except as otherwise expressly provided in this agreement, the Assets shall include only the following assets owned by Seller at the time of closing.
   A. Machinery and Equipment.

All machinery and equipment, furniture and fixtures, and the like as set forth in Exhibit B attached hereto.

B. Tools, Dies, and Fixtures.

All tools, dies, and fixtures owned by the Seller.

C. Inventories.

All inventory, including raw materials, work-in-process, finished goods, repair parts, and supplies; all inventory records; and all outstanding purchase and sales orders.

D. Accounts Receivable.

The Buyer will use best efforts to collect all accounts receivable and pay those receivables as collected to the Seller within ninety days of closing in accordance with an agreed-upon list of such receivables as found on Exhibit E as of the date of closing. Upon demand of Seller, Buyer will reassign for collection of uncollected receivables ninety days after the closing.

E. Corporate Name and Trade Names.

All processes, patents, patent applications, trademarks, signs, advertisements, trade names, copyrights, drawings, and logos, including the name "Carlisle, Inc."

F. Customer Lists and Contracts.

All customer lists, files excepting accounting records, licenses, permits, contract rights, and sales backlog as found on Exhibit C, and telephone and fax number _____. Seller will provide buyer with access to Seller's accounting records upon reasonable notice for customary business purposes.

G. Goodwill.

The goodwill of the Seller.

Excluded from the sale shall be all cash, bank accounts, utility security deposits, and prepaid expenses and the land and buildings, which shall be leased to Buyer by Seller in accordance with the Lease attached hereto as Exhibit A.

2. Liabilities.

Buyer agrees to assume up to $_____ of Accounts Payable in accordance with Exhibit J. Buyer is specifically not assuming any other liabilities whatsoever of Seller, including without limitation, all taxes of whatever kind or nature, accrued or payable by Seller to any taxing authority prior to and including the closing date, all of which the Seller agrees to pay.

3. Closing Date.

The closing will take place no later than 1:00 P.M. _____ _____, at the offices of Seller or at such other time and place as the Buyer and Seller may hereafter agree upon. Adjustments and prorations shall be made effective the end of business _____.

4. Purchase Price.

A. Price.

The purchase price to be paid for the Assets is Five Hundred Thousand ($500,000) Dollars, which sum shall be paid as follows:

Certified or bank check at closing	$200,000
Buyer's promissory note per paragraph 6	200,000
Accounts Payable per paragraph 2	100,000
TOTAL	$500,000

B. Allocation.

The purchase price for the Assets shall be allocated as follows:

Inventories	$100,000
Machinery and Equipment	$200,000
Goodwill	$50,000
Accounts Receivable per paragraph 1(D)	$150,000
TOTAL	$500,000

5. Personnel Agreements.
   A. Noncompetition Agreement.
      Stockholders will enter into a noncompetition agreement with the Buyer, in the form attached as Exhibit D.
6. Buyer's Note at Closing Date.
   In part payment of the purchase price, Buyer shall make and deliver to Seller at the Closing Date a negotiable promissory note in the amount of Two Hundred Thousand ($200,000) Dollars, bearing annual interest at eight (8.0 percent) percent, for sixty (60) months and requiring equal monthly installments of interest and principal beginning thirty (30) days after the closing contemplated herein. Such note shall be secured by a first security interest in Machinery and Equipment acquired and shall be personally guaranteed by Buyer in the form attached as Exhibit H. The form of said note and security agreement, and UCC financing statements are attached hereto as Exhibits F and G.
7. Seller's Use of Name.
   It is understood and agreed that Seller will not use the name "Carlisle Inc." to pursue any business interests nor will Seller sell, lease, or convey usage of its name to any entity or individual.
8. Seller's Representations and Warranties.
   A. Corporate Authority.
      Seller is a corporation duly organized, validly existing, and in good standing under the laws of the State of Massachusetts and has the right and authority to enter into this agreement and carry out the terms and conditions hereof applicable to it and the execution, delivery, and performance of this agreement will not violate or conflict with the provisions of the Articles of Organization or Bylaws of the Seller.
   B. Agreement Default.

Seller as a result of the Closing will not be in default under any agreement or other commitment to which it is a party or by which it is bound.

C. Financial Statements to Buyer.

Seller has delivered to Buyer the Financial Statements through _____. Said Financial Statements are true and complete. Seller shall provide interim financial statements for the period ending ___ _____ as soon as practicable after closing.

D. No Material Change.

Since _____, there has not been, to Seller's knowledge, any material change in financial condition, assets and liabilities, or business, other than changes in the ordinary course of business.

E. Tax Returns, Audits, and Tax Payments.

Within the times and in a manner prescribed by law, Seller has, and shall have through the closing date, filed all federal, state, foreign, and/or local tax returns required by law and has paid all taxes (including without limitation, income, franchise, sales, use, meals, transfer, payroll, and ad valorem taxes), assessments, and penalties due and payable with respect to the Business of the Seller. The Seller is not delinquent in the payment of any other governmental tax, assessment, or other charge.

F. Marketable Title.

Upon the transfer of the assets at closing, Buyer shall acquire title to such property free of all liens and encumbrances and free of all claims of third parties.

G. Good Condition.

To Seller's knowledge and except to the extent disclosed to Buyer or known to Buyer, all Seller's equipment and similar tangible personal property are in good condition and repair, consistent with the age and remaining useful life thereof, and their use is in conformity with all applicable laws, ordinances, and regulations. The Assets are being sold in "as is" condition, and any and all warranties from manufacturers or dealers in existence at date of sale are included in the sales price. Buyer acknowledges that Buyer has been provided a full and complete opportunity to inspect the Seller's machinery and equipment and similar tangible personal property, is satisfied with the results of all such inspections, and that the Seller and Stockholders have made no warranties or representations with respect thereto.

H. Customer Commitments.

Attached as Exhibit C is a list of all presently existing customer commitments to which Seller is a party or by which it is bound. To Seller's knowledge, all such commitments are valid and enforceable in accordance with their terms.

I. Litigation.

To the Seller's knowledge, there is no pending or threatened action, arbitration, suit, notice, order, real estate tax contest, or legal, administrative, or other proceeding before any court or governmental agency, authority, or body, against, or affecting Seller, either directly or indirectly, with respect to the Assets pending or threatened that will survive the closing. There is no order, writ, injunction, or decree of any federal, state or local, or foreign court, department, agency, or instrumentality that directly or indirectly relates to the Assets. Seller has complied and is complying in all material respects with all law, ordinances, and government rules and regulations applicable to it and its properties, assets, and business.

J. No Untrue Representation.

To Seller's knowledge after inquiry, no representation or warranty by Seller in this Agreement, or certificate furnished or to be furnished to Buyer pursuant hereto or in connection with the transaction contemplated hereby, contains or will contain any untrue statement of a material fact.

K. Continuation of Truth.

The representations, warranties, and covenants set forth in this agreement will continue to be true in all respects as of the closing date and shall survive the Closing.

L. Licenses Obtained.

All government licenses, permits, and authorizations necessary for the ownership of Seller's properties and the conduct of its business as currently conducted are listed on Exhibit I, and Seller has all such licenses, permits, and authorizations.

M. Liabilities.

At the closing there will be no liabilities, commitments, or contingencies of Seller whether accrued, secured, or determinable that encumber the assets other than those expressly assumed by Buyer under the terms of this Agreement.

N. Continued Business.

Seller is not aware of any reason why its customers, subcontractors, or suppliers will not continue to do business with the Buyer after the closing in the same manner in which they have done business with the Seller prior to the Closing. This does not assure or imply that the existing customer base will be retained after the closing.

O. Stock Ownership.

The Stockholder named herein owns One Hundred (100 percent) Percent of the outstanding stock of the Seller.

P. Absence of Certain Changes.

Since the date of this Agreement and as of the Closing, there shall not have been any:

(a) Transactions by Seller affecting the Assets except in the ordinary course of business.

(b) Material adverse physical change in the Assets.

Q. Profits Pending Closing.

Profits from the date of this Agreement up to and including _____, shall be the property of the Seller.

9. Buyer's Representations and Warranties.

A. Corporate Authority.

Buyer is a corporation duly organized, validly existing, and in good standing under the laws of the State of Massachusetts and has the right and authority to enter into this agreement and carry out the terms and conditions hereof applicable to it and the execution, delivery, and performance of this agreement will not violate or conflict with the provisions of the Articles of Organization or Bylaws of the Corporation.

B. Agreement Conflict.

This Agreement does not conflict with the Buyer's bylaws, corporate charter, or any other internal requirement of the Buyer. _____

____ individually and collectively, are subject to no agreement or other constraint that conflicts with their carrying out the terms of this agreement.

C. No Government Approvals.

The transaction contemplated by this agreement does not require any state, local, or federal government approval.

D. Inspection of Assets.

Buyer acknowledges that he had an opportunity to inspect and actually did inspect all of the assets sold under this agreement and is satisfied with the results of such inspection.

E. No Untrue Representation.

Buyer's warranties and representations contained in this agreement are true as of the date of the agreement and shall continue to be true in all material respects up to and including the date of closing. This provision shall survive the closing.

10. Indemnification.

The Seller hereby agrees to indemnify, defend, and hold the Buyer harmless of and from any and all debts, liabilities, costs, and expenses of any and every nature whatsoever resulting from the breach or violation of any obligations. representations, covenants, or warranties of the Seller contained in this agreement and from any liability or obligation of the Seller arising out of the Seller's ownership or sale of the Assets or the Seller's operation of the business except for those accounts payable assumed by the Buyer pursuant to paragraph 2 of this agreement and as specifically identified in Exhibit J. Except as specifically set forth in said Exhibit J, the Buyer shall not and does not assume any other of the liabilities or obligations of the Seller.

The Seller, at its own expense, shall have the opportunity to be represented by counsel of its choosing, and control, at its expense, the defense of any claim that may be brought against the Buyer in respect of which the Buyer may be entitled to indemnifications. The Buyer shall promptly give written notice to the Seller of any such claim. In the event that the Buyer does not receive written notice from the Seller within fifteen (15) days of such written notice, the Seller shall be deemed to have waived the right to be represented by counsel.

In the event the Seller breaches or violates any provision contained herein, the Buyer shall have a right to set off against any payments due Seller under this agreement, under a Note of even date in the amount of $200,000, or against any payment due _____ under a noncompetition agreement between the Buyer and _____, an amount equal to the amount of any claim successfully brought against the Buyer as a result of said breach or violation if Seller elects to defend the claim or the amount of damages suffered by the Buyer if the Seller elects not to defend. Prior to such setoff by the Buyer, the Buyer shall give fifteen (15) days written notice to the Seller setting forth therein the reason(s) for said setoff. The Buyer shall exercise such right of setoff by applying such damages against payments due the Seller as they fall due pursuant to the promissory note referred to in paragraph 6 of this agreement and against payments due under the noncompetition agreement referred to in paragraph 5 of this agreement.

Any notice sent to the Seller should be mailed, postage prepaid, registered or certified mail, return receipt requested, or delivered by overnight carrier and addressed to the parties at their respective addresses as set forth in the Agreement, with a copy in case of notice to the Seller sent as follows:

To Seller's attorney: Name

                              Address

                              City

11. Condition of the Closing.

    A. Conditions of Sellers' Obligations.

        (a) Payment.

            Buyer's delivery to Seller at the Closing Date of payment in the amount of Two Hundred Thousand ($200,000) Dollars payable by Certified or Bank check without intervening endorsements.

        (b) Buyer's Note.

            Buyer's delivery to Seller at the Closing Date as defined herein of a promissory note in the amount of Two Hundred Thousand ($200,000) Dollars.

Security Agreement and Financing Statements.

Buyer's delivery to Seller of a security agreement and UCC financing statements as set forth in paragraph 6 and Exhibits F and G.

Buyer's Guarantee.

Buyer's delivery to Seller of a Guarantee from _____ as included in Exhibit H.

Detail Accounts Receivable Listing.

Buyer's and Seller's written agreement of the detail accounts receivable as of date of closing as set forth in Exhibit E is included herein.

True and Complete.

The representations and warranties of Buyer shall be true and complete in all respects, and Buyer shall have performed and complied with all agreements and conditions required by this agreement.

B. Conditions of Buyer's Obligations.

Buyer's obligations at the closing shall be conditional upon the following:

(a) True and complete.

The representations and warranties of Seller shall be true and complete in all respects, and Seller shall have performed and complied with all agreements and conditions required by this Agreement.

(b) Bill of Sale.

Seller's delivery to Buyer of a bill of sale and all other instruments necessary to convey to Buyer good and marketable title to the Assets.

(c) Noncompetition.

The signing of a Stockholders' noncompetition agreement in the form of Exhibit D.

(d) Lease.

The signing of a Lease acceptable to Buyer and Seller in the form of Exhibit A.

(e) At the closing Seller will deliver to Buyer:

(1) List of commitments and customers.

An updated list of contracts relative to Exhibit C, which list shall not vary significantly from its present form except in the ordinary course of business.

(2) Instruments.

Appropriate instruments, including Bills of Sale, and assignments transferring and conveying to Buyer, good and marketable title to the Assets.

(3) Vote of stockholders.

A certificate of Vote, duly executed by the Clerk of Seller, as to the due adoption by the Stockholders and the Board of Directors of Seller of a resolution authorizing the transactions contemplated of Seller by this agreement.

12. Seller's Conduct of Its Business Prior to Closing.

Seller agrees that it will make no changes in the Assets and will incur no liabilities or obligations between the date of this agreement and the closing date except changes, liabilities, and obligations arising or occurring in the ordinary course of business. Seller agrees that it will use its best efforts prior to the closing to maintain and preserve its business and to retain good working relationships with its suppliers, distributors, customers, and others with whom it deals.

13. Bulk Sales Act.

The Seller has provided Exhibit J setting forth all creditors, claimants, or others that may have claims or liens upon any of the assets to be transferred herein. Notification will be given to creditors of record. The parties agree to waive compliance with all the provisions of Article 6 of the Uniform Commercial Code dealing with bulk transfers.

14. Broker's or Finder's Fee.

Buyer and Seller agree that no broker or finder is involved in the sale of assets other than _____ of _____ _____ and _____ of _____.
A broker's commission of $_____ to _____ ___ shall be paid at the closing by Seller if the sale hereunder contemplated is consummated and the purchase price is received by Seller.

15. General.

A. Written Notice.

All notices and other communications hereunder shall be in writing, and given by delivery or mail (by overnight carrier providing a receipt or facsimile followed by first-class mail, postage prepaid) to a party at its address set forth at the beginning of the Agreement or at such changed address as a party may have furnished to the other party in writing at least ten (10) days prior to the effective date thereof.

B. Severability.

If any provision in this Agreement shall be deemed unenforceable or void as a matter of law, such circumstance shall have no effect on the surviving portions of the Agreement, each of which shall have full force and effect. Buyer and Seller shall be required to use their best efforts to agree upon and replace any provision that has been declared legally void or unenforceable.

16. Miscellaneous.

A. Binding effect.

This agreement is binding not only upon Seller, Stockholders, and Buyer, _____ but also upon Seller's, Stockholders', and Buyer's respective successors, heirs, executors, administrators, and assigns.

B. Governing law.

The laws of Massachusetts as of the date appearing below shall govern the interpretation and enforcement of this agreement.

C. Modifications.

No modification of this agreement shall be binding unless in writing and executed by all parties with the same formality as this Agreement.

    D. Entire agreement.

This agreement represents the entire and integrated agreement of the parties and supersedes all prior oral and written negotiations and agreements.

    E. Liquidated Damages.

Upon failure of the Buyer to fulfill Buyer's obligations under this Agreement, the deposit may be retained by the Seller as liquidated damages for any such default. Such deposit will be held by counsel for the Seller.

Effective as of _____

_____   _____

Witness   RST, Inc. FKA a Carlisle Inc.

_____

President

_____   _____

Witness   _____

    Stockholder of RST

_____   _____

Witness   _____

    Buyer

_____   _____

Witness   _____

    Buyer

_____

President

Exhibits contained herein:

A   Lease
B   Machinery & Equipment
C   Customer Lists & Contracts
D   Noncompetition
E   Listing of Accounts Receivable
F   Buyer Note & Security Agreement
G   UCC Financing Statements
H   Guarantee
I   Licenses & Permits
J   List of Creditors

CHAPTER 27

Case Studies of Buyers

NEVER GIVE UP

John Ela was a very capable entrepreneur/businessman searching for a company to acquire. Almost two years after identifying the company he wanted to acquire, he finally persuaded the three different family owners to come to terms with him—but not before the negotiations "blew up" three times. For nearly seventeen months, John Ela worked full time on completing the transaction. While the effort ended in a successful closing, a person with less tenacity than John Ela would not have succeeded.

The Search

John had more than twenty years of experience as a CEO. He had an ideal background as an operator to attract other equity investors. Graduating with a Masters degree from business school, he then worked for a division of Exxon Corporation. For ten years he was with Dynatech Corp. (NYSE) and during one point he was CEO of a division which he turned around from a $1 million write-off into a business that eventually sold for $18 million. Later he became president of a $5 million manufacturer of air compressors and subsequently president of a $10 million multichannel marketer/manufacturer of products for backyard nature enthusiasts.

In 2004, John started his own consulting practice focusing on four segments:

1. Improve business strategy and execution.
2. Implement business process improvement.
3. Facilitate cultural change.
4. Create branding awareness.

In 2005, he started searching for his own business to acquire while he was a practicing consultant by seeking a CEO position, offering to help fix or buy the target company. John's second method for the hunt was to contact different types of advisers to companies, i.e., attorneys, bankers, consultants, and accountants. Along the way, John broadened his search criteria from manufacturing companies to include value added companies such as distributors providing installation services as well.

Finally, it was an accounting firm that recommended John visit EPOCH Corporation. By this time, John had spent twelve months searching for a business to buy having previously entered into three letters of intent with other companies, all of which failed because either the owners couldn't afford the loss of annual income postclosing, the owners were ultimately unrealistic on the purchase price, or the owners refused any contingency payments. In none of these situations were the sellers being advised by an intermediary.

The Deal

EPOCH is coincidently located in Pembroke, next to John's hometown in Concord, New Hampshire. The three owners had previously worked for Key Lock Homes, a modular home manufacturer in Hooksett, New Hampshire, and established EPOCH in 1983. With the exception of one co-founder, Doug Basnett, who remained as a shareholder and COO, the others wanted to retire.

Since EPOCH has revenues of $15 million with 115 employees, John needed some institutional equity and debt to finance the acquisition. He had previously developed a database of thirty to forty private equity groups, a subset of which EPOCH fit within their investment profile including their interest in investing in New England. John boiled the list down to five groups and finally settled on Ironwood Equity Fund. Ironwood liked the deal for the following reasons:

Modular homes are gaining market share throughout the country with a 20 percent increase between 2002 to 2004 from 36,000 units to 43,000. With the exception of the "mud-season" the business is not seasonal and EPOCH focuses on the high end of the market.

Ironwood was very impressed with John and his management capabilities.

The valuation was reasonable with an EBITDA multiple of less than five.

For the next seventeen months, John negotiated the transaction with the owners who throughout the process did not have the benefit of an investment banker or M&A adviser. Surprisingly, the original price was not changed nor attempted to be renegotiated. The difficulty in coming to complete agreement by both parties on the Purchase & Sale Agreement was the interpretation of the deal process, and the subsequent misunderstandings. During this period of time, most of the employees thought that John was a consultant for EPOCH, but in actuality he had complete access to the company's records as part of his due diligence investigation. By the time the negotiation blew up for the third time, John felt that this year-and-a-half-long ordeal would never be resolved. He had been totally committed to this *one* deal and had no other options.

Finally, John's perseverance paid off and after twenty-nine months spent on this project, the deal closed on July 31, 2006. "In many ways," John explained, "it took the three blowups to crystallize everyone's mind of bridging the various gaps."

Postacquisition

To better understand the business, it is important to realize the business model. EPOCH homes are built inside the company's factory in large modules. From the date of order, the delivery is in five to ten weeks, and the independent EPOCH builder finishes the construction in another four to ten weeks. Excluding the land, roughly half the cost of the house is attributed to EPOCH, the other half to the builder. The average price of these houses leaving the factory is $150,000 with average annual production of 100+ units, or $15 million in the aggregate.

Soon after the close, John started to apply his skills toward improving the company. John was asked specifically what he personally believed to be his major attributes as a CEO. He listed five key factors:

1. Ability to change the company's culture
2. Emphasizing customer focus
3. Streamline internal processes
4. Facility to see the big picture, yet handle the details as well
5. Implement cross-functional teams among the staff

In order to improve the company's profitability, John expects to spend 60 percent of his time developing the team approach in order to increase efficiency and productivity. With 115 employees, of which eighty-five are in the plant, coordination is imperative to produce a custom modular home on budget and on time. The other 40 percent of John's time is spent on sales and marketing supporting the forty to fifty builders in New England who are independent EPOCH builders. While the current real estate market is trending down, it is not a long-term concern for John, because he expects EPOCH to increase its market share. EPOCH has a big advantage over the "stick" built homes where the builders use a vast assortment of subcontractors and where the quality suffers from their revolving workforce.

Perhaps the above transaction would have gone more smoothly if the sellers were represented by professional M&A advisers. On the other hand, John was sufficiently experienced and capable to act as his own investment banker and above all he had the persistence and tenacity to prevail against seemingly unbeatable odds. During the seventeen months of constant courting and negotiation, he worked inside the company performing due diligence and becoming more knowledgeable about the company and the industry. In the end, a successful conclusion was reached, but not without extensive trials and tribulations.

Lessons Learned

- Understand the industry to succeed postclosing.
- If the seller is not being represented by a professional intermediary, the good news is that you are not competing with another buyer. The bad news is that the seller's inexperience in doing M&A deals often leads to confusion and indecision. If the latter occurs, then your tenacity and persistence must prevail.
- With an extended period of courting and negotiating, take advantage of this time to really get to know the company and its industry so that postclosing the transition will go more smoothly.

THE POWER OF TWO

Most individuals who are desirous of acquiring a business approach the project as a solo enterprise. The following situation involves two fellow employees who worked for the same *Fortune* 500 company and left together to form Acquity Partners as an entity to acquire a business. While their business skills were different, their respective attributes were complementary.

Background on the Buyers

Tim Cabot was CEO of the Plastic & Ink division of Cabot Corporation, which is a niche business with high margins and modest sales. Bob DeAngelis was CFO and marketing manager for the Carbon Black division of Cabot Corporation, which is a commodity business with low margins but $500 million in annual revenues.

Both Tim and Bob had each been employed at Cabot Corporation for fifteen years pursuing different careers. During the early 1990s, the company's CEO, Sam Bodman, was their respective mentor imparting a very entrepreneurial attitude. When Bodman left the company to become George W. Bush's Secretary of Energy, the company's culture changed, becoming more centralized. Realizing that the middle management would have less autonomy and less responsibility, Tim and Bob decided to strike out on their own and find a business to buy.

The Organization Process

As individual buyers, Tim and Bob packaged themselves as an acquisition company, Acquity Partners, run by experienced operating people with a specific focus in the chemical and adhesive industries. They gave themselves a two-year time horizon to complete a transaction. While they both had some equity for an acquisition, they realized that if they were to acquire a reasonable size business with sales that they would need to partner with a private equity group and/or financial institution. They also realized that they needed M&A counsel for valuing, structuring, and arranging for the financing.

Buying a business can be a full-time job. Without the resources of a big company, they had to rely on all the help they could muster from other people. Both Tim and Bob established an office in their respective homes, rolled up their sleeves, and worked eight to ten hours per day. One of the advantages of having a partner in this situation was their ability to motivate each other and set a rhythm in their work schedule. Once they became organized, Tim and Bob were able to review five deals per week over a six month timeframe.

Becoming M&A Partners

The first major challenge was to engage an investment bank and a financial partner with whom they could work well together. Most investment banks in the lower end of the middle market are accustomed to representing sellers and maybe complete only one buy-side assignment per year. Realizing that Tim and Bob would have to use their industry connections to surface most of the leads, they retained Consilium Partners of Boston as their investment bank. This decision proved to be a smart move, particularly in capitalizing on their expertise in valuing and structuring deals, but further in their introduction to Seacoast Capital which provided the financing. Seacoast was particularly perceptive and sanguine to appreciate the merit of both Tim and Bob's operating background relevant to their target companies.

Achieving Goals

Geography was not a barrier to their acquisition search as they pursued a $25 million polymer company in South Carolina and a $50 million chemical company in North Carolina. Tim and Bob learned to quickly "price-out" the deals as in the latter case the seller was using them as a stalking horse in effect to refinance the company. However, once Tim and Bob had their acquisition team in place, they moved quickly and decisively. After twenty-five offers to buy companies, Tim and Bob zeroed in on Katahdin Incorporated of Natick, Massachusetts, which specializes in producing medical finishes and industrial coatings in Teflon and hard anodizing processes.

Katahdin was a company owned by a private equity group that felt it was time to sell to achieve a liquidity event for their investors. The company was not so profitable that it attracted a lot of attention from buyers as the only other bidders were another individual and a competitor. Luckily, the intermediary representing the seller did not realize and/or exploit the tremendous "upside" of the business. Over 50 percent of the $10 million in sales were from the Teflon coating business, of which 50 percent were from medical device customers—a fast growing sector.

Tim and Bob continue to work well as partners postacquisition. It is one of those great success stories resulting from hard work, smart implementation, and a vision.

Lessons Learned

- Put a strong acquisition team together.
- If the time from the letter of intent to closing is delayed because the seller is not prepared for a ninety-day (or fewer)

due diligence period, take that time to learn more about the company so you can develop a comprehensive postclosing business plan.

- Just as Ron Reagan stated, trust but verify information given to you.

PERSISTENCE PAYS OFF

Phil Harris, age fifty-one, of QuadTech in Bolton, Massachusetts, bought this business from GenRad, an old-line electronics testing manufacturer. The company's base business is impedance bridges and standards as well as stroboscopes, with a total of $10 million in sales. A new series of precise testing equipment selling for approximately $8,000 to $12,000 each should add another $2 million to $3 million of sales in Phil's fourth year of ownership.

Putting the Acquisition Plan in Motion

Phil had a classic business background that included Wharton Business School, Xerox, and a position as a division manager of Wang during that company's growth years. Phil realized that he needed financial credibility to buy a middle-market manufacturer, and so he aligned himself with Hambro Venture International, a well-known worldwide venture capital organization. It was a win-win situation for both parties. Phil took an office at Hambro and used its support system as well as its name. Phil's mission was to find the company, negotiate, and close the deal. His arrangement was that he would be president of the acquired company and own a minority interest. Hambro would provide most of the equity and own a majority of the business.

Phil's second order of business was to establish a target mailing list, and so he went to Dun and Bradstreet with three specific criteria: geographically forty miles west of Boston, sales over $5 million, and business in a given range of Standard Industry Codes (SIC). Supplied with 1,000 names of presidents and their companies, Phil realized he had to hit prospects' hot buttons. With the help of an executive from a large advertising agency, Phil carefully crafted a letter that stated he was seeking a business exactly the same as theirs, that he had previously managed a business, that he had financing capability, and that further discussions would be held in high confidence. What was really different, however, was that Phil included a photograph of himself with his jacket off and his shirt sleeves rolled up, implying that he was a take-charge, man of action type. Each letter was personally signed, and each envelope had a postage stamp.

Normal response rate for this type of mailing would be 1 percent, but Phil received an unbelievable 9 percent response. As the telephone began ringing off the hook, Phil was left in the embarrassing position of talking to people who were responding to his personalized letter, yet he couldn't bring up the name and company on the computer screen fast enough to have an intelligent conversation. He therefore had his secretary take all his calls so that he had time to check the target company's profile before calling back.

At the same time Phil was sending out letters, he borrowed the huge Rolodex of the managing partner of Hambro's Boston office. He worked incredibly hard, prospecting and visiting four or five companies a day, but when his leads dissipated, he realized that he had to add an incentive. Phil offered people a $10,000 reward if they merely gave him a name of a company that might be for sale, provided, of course, that there was an ensuing purchase of the company. Additionally, Phil maintained a list of 300 people with whom he networked. Because the list was so large, he would send out letters periodically saying that he was still looking and please continue to remember him.

Road to Success

There were a number of reasons why Phil succeeded, but none compared to his persistence. He pursued one company for nine months and thought for sure that he had a deal, but it fell apart because the seller did not like the terms of the subordinated debt financing. He learned to quickly qualify the prospective sellers by "schmoozing" on the first visit, gathering financial information at the second meeting, and making an offer with a letter of intent at the third. However, Phil still had not bought a company after all his effort. He was facing self-imposed pressure and was close to considering himself a failure. Instead of easing up, though, Phil increased his knowledge of M&A by reading numerous books on the subject, listening to tapes, and enrolling in accounting courses, even though he was a Wharton graduate.

After two years and two months, Phil and Hambro, with the introduction of an intermediary, bought the precision product line, with sales of $10 million, from GenRad. Phil had looked at 250 companies, and liked twenty of them. He made offers for ten companies and negotiated with four others before he hit the jackpot with GenRad. Asked what he would do differently if he could do it over again, without hesitation Phil said that he would have narrower criteria and would focus on corporate spinoffs by concentrating on contacting directors of corporate development of larger companies with small divisions.

Lessons Learned

- Concentrate on corporate divestments, as there is a greater probability of doing a deal with a committed seller. Many owners of privately owned companies have "seller's remorse" and become overly emotional about transferring ownership.
- Communicate your focus on definite acquisition criteria, especially as they pertain to an industry. Just as job seekers might change the "objective" statement on their resume to suit a particular interview, impress your contacts with a narrow focus.
- Organize yourself for the acquisition search as if this were a sales and marketing assignment, for in fact you are seeking a customer and selling yourself.
- Persistence pays off.

LINING UP YOUR INVESTORS FIRST

Tom Tremblay, then age forty-two, a former venture capitalist, established a buyout company. Tom had an engineering and business school background. From his venture capital experience he was accustomed to valuing, structuring, and negotiating deals. In his quest to buy a company on his own, however, he lacked two important ingredients for success: capital and credibility in the eyes of potential sellers. As a relatively young man with a newly acquired house, a wife who had retired from her job, and three young children, Tom was not able to go without income for the duration of the search and still provide sufficient equity to do a deal.

Working Together Toward a Single Goal

Creating a buyout company was Tom's vehicle for raising capital and gaining credibility. For the first few months, he contacted personal and business friends who he felt would be interested in being co-investors. The funding was set for two stages; first, to pay Tom a base salary plus basic out-of-pocket expenses during the search, and second, to invest capital to acquire the company. Tom obtained twelve investors to participate in the first phase of funding. These investors had the option to invest significantly more money in the second phase or pass on the deal.

Several of the investors served as a quasi-board of directors, as Tom called on them for their insight on various deals and would occasionally take one of them to a target company that was of particular interest. Asked what motivated the investors to put money in his project, Tom responded, "A third believed in the enterprising concept of backing an energetic entrepreneur, a third felt it was a sound businessman's risk, and the final third were a combination of both." Perhaps the most insightful information I received from this interview was Tom's comment that putting the investor group together was one of the more straightforward parts of the entire acquisition.

Give Yourself Credibility

With the capital portion fulfilled, the next necessary ingredient to add was credibility. Knowing that there is a tight universe
of corporate sellers within Tom's target companies, he realized he
needed to be able to deliver his message with credibility. Therefore, Tom printed a brochure that included:

The company's mission
His background
Names of the directors and advisers
Names of law and accounting firms
The type of companies being sought

Additionally, Tom did not make the mistake made by so many
individual buyers. He established an office away from his home
in a highly visible business community. In his case, it was in the
center of Boston's financial district. Once he had established it,
he compiled his computer database of desired target companies.
He sent as many as four separate mailings to each of these companies. Tom also had a mailing list of 600 intermediaries such as
lawyers, bankers, and accountants and a fax list of 300 intermediaries that could be "broadcast to" through a fax modem. Getting
attention was the name of the game during the search process, and
the *Worcester Telegram* and the *New Hampshire Union Leader*
picked up his story and published it.

This story reaffirms what one hears so often: in buying a company, persistence is often the overriding reason for success. From
the initial contact to the successful closing date, it took Tom two
years to complete the sale. Initially the company was introduced
to Tom by a marketing consultant who did public relations for the
company. The profile of the company fit Tom's criteria perfectly:

Manufacturer of a trademarked industrial product
Profitable sales of approximately $2 million
4,000 customers total, including 2,000 distributors

National accounts such as Frito Lay and Johnson & Johnson
Growth even through the recession
Solid product reputation

The eighty-nine-year-old founder and owner of Guardair Corporation had not begun to explore selling the business before Tom
arrived on the scene. Then the following series of events took
place, which is worth noting.

1. Tom stayed in touch with the owner, but the situation did
   not change from their original encounter until six months
   later. The owner's eldest son died, forcing the owner
   to devote himself full time to the business. The owner
   called Tom, expressing his interest in selling.
2. Like those of the other potential buyers, Tom's valuation
   was nowhere near the owner's price. But he kept in constant touch.
3. Tom was close to a verbal agreement with the owner and
   a closing appeared imminent; however, the widow of the
   owner's deceased son fiercely objected, preventing Tom
   (or any other buyer, for that matter) from getting clear title.
4. Nine months passed without any further headway, but then
   the two parties started to negotiate again. One month later,
   the founder had a stroke and the bookkeeper left.
5. A second son who had been filling in for his father took
   over the negotiating process. Although he was somewhat
   familiar with the business, he was unfamiliar with the
   process of selling a business. Therefore, Tom had the
   arduous task of re-creating the negotiating process and
   convincing the seller that various adjustments were in
   order. In any event, the closing finally did take place, but
   not without enormous patience, persistence, and persuasion. Nine of Tom's original investors ultimately became
   stockholders of the company.

From Beginning to End

The search and acquisition process took Tom two years. He had reviewed 275 companies and made six offers during this time. Asked what sage advice he could impart to other buyers, Tom commented that he thought it best to be objective and less ambiguous during the letter of intent stage. You can often get caught up with the spirit of getting the deal done, but you should precisely spell out price adjustments for old inventory or dubious accounts receivable.

The different perspectives on the company's value as translated into the perceived selling price and the perceived buying price are almost always a major stumbling block. As outlined in the chapter about negotiating, rational objective data shared by buyers with sellers is one of the most powerful arguments. In the years I have known Tom, I have often heard him respond to an overpriced deal by asking, "How do you finance it?" I am sure he used this rationale in order to convince the owners that their family business had to be priced accordingly. In this case, as in most buyouts, the investors need a certain rate of return on their equity investment and the bank needs a certain debt coverage and payout level in order to go forward.

This acquisition certainly lived up to its potential with revenues increasing over five times in twelve years, partly aided by several small acquisitions.

Lessons to Be Learned

- Get your database in order: targets, intermediaries, contacts, etc.
- Very few companies are really for sale. If you stumble onto one, full court press.
- Worry about finding a good deal. Financing dollars will follow good deals.

TURNING A FALTERING BUSINESS INTO A SUCCESS

In 1960 Franklin Wyman Jr., then age forty-one, was controller of a well-known old-line Boston retail chain, R.H. Stearns & Co. Frank had a penchant for sweets, and so he frequented Bailey's of

Boston, an ice cream parlor, restaurant, and candy store. Bailey's manufactured its own candy and ice cream products.

While Bailey's had a superior reputation for quality and value, the store was faltering, and there were rumors that the business might be liquidated. Frank felt that Bailey's would be a fun business to own, and so he put together an investor group of three other business friends and approached Bailey's attorney. After two years the owner finally accepted Frank's "low-ball" offer. With only $7,500 of Frank's money plus his partners' investments, they bought a well-established food emporium with annual sales of $250,000.

Unlike most business buyers, Frank retained his other job. In fact, soon after he bought Bailey's, he was promoted to manager of R.H. Stearns' branch stores. Operating two businesses consumed ninety hours a week of his time, but was necessary to pay the educational costs for his four children at prep school and college.

Expanding the Business

Over the years, Frank bought out his three other partners and started to expand the restaurants, first opening one on Temple Place next to a busy area between the Provident Institution of Savings and the famous Locke-Ober five-star restaurant.

During the twenty-three years of growing the business, Bailey's had become a significant part of Frank's life. He increased the number of stores from one to nine and sales from only $250,000 to $4.6 million. All four of his children had worked in the business at one time or another, and Frank had become a minor local celebrity with his frequent radio and television advertisements.

Selling the Bought Business

In 1982, at age sixty-two, Frank realized that neither of his two sons was interested in taking over the business and that perhaps he should consider cutting back on his six-day work week. A mutual friend introduced Frank to an executive from Fanny Farmer, a national chocolate producer. Within nine months,

Frank had become a seller of his own business, receiving over $1 million for the company, a handsome return on his very modest original investment. One-third of the purchase price was notes substantiated by a letter of credit from the Bank of New England. Instead of being elated with the transaction, Frank was depressed. He describes the loss of his life's most rewarding piece of work as similar to giving up a child for adoption. Perhaps it is hard to understand for someone who has not owned his own business. In fact, some owners withdraw from closing the deal because of their attachment to a business that has provided close personal relationships and a feeling of importance and accomplishment.

The Dangers of Acquiring

The saga of Bailey's continued, and like the cat that has nine lives, Bailey's got another owner in 1987 when Frank's successor was unable to run the business with the same attention to detail, promotional flair, and tight employee relationships. Ironically, Frank was chairman and part owner of a small investment banking firm when his successor at Bailey's decided to bail out of a business that had become more than he could handle. O'Conor Wright Wyman of Boston accepted the "for sale" assignment even though Bailey's was hemorrhaging badly, with declining sales, negative book value, $800,000 in long-term debt, and restaurant leases expiring. Faced with a rapidly declining business and mounting debt, the owner had to sell Bailey's quickly or face corporate and personal disaster.

O'Conor Wright Wyman valued the business and prepared a selling memorandum. For several decades the firm had successfully transacted M&A deals for clients both here and abroad, but this assignment looked to be one of the most difficult. Partly from a feeling of desperation and partly from instinct, the firm placed an advertisement in the *Wall Street Journal*. Serendipitously, a successful executive from another fast-food chain responded. Within six weeks from the beginning of the assignment, Bailey's was sold to this executive for the asking price, which was more money than the seller or O'Conor Wright Wyman expected.

While the buyer had been enormously successful with another restaurant chain, he tried to change the corporate culture of Bailey's, a Boston institution since 1873. Within two years of his purchase, the company was substantially out of business and no longer a Boston landmark. The following excerpt is taken from the O'Conor Wright Wyman brochure as a forewarning to those intending to acquire a business: "During the last two decades nearly one-half of all acquired or merged companies were less profitable after the acquisition or merger than before. Though the number of such transactions reached an all time high, nearly one-third were dissolved by the end of this dynamic period."

This is a story of both success and failure—the same business over a period of one hundred years encompassing five different owners.

Lessons Learned

- Success in buying a business will do no good if the owner is not able to run it.
- Buyers should go slowly when making changes in a newly acquired business. They should never assume that because they were successful in one business, they will have all the answers in another business.
- A seller who has never sold a business should not be afraid to employ an intermediary. The cost is more than justified by the increased price the seller can generally obtain when the company is packaged and a systematic search for a synergistic buyer is conducted.
- The seller should begin the planning for a transition in ownership many years before the event takes place.

CHAPTER 28

Pearls of Wisdom

Throughout this book, different issues involved in buying a company are addressed in separate chapters. Cumulatively the text should be helpful to you in completing a transaction. In this chapter, however, I have brought together the important nuggets of information; hence its title.

From an experienced dealmaker's perspective, Andre Laus, managing director of the Recovery Group in Boston, a firm specializing in turnaround and corporate improvement, has the following comments for buyers:

> *Profits, profits, profits: Like the analogy of the ingredients for successful real estate acquisitions, location, location, location, companies with consistent profits over a long time period are usually the best acquisitions. Reliability of earnings, year in and year out, is more important for most buyers than the total magnitude of earnings if the earnings are inconsistent. A very successful group with which I was previously associated acquired over a dozen midsize companies in less than ten years. Part of their success is attributed to the majority stockholder's criterion of acquiring only companies with ten years of unbroken profitable earnings. Such standards place a greater burden on the acquisition process, but the postacquisition results have been most rewarding.*

Additionally, the corporate culture that no cost is too small to address, cumulatively results in noteworthy profits. From a buyer's perspective, continuous cost management results in more profits, just as increasing sales usually results in greater profits. Management should focus on both items with equal emphasis.

The quality of working capital: Working capital (current assets less current liabilities) should be viewed skeptically and beyond the immediate implication of the numbers. For example, if there is an excessive amount of receivables over ninety days, it may be indicative of the industry, the quality of the customers, or the company's

own lack of financial discipline. Either way, the extent of this item may cause a buyer to reconsider the potential acquisition.

Also, inventory is an important component of working capital. Most businessmen analyze inventory with regard to annual turnover, but few people focus on the equally important issue of what percentage of the orders are shipped complete or if a system to measure customer order fill exists at all.

Strong customer orientation: Many of us have read Tom Peters' famous book *In Search of Excellence*, which keeps focusing on the importance of the customer in the eyes of "all" employees of the company. Some progressive companies have a customer council that meets quarterly. Buyers should be looking for companies that are customer-driven, as this is indicative of future success.

Strong employee orientation: Employee training programs, employee empowerment, and employee respect are all indications of a company that probably believes its most important asset is its people. Not a bad philosophy! An incidental tip is to look at the company bulletin board, which reflects how management feels about its employees. And, above all things, look at the men's washroom. If it isn't clean, reconsider buying the company. The employees probably do not take pride in their company, their products, or themselves—and the company accepts it.

No problems with the company: Within reason, buyers should try to avoid buying companies with serious problems. Of course, all companies have some problems, but before a new owner can start growing his new acquisition, he should heed the advice of Roy Little, the famous capitalist and owner of Narragansett Capital. Before seeking ways to grow a company, first concentrate on avoiding catastrophe, and second, be sure to keep the ship on a straight course. After those two points have been achieved, then one can focus on ways to grow the company.

In addition to Andre Laus's "pearls of wisdom," I have forty-six recommendations of my own:

1. A buyer should be talking with at least four or five potential sellers at any one time and actively negotiating with two or three.
2. Memoranda to oneself following each meeting, detailing the points discussed and minor or major matters agreed upon, are invaluable in keeping discussions on course.
3. Avoid introducing your attorney into discussions with principals before the elements of a business deal have been agreed upon. As soon as the buyer introduces such an expert into discussions, the seller does likewise. Since attorneys must protect the technical aspects of their clients' positions, more transactions have failed because of the premature introduction of such specialists than have been made.
4. Don't make a ridiculously low offer that will insult the owner.
5. Don't negotiate complex deals.
6. Don't get hung up on assets; be a cash flow buyer. Lenders tend to look at fixed assets, while buyers concentrate on cash flow.
7. Keep the buying process moving as fast as possible. The buyer who is able to make rapid analyses and decisions will benefit from the momentum.
8. For any given deal, there is a limited window of opportunity. If you spend too much time raising equity after the target company is "in play," the window will close.
9. If you are having difficulty raising the necessary equity to complete the transaction, suggest that the seller keep the accounts receivables, the real estate, or even the machinery. Sellers can lease the equipment to the buyer.

10. If you plan to borrow money against machinery and equipment for your acquisition financing, your banker will need to have an official liquidation appraisal on the machinery and equipment. Anticipate this and have the appraisal done early instead of later so that the momentum of completing the deal is not lost.

11. Predetermine your acquisition borrowing power so that your financing will not come up short at the critical juncture of the transaction. For example, the following percentages are normal borrowing ranges:

Accounts receivable (90 days or less)	70–85%
Inventory (not work in process)	25–60%
Machinery & equipment (of forced liquidation)	50–80%
Land & buildings (of market price)	60–80%

12. Remember the rule of one-third: After an equity investment of one-third of the purchase price, the cash flow must provide the CEO/owner's salary, a return on investment, and enough money to service the debt.

13. Besides profitability, some successful buyers often concentrate on the following ingredients:
    • Strong and committed management
    • Steady and predictable business in noncyclical industry
    • Substantial market share
    • Admirable corporate culture

14. Agree at the outset that the party that is acquiring the business will draft all the documents and the selling party will then review and make comments. Not only does this sequence provide order for the transaction, but it is to your advantage as the buyer to draft the documents based on your understanding in your own language.

15. When buying a company, target an industry, product, or service that is on the upswing. Conversely, few acquisitions succeed if the industry, product, or service is on the downswing.

16. The announced reason for the sale of companies is rarely the real reason. Investigate, take your time, and listen carefully. If you are getting bad vibes about the deal, get out of the transaction quickly.

17. In order for your attorney to be a dealmaker instead of a dealbreaker, don't expect him or her to win every point in contention.

18. Sellers are often selling their legacy, and so the dynamics of the sale are often more important than the top bid. The preferred buyer, in the eyes of the seller, is not necessarily the high bidder, but rather the one who has the best intentions, the best chemistry, and/or the best credentials. Buying businesses goes beyond the numbers. Unfortunately, many buyers drop the ball in romancing the seller.

19. A buyer's insensitivity to the owner of the selling company can destroy a deal. Be sensitive to the seller's attachment to the company and its employees, customers, and vendors.

20. Most deals take time to complete, usually from two to five months after the letter of intent. While you have to exercise some degree of patience, you must remember that 50 percent of all deals fail to close after reaching the letter of intent stage. It is very important to keep the momentum going, and it is imperative that you retain experienced counsel in closing deals. Most sellers, somewhere along the line, get cold feet, and so buyers must maintain the seller's interest.

21. Nonnegotiable items should be pointed out early in the negotiation, such as an asset versus a stock sale or that the seller's paper will be subordinated to the bank.

22. For companies without audited statements, make sure you substantiate their financials with their tax returns. You can justify paying less for a company if the statements are not audited, because the figures are not verified by the accountant.

23. The older the business, the better established it is and the stronger its customer and supplier relationships.

24. The more industries in which the company sells its product, the more protection it has from cyclicality and/or an industry downturn.

25. The tax objectives of a buyer and seller are at opposite ends of the spectrum in an acquisition. The seller's goal in structuring a buyout is to maximize the after-tax cash in his or her pocket, while the buyer's goal is to maximize the seller's assets that can be depreciated or amortized.

26. The best growth companies, if a reasonable size (over $10 million in sales), usually are heavily pursued by numerous private equity groups that have an overabundance of capital to invest.

27. Buying companies is usually cheaper than trying to grow them from scratch.

28. From a buyer's standpoint, a business is worth less if it is a subchapter S corporation because of the lower book value resulting from the earnings flowing through to the owners. A lower book value is also going to reduce the leverageability of the transaction.

29. Try to get very close to the other principal because there is a strong possibility that his or her advisers are not experts in mergers and acquisitions. Additionally, the potential seller is apt to receive some opinionated advice from friends that invariably increases the seller's insecurity about the deal. Meeting alone with the other principal, even during the final negotiation, will frequently improve the chance of not having the deal derailed by the sellers' advisers.

30. If the buyer is not receiving information that was requested from the seller, it is an indication of a possible coverup of facts. The buyer should consider other companies instead.

31. A critical issue in buying a business is access to capital.

32. Management: the most important issue you need to consider is whether the owner is the reason for the success of the business. If the owner leaves, can you fill this role?

33. Seller financing is a popular means of structuring the deal and is used in over half of the transactions completed.

34. Be sure that the CEO has the legal authority to sell the business as this authority may rest with the board of directors, a majority stockholder, a bank with a lien on the business, etc.

35. Knowing the strengths of a business is as important as, or perhaps more important than, understanding its weaknesses. Focus on the target company's competitive edge.

36. The art of the business acquisition process begins with techniques to find a large number of business deals and to find them before they come on the market.

37. Many people do themselves a disservice by looking at all deals that might be interesting. Targeting industries, types of businesses, size and geographic location makes your search more efficient and more likely to succeed.

38. It is imperative that you follow up with anyone who gives you a referral. Report back to the person giving the referral, indicating what transpired. Not only is this professional courtesy, but it will lead to more referrals from the same source.

39. Make generous use of appraisers, i.e., corporate, real estate, equipment, etc. The appraisals will keep you from overpaying.

40. Price doesn't kill deals—terms do.

41. From a seller's perspective, if the deal falls through, a great deal of confidential information has been given to the wrong people. Therefore, the more discreet the buyer is with confidential information, the more confidence the seller will have with the buyer.

42. Act with absolute clarity in all of your negotiations so that the potential dealbreakers surface as early as possible and can be dealt with for as long a period of time as possible rather than at the eleventh hour.

43. In negotiations concerning a promissory note, the interest rates and payment schedules are key issues. Interest rates often will track rates of commercial lenders. Parties also

should evaluate various amortization options, including interest-only periods and balloon payments, as alternatives to equal installments of principal and interest over a given term.

44. In negotiating, if the seller wants a stock sale instead of an asset sale for tax reasons, then the buyer should request a lower selling price. If the seller wants a fully collateralized note from the buyer, then the acquirer should negotiate a lower interest coupon.

45. The biggest dealbreaker is usually the disparity of the price between the buyer and seller, and the negotiation is usually a colloquy to bridge the difference. To broach this, the buyer could say: "This is the way I see the valuation. What do you see?"

46. As a buyer, ask the seller these three provocative questions: a) How do you grow the company? b) What is the company's competitive advantage? c) If you had a million-dollar windfall in the company's checking account, what would you do with it?

CHAPTER 29

Conclusion

Finding a business to buy is a lengthy process. Ultimately, buying a business is the culmination of analyzing, negotiating, financing, and implementing your professional and personal skills and resources.

In the case studies of successful buyers in Chapter 27, the individuals were resourceful, committed, and tenacious in their quest to own their own company. For every successful acquirer of a company, there may be ten others who are unsuccessful. This latter group fail to buy a company for a myriad of reasons, but of equal concern are those who buy a company and then fail thereafter. This book is an attempt to bring some of my knowledge and the experience of others to those interested in buying a business.

Partly because large companies have recently restructured by laying off thousands of senior managers and partly because of the desire of many businesspeople to be entrepreneurial, the demand for middle-market companies far exceeds the supply. However, most business schools do not teach people how to buy a company. Working for a manufacturing company does not necessarily properly prepare you to buy or run one. Being a corporate executive of a *Fortune* 500 company is far different from being a CEO of a middle-market company with a small support staff, long hours, tedious tasks, and tight finances. Owning your own business can be particularly taxing on your marriage.

This book, while comprehensive, does not alleviate the need for a buyer to surround himself or herself with excellent advisers—intermediaries, transaction lawyers, accountants, corporate appraisers, tax consultants, etc. Because businesses are difficult to properly value, it is often prudent to have an independent valuation. The $2,000 to $10,000 you spend on this upfront expense could be just a drop in the bucket compared to what you might save in the final price. Such an appraisal helps buyers enormously in the negotiating process. In the final analysis, the business you acquire should be able to generate sufficient earnings to service the debt, pay you a competitive salary, and provide an annual return on investment of 20 percent or more.

In spite of all the books you may read on the subject of buying a business and all the expert advice you will receive, your gut instincts may ultimately be the most important factor determining what, if any, business you should acquire. While it is human nature for most people to be trusting of others, the stakes are high when it comes to buying a business, and so I urge you to be sure you know why a person is selling a company. The owner truly may be burned out or bored, but he or she also has the advantage of knowing more about the business and probably more about the company's industry than you do. Therefore, it is important to do the best you can to determine why the owner is selling. It is also important to spend enough time and effort on due diligence—not just number crunching, but product and market analyses. It may be better to spend more money for a healthy company than less money for a sick company. And finally, beware of the seller who insists on all cash at closing. If the seller agrees to help you finance the acquisition by having some of the purchase price paid in the form of a noncompete agreement, a consulting agreement, and/ or notes, the seller is your quasi-partner through the transition period, and you have retained a form of leverage in case there are any skeletons in the closet.

Throughout the book we have shown that acquisitions are difficult, but obviously doable if the potential buyer uses all of his or her resources, relies on advisers, and is relentless in the search for a company to buy. Individual buyers usually have to meet the acid test when acquiring a company: pay themselves market-rate salaries, service the debt, and achieve a satisfactory return. Often the individual buyer is bidding on a business against a corporate buyer that can justify a higher price based on future synergism of the two companies, elimination of duplicate staff, economies of scale, and the benefits of selling new products through the same distribution channel.

The vicissitudes in doing a deal are enormous. For example, you must analyze the industry and the company in order to properly value the business, so that you can finance the transaction that will lead you to the negotiations, due diligence, and closing. You may be buying a company for the first time, but as Merrill Halpert of the Charterhouse warns, "Time works against you. The longer it takes to pull a deal together, the greater the possibility of the deal falling apart." When the momentum is lost, the deal is dead.

In many cases, it is more difficult to buy a small company, because the business probably does not have audited statements, and at first, you may not know exactly what you are buying. Surprisingly, most small businesses are not sold with all their assets and liabilities. If you insist on an asset sale rather than a stock sale, the seller's lawyer will probably advise the client to increase the price. Be prepared to find out what assets are to be withdrawn and what debt obligations are to be assumed. When the preceding items are resolved, will there be adequate working capital left to properly run the business?

I have offered numerous approaches and techniques for successfully doing a deal. While the case studies clearly show that most of the successful acquirers of companies were tenacious, two of the other attributes you need to successfully complete a deal are simply human qualities. One is to use your intuition as to what is right and what is wrong. The other is common sense. For example, if you buy a company in an industry with which you are not familiar, you are asking for trouble. Thoroughly understanding the industry in which your acquired company operates is not imperative, but it is a definite advantage.

Ideally you will want to acquire a business that has the following characteristics:

- Profitable, with a historical record of stable earnings
- Strong middle management that is willing to stay on

- Good market position in a niche business
- Strong growth rate with continued upside
- Affordable price

The above checklist is near utopian. Such a company may not be available for you to acquire. In fact, the problem most individual buyers have with acquiring middle-market companies is that they are almost paranoid about the "warts" on the businesses. Almost all companies have some warts. What the buyer should concentrate on is the core competency, the core skills, and the core business of the company.

If you have come this far in the book, I applaud you for your efforts. If executed correctly, buying a middle-market company can be one of the most exhilarating and challenging episodes of your life! Good luck and God bless you.

Russell Robb at russellrobb@verizon.net

Supplemental References

Albo, Wayne P., and A. Randal Henderson. *Mergers & Acquisitions of Privately Held Businesses* (Canadian Institute of Chartered Accountants, 1987).

Bazerman, Max H., and Margaret A. Neale. *Negotiating Rationally* (New York: The Free Press, 1993).

Crouch, Holmes F. *Selling Your Business* (Saratoga, CA: Allyear Tax Guides, 1994).

Ernst & Young. *Mergers and Acquisitions* (New York: John Wiley & Sons, 1994).

Evans, Frank C. and Bishop, David M. *Valuation for M&A: Building Value in Private Companies* (New York: John Wiley & Sons, 2005).

Fifer, Bob. *Double Your Profits in 6 Months or Less* (New York: Harper Business, 1994).

Freund, James C. *Smart Negotiating* (New York: Fireside—Simon & Schuster, 1993).

Ilich, John. *Deal Breakers & Break Through* (New York: John Wiley & Sons, 1992).

Joseph, Richard A., Anna M. Nekoranec, and Carl H. Steffens. *How to Buy a Business* (Chicago: Enterprise Dearborn, 1993).

Klueger, Robert F. *Buying and Selling a Business: A Step by Step Guide* (New York: John Wiley & Sons, 1988).

Knight, Brian. *Buy the Right Business—At the Right Price* (Dover, NH: Upstart Publishing Company, 1990).

Mancuso, Joseph R. *How to Get a Business Loan* (New York: Fireside—Simon & Schuster, 1990).

Mancuso, Joseph R., and Douglas D. Germann, Sr. *Buying a Business (For Very Little Cash)* (New York: Fireside—Simon & Schuster, 1990).

Marren, Joseph H. *Mergers & Acquisitions—A Valuation Handbook* (Homewood, IL: Business One Irwin, 1993).

Myss, Joseph E. *Divestiture Strategies for Owners of Private Businesses* (Wayzata, MN: Joseph E. Myss and Associates, Inc., 1994).

Peterson, C. D. *How to Sell Your Business* (New York: McGraw-Hill Publishing Company, 1990).

Post, Alexandra M. *Anatomy of a Merger* (Englewood Cliffs, NJ: Prentice-Hall, 1994).

Pratt, Shannon. *Valuing Small Businesses and Professional Practices* (Homewood, IL: Dow Jones Irwin, 1986).

PricewaterhouseCoopers. *The Buying and Selling a Company Handbook.* (New York: PricewaterhouseCoopers, 1995).

Reed, Stanley Foster. *The Art of M&A—A Merger Acquisition Buyout Guide* (Homewood, IL: Business One Irwin, 1989).

Robb, Russell and West, Thomas, Editors. *The Best of M&A Today* (Westford, MA: Business Brokerage Press, 2003—only available through www.bbpinc.com).

Rock, Milton L. *The Mergers & Acquisitions Handbook* (New York: McGraw-Hill Book Co., 1987).

Sherman, Andrew J. and Hart, Milledge A. *Mergers & Acquisitions From A to Z* (New York: Amacon, 2006).

Silver, A. David. *The Middle Market Business Acquisition Directory and Source Book* (New York: Harper Business, 1990).

Slee, Rob. *Private Capital Markets* (New York: John Wiley & Sons, 2004).

Snowden, Richard W. *The Complete Guide to Buying a Business* (New York: Amacom, 1993).

Welch, Jack. *Winning* (New York: Harper Collins, 2005).

Woolf, Bob. *Friendly Persuasion* (New York: G. P. Putnam's Sons, 1990).

Index